Journalism at the End of the American Century

Journalism at the End of the American Century, 1965–Present

JAMES BRIAN McPHERSON

The History of American Journalism Series, No. 7
James D. Startt and Wm. David Sloan, Series Editors

Westport, Connecticut
London

Library of Congress Cataloging-in-Publication Data

McPherson, James Brian, 1958–
    Journalism at the end of the American century, 1965–present /
James Brian McPherson.
       p. cm. – (The history of American journalism, ISSN 1074–4193; no. 7)
    Includes bibliographical references and index.
    ISBN 0–313–31780–1 (alk. paper)
    1. Journalism—United States—History—20th century.
    2. Press—United States—History—20th century.
    I. Title. II. Series.
    PN4855 .H57 2003 no. 7
    [PN4867]
    071'.30904–dc22   2006009794

British Library Cataloguing in Publication Data is available.

Library of Congress Catalog Card Number: 2006009794
ISBN: 0–313–31780–1
ISSN: 1074–4193

First published in 2006

Praeger Publishers, 88 Post Road West, Westport, CT 06881
An imprint of Greenwood Publishing Group, Inc.
www.praeger.com

Printed in the United States of America

∞

The paper used in this book complies with the
Permanent Paper Standard issued by the National
Information Standards Organization (Z39.48–1984).

10 9 8 7 6 5 4 3 2

Contents

Series Foreword

Since the renowned historian Allan Nevins issued his call for an improved journalism history in 1959, the field has experienced remarkable growth in terms of both quantity and quality. It can now be said with confidence that journalism history is a vital and vitalizing field full of scholarly activity and promise.

The new scholarship has widened the field's horizons and extended its depth. Today, especially with new bibliographic technologies at their disposal, journalism historians are able to explore literature pertinent to their studies to a greater extent than was previously possible. This expansion of literary sources has occurred in conjunction with other advances in the use of source materials. Today's historians incorporate primary and original records into their work more than was common when Nevins issued his call, and they also utilize sources produced by the electronic media. As the source foundation for journalism history has grown, so has its content also undergone a substantive expansion. Previously neglected or minimized subjects in the field now receive fairer and more concerted treatment. Contemporary journalism history, moreover, reflects more consciousness of culture than that written a generation ago.

Growth, however, has created problems. Abundance of sources, proliferation and diversity of writing, and the stimulation of new discoveries and interpretations combine to make scholarship in the field a formidable task. A broad study covering journalism history from its beginnings to the present, one combining the rich primary materials now available and the older and newer literature in the field, is needed. The History of American Journalism series is designed to address this need. Each volume is written by an author or authors who are recognized scholars in the field. Each is intended to provide a coherent perspective on a major period, to facilitate further research in the field, and to engage general readers interested in the subject. A strong narrative and interpretive element is found in each volume, and each contains a bibliographical essay pointing readers to the most pertinent research sources and secondary literature.

The present volume, the seventh and final one in the series, examines journalism during the most recent forty years, from 1965 to the present. The press found itself in a media world vastly different from any that had existed up to that point. More challengers, including the Internet and 24-hour cable television news, threatened to unseat newspapers from their traditional leadership role as providers of news. Journalism at the same time faced changes of historic importance in American culture, politics, and business. As the other volumes in the series have done, this volume focuses on the nature of journalism during the years surveyed, chronicles noteworthy figures, examines the relationship of journalism to society, and provides explanations for the main directions that journalism was taking.

Preface

American journalism today can be generally described as pervasive, entertaining, and mistrusted. In some ways, it is the best journalism Americans have ever seen. In other ways, the modern news media fall short of the ideals held by most of those who love journalism, and far short of the promise they once seemed to offer in terms of helping create an enlightened democracy. The turning point may have come in the late 1960s and 1970s, which were among the most turbulent and interesting years in America. Journalism of the period reflected the turbulence, and contributed to it. By the late twentieth century (commonly referred to as "the American Century") the American news media were everywhere, both more expansive and more intrusive than ever before. As the world prepared for the "New Millennium," satellites and computer technology allowed Americans to see news from far-off places with an immediacy never previously known. At the same time, putting events in context became increasingly challenging. Increasing corporate concentration, globalization, and new technology meant that news was presented through new media, in new formats, literally around the clock.

In the early years of the period discussed in this book, Vietnam and Watergate joined other societal factors in contributing to a perceived "need" by consumers for news that was current, emotionally gripping, and increasingly confrontational. The same period also saw a movement toward alternative journalism, a movement that largely fizzled but which prompted change among mainstream news media. Oddly, despite (or perhaps somewhat because of) the increasing amount of news through-out the period, general public understanding of many social and political issues and, many would say, the depth and reliability of the news discussion decreased. The press contributed to a diminishing trust of government and societal institutions, and then perhaps ironically found itself among those institutions struggling to maintain credibility.

This volume examines significant changes in journalism that occurred during and after the mid-1960s, discussing how those changes contributed to the expanding reach of news and the diminishing trust in both journalists and those they cover. Technological advances ranged from satellites and computers to photocopy machines, videotape, and digital cameras. Business trends included increasing corporate concentration and cross-promotion. Legal factors played a role, as the Supreme Court decided several key First Amendment cases in the 1970s, and governmental deregulation permitted significant changes in the business of news. The final effects of those changes remain unknown. Americans began to rely more on television, then later in many cases on the Internet, than on newspapers for their news. Entertainment values increased in the presentation of news including in print journalism content and layout, and definitions of news broadened. The business became increasingly inclusive of women and minorities. Two U.S. presidents faced possible removal from office, largely because of press revelations.

Each chapter herein covers a general theme that became prominent during the period discussed. Key events within those themes appear in general chronological order of importance, though with an overall time period of less than forty years, a historical blink of an eye, naturally time periods of various chapters overlap. One trend typically began before another ended, and many of those trends continue even today. Some trends ran throughout the time covered by this book, while others arose and faded during a briefer period. As with any approach, this one admittedly is imperfect, and some readers might prefer a stricter chronological approach. Still, unless one sticks to presidential terms or the Olympic Games, history rarely happens in neat chronological packages.

Because it deals with recent history, a potential weakness of this book is a lack of perspective—perspective that only the passage of time can provide. Indeed, some historians argue that many, if not most, of the events discussed here are too recent to be considered "history." On the other hand, it seems that one's perspective of what qualifies as history sometimes depends on which war one happened to be born after. For those who happen to be older, it is worth remembering that for most college students who read this, the explosion of the Space Shuttle Challenger and the first Persian Gulf War are but dim memories. Those students have never known a world without microcomputers, videotape, satellites, USA Today, or CNN, all of which contributed to significant changes in journalism after 1970.

Changes in journalism and technology also mean that this book differs from other volumes in the History of American Journalism series in other ways. This work benefits from the fact that a multitude of scholars have devoted extraordinary effort to trying to understand and explain the workings of the news media, producing thousands of well-researched articles about the art and practice of journalism. For example, one journal alone offered almost 2,000 articles related to journalism and mass communication during the twenty-five years from 1971 to 1996. Though especially in recent years many of those journal articles say at least as much about the values and vagaries of contemporary academic research as they do about journalism, many offer valuable insight about the news media. Many findings from that research are cited in this book, providing a type of context not often available for writers of "older" history. Even newer than most academic journalism journals is the Internet, which became not just a subject but also a key means of research. This is an exciting time to be a researcher, with the ability to bring sights and sounds of the past literally into one's office in ways that only recently were unimaginable.[1]

It is true that the full impact of many post-1965 events cannot yet be determined. With time, some incidents and people will seem more important than they do now, others less important. That process will occur in part because of choices made in early attempts such as this one, though it is not the first, to select, record, and analyze the events deemed most significant. Also, because some of the individuals discussed and quoted here continue to be involved in journalism, they have had less time to contemplate (or write about) their own activities. Their views may be colored by current personal or industry realities.

Journalism often is called "the first draft of history." This volume provides at least a slightly later, more reflective draft, though I harbor neither the illusion nor the desire that it will be the last or best version. A few years ago, the first book of this seven-volume series brought forth a history of the American press from 1690 to 1783 and revealed new details about events from 300 years earlier. That volume was built on the work of past historians, and future historians will build upon it. History does not end, in either its expanding breadth or in our depth of understanding. That complexity makes history both more interesting and more worthwhile as a topic of study.

Many people contributed in various ways to this volume. At the inevitable risk of forgetting some, let me take this opportunity to mention some of the most important (while noting, of course, that I acknowledge full responsibility for errors or omissions). Series editors Jim Startt and David Sloan and Praeger editor Hilary Claggett have been insightful, helpful, patient, and kind. Numerous librarians in various locations, especially those at Whitworth College, the Library of Congress, and the Wisconsin Historical Society, have helped me find and make sense of information. Whitworth College and Peace College helped fund my research. Historians LeRoy Ashby, Mary Cronin, and especially Tom Heuterman served as valuable mentors while I was learning to "do history"; I am blessed to consider them, along with many members of the American Journalism Historians Association, as colleagues and friends. Friend Marti Ford read much of the manuscript, and she and Michael Kyte provided great moral support.

Closer to home, I owe deep gratitude to my parents Jim and Edna, who more than anyone else prompted and nourished my love of learning and books. Brother Guy read every word of this manuscript and provided valuable academic and literary advice. Sister Carol is unfailingly honest and encouraging. "Kids" Grace, Kathy, and Gary helped keep me on track in numerous ways. Ruthie and Larry contradict in-law clichés with their support and friendship. Granddaughter Brooke is simply light and joy. And my wife, Joanna—my best editor and my best friend—for more than two decades has made life infinitely more fun and more interesting, and has through her love and understanding ultimately made this book and all of my most difficult work both possible and worth doing.

NOTE

1. Daniel Riffe and Alan Freitag, "A Content Analysis of Content Analysis: Twenty-Five Years of *Journalism Quarterly*," *Journalism and Mass Commu-nication Quarterly* 74 (Autumn 1997): 515–524.

CHAPTER 1

The Press and Social Battles

In August 1965, fires were intentionally set in two relatively unknown neighborhoods, an ocean apart. First, CBS cameras recorded American soldiers as they used Zippo lighters to burn a Vietnamese village. The same month, viewers saw rioting leave much of the Los Angeles neighborhood of Watts in flames. The two events demonstrated that America's twin struggles of the mid-twentieth century—civil rights at home, and the Vietnam War abroad—were far from over. They also helped illustrate why more Americans were now turning to television for most of their news than to their newspapers. That increasing "threat" of broadcast news, coupled with inescapable societal conflict, helped propel newspapers into new ways of reporting and presenting news—and prompted what might have been the best and most varied journalism of American history.

Though the military had been there in an advisory capacity much earlier, American ground troops arrived in Vietnam in 1965. Television news crews came with them. Those reporters, and the conflict itself, differed from those of previous wars in a number of ways. Many of the reporters seeking action were veterans of civil rights battles in America and perhaps less inclined to trust government officials than had been the reporters in other wars. Some print reporters definitely questioned the words and motives of military and political leaders more than those leaders, based on previous war experience, might have expected. Most important, though, was the fact that Vietnam was the first true television war. Americans did not have to lean toward their radios, waiting for Edward R. Murrow, H.V. Kaltenborn, or George Hicks to tell them what was happening, as they had during World War II. Instead, they leaned over TV dinners to see and hear Americans screaming in pain—and inflicting pain—on the nightly network news, which in 1963 had expanded from fifteen minutes to a half hour. And thanks to Telstar, launched in 1962, and later communication satellites, viewers could witness the pain soon after it was inflicted.

Because of the numbers of reporters, improvements in equipment, and unprecedented access, the American press probably covered the Vietnam War better than any war before or since. Some have argued that through the use of graphic images and the repeated reporting of death totals the news media sabotaged the American war effort. The most famous example is Morley Safer's 1965 report from Cam Ne, in which American soldiers used their lighters to burn down 150 houses. Enraged, President Johnson called CBS News President Frank Stanton to demand, "Frank, are you trying to fuck me?" Johnson knew the power of moving pictures, having earlier that year become the first U.S. president to give a State of the Union Address on prime-time television. Still, Safer had been invited on the mission by the Marines, who as they saw it simply were doing their job. Journalists also regularly reported heavy death tolls, and though military leaders distorted the figures the numbers still had a demoralizing impact. When the dead were American soldiers, American leaders and viewers complained.[1]

Even so, burning villages and blood continued to be staples of the television war. Television correspondents found that the most graphic images, especially those that focused on injured or killed Americans, were most likely to get on the air in the precious minutes each evening devoted to the war. On the print side of journalism, newsmagazines provided some of the most memorable images, though not as many of them as critics "remembered" after the fact. Their photos did not become more graphic as time went on. Oddly, perhaps the images that became most memorable did so because Americans actually saw relatively few similar images. In fact, graphic photos were far less common than were the types of horrifying incidents those photos depicted.[2]

At the same time, rugged living conditions coupled with the graphic nature of the war coverage caused some correspondents to question their own ethics—and the ethics of the war effort. Even correspondents who went to Vietnam favoring the war sometimes changed their minds after they found themselves surrounded by lying bureaucrats and death. "I wasn't in Vietnam more than three months when I realized this war was wrong," recalled journalist Jurate Kazickas, who had initially supported the war effort.[3] But reporters did not need to go into the jungle to become cynical. Journalists came to refer to daily briefings by military officials in Saigon as the "Five O'Clock Follies."[4]

Vietnam has been termed the first and last uncensored war, though censorship actually varied throughout the war and sometimes depended on who was in charge of a military operation. Some officers gladly took reporters on missions while others refused. One anonymous journalist was quoted as saying, inaccurately and hyperbolically, "This is the first war in American history in which newsmen are being barred from the battle area—in this case, air strikes, air bases and the fleet—to talk freely to the men involved." Associated Press General Manager Wes Gallagher complained: "Barring correspondents from free access to air bases and other military installations and providing a military 'escort' for every correspondent is clearly aimed not at security matters but at controlling what American fighting men might say. Such controls exceed anything done in the darkest days of World War II."[5]

Still, especially compared with later military efforts, the news media enjoyed remarkable freedom in Vietnam—probably largely because they had been so supportive of the war effort early on. For example, *Editor & Publisher* noted that at least one newspaper refused to put antiwar demonstrations on its front page, arguing: "We hope ALL Americans will soon realize, despite some of the leftist propaganda organs which say the contrary, that if America is to remain the leader of the Free World, the greatest nation in the world, this country must fight in Southeast Asia to halt the aggressor whose goal is world-wide communism and nothing less. And in plain English, that means world-wide slavery."[6]

Though many correspondents never left the city of Saigon, and others took the field only briefly, some surprised soldiers by their willingness to live in close contact with the military men they covered. Sometimes reporters also died with them—one writer reported hearing that combat photographers suffered the highest loss of life in the 1st Signal Brigade during one year of the war. More than fifty journalists, including two women, died in Vietnam during the conflict. Some shot back. "I know [shooting] is not my job, but part of my job is gaining the confidence of the troops I cover," noted *New York Times* correspondent Charles Mohr. "And I am reasonably convinced that had I prissily refused to shoot, they would have refused to take me along the next day."[7] Mohr also wrote that *Times* correspondent Johnny Apple "became so proficient with an M-16 rifle that the First Cavalry Division presented it to him."[8] Apple came so close to being shot that a bullet split the back of his trousers while he lay on his stomach. For his part, Mohr also said he "spent far more time running than shooting."[9]

Gun-wielding correspondents were only one issue that called reporters' ethics into question. The Newspaper Guild (the largest newspaper employees' union) faced credibility problems in 1967 after accepting nearly $1 million in Central Intelligence Agency subsidies for international programs. That action cast doubt upon the trustworthiness and independence of journalists working abroad, making an already-dangerous job potentially even riskier.

Until late in the war, newspapers generally reported the news from Vietnam matter-of-factly, avoiding the type of interpretation that would become common a few years later. Few opposed the war at first, and some newspapers began carrying a new pro-military syndicated comic strip, "Tales of the Green Berets." Later the tone changed. By mid-1967, newsmagazines were calling the conflict a stalemate, prompting Johnson to try to win media support for the war by allowing selective access to previously off-limits intelligence documents. Even so, many reporters in Vietnam opposed the war, and found that editors at home did, too. TV correspondent Liz Trotta wrote that she "was shocked to learn that if you did twenty interviews in the field with GI's, chances were those who knocked the war would survive the editor's scissors."[10]

A few news people opposed the war effort even at the beginning. One, famed columnist Walter Lippmann, debated it regularly with Joseph Alsop in the *New York Herald Tribune*. Besides nightly news reports, the three national networks (ABC, CBS, and NBC) aired numerous documentaries and hearings related to the war, and some of the sources in those reports questioned U.S. policy. Among Americans not working in the media, multitudes of protesters demonstrated throughout the conflict, often—especially in the later years—finding themselves in the news. College students engaged in antiwar rallies, "sit-ins," and "teach-ins," activities that many journalists (and the FBI) regarded as potentially dangerous, or, at best, silly.[11]

"I picketed with 'Peaceniks,'" one journalist wrote about his two months "under cover," during which he participated in "demonstrations against the war in Viet Nam, against poverty and against 'police brutality.'"[12] The resulting twelve-part series ran in more than fifty newspapers around the country. Journalists covered many college protests, and on May 4, 1970, all eyes turned to Kent State University. "Four students in a crowd pelting National Guardsmen with bricks and rocks were shot to death at Kent State University Monday when the troops opened fire during an antiwar demonstration. Two of the dead were coeds," read the Associated Press lead.[13] The *New York Times* was less inclined to blame the dead: "Four students at Kent State University, two of them women, were shot to death this afternoon by a volley of National Guard gunfire."[14]

Some antiwar protesters came from the military itself. A few started their own newspapers, supporting the efforts of groups such as Viet Nam Veterans Against the War. That group, founded in 1967, five years later boasted "over 30,000 members (not including the dead) and thousands of civilian supporters."[15] Similar to other "alternative publications" of the time, the military antiwar publications carried a mix of news, pictures, cartoons, and poetry such as a grim fourteen-stanza "collective poem" for which each stanza ended, "Napalm sticks to kids." The poem also described what became one of the powerful images of the war, a 1972 photo of a napalmed 9-year-old girl running naked down a road. That photo and a few others came to signify the horrific realities of war and contributed to antiwar sentiment that grew over time. An Associated Press photo and NBC both showed the execution of a Viet Cong guerrilla by a South Vietnamese general during the 1968 Tet offensive. The NBC report, featuring "the world's first televised death," drew a huge audience.

Another set of images was so horrifying that the photographer had trouble selling them. Finally, in late 1969, the *Cleveland Plain Dealer* and *Life* magazine ran stories and photos from the My Lai massacre, in which American soldiers killed scores of Vietnamese civilians, in 1968. Media historian Rodger Streitmatter later argued: "It was the racist nature of the fighting, the treating of the Vietnamese 'like animals,' that led inevitably to My Lai, and it was the reluctance of correspondents to report this racist and atrocious nature of the war that caused the My Lai story to be revealed not by a war correspondent, but by an alert newspaper reporter back in the United States—a major indictment of the coverage of the war."[16]

The massacre occurred after a U.S. Army company, which had suffered several casualties in trying to fight the elusive Viet Cong, entered the Vietnamese village of My Lai and began slaughtering apparently unarmed villagers. American soldiers killed more than 300 people—including old men, women, and children—with bullets, bayonets, and grenades. The story came out because a former soldier, who heard about the incident from other soldiers, tried to prompt investigations by Congress, the White House, and the Pentagon, and then told his story to reporter Seymour Hersch. Lt. William Calley was charged with murder a couple of months before the story appeared in America. He was convicted and sentenced to life in prison, but served less than five years. Polls found that most Americans disagreed with the verdict, apparently convinced that Calley was made a scapegoat in the incident. Even so, two weeks after the verdict came the first opinion poll in which the majority of Americans opposed the war.[17]

The My Lai massacre may have gone unnoticed by the press for more than a year, but the news media heavily covered another 1968 event. In the bloody Tet Offensive, the Viet Cong surprised American forces but were beaten back, suffering heavy losses. Dramatic network coverage managed to portray the battle as a victory for the Viet Cong, despite evidence to the contrary. Newspaper coverage of Tet may have been a bit more accurate than that of the networks, but it did little to stem the view that Americans had lost the battle. *Washington Post* Bureau Chief Peter Braestrup later concluded, "Rarely has contemporary crisis-journalism turned out, in retrospect, to have veered so widely from reality."[18] After the battle Walter Cronkite, the most-trusted news anchor (perhaps the most-trusted man) in America, traveled to Vietnam and then stepped out of his anchor role to somberly tell Americans that the war seemed "mired in stalemate." He later noted that the broadcast was only the second or third time he had offered a personal commentary. Within a few weeks, the American majority shifted from favoring the war to opposing it.[19]

Lyndon Johnson, blamed for the morass, announced that he would not run for reelection. Still, many of those in opposition showed up on the streets of Chicago in August, where the Democratic Convention erupted into several days of rioting. During the convention, police officers beat hundreds of protestors and dozens of journalists in the streets. CBS, ABC, NBC, *Life, Newsweek,* and several newspapers all had reporters or photographers beaten. A national audience saw a security officer punch CBS reporter Dan Rather on the convention floor, and activist Dick Gregory quipped, "I never thought I would see the day when it is more dangerous to walk along the street with a camera than with a beard."[20]

The *Chicago Tribune,* the city's largest newspaper which carried the front-page slogan "The American Paper for Americans", did little to quell concerns about violence. Stories and editorials alike conveyed a discernable conservative anti-"hippy" bent. An editorial on the first day of the convention revealed Democratic candidate Hubert Humphrey's childhood nickname of "Pinkie," noting, "But if readers jump to the logical conclusion that this appellation had something to do with Humphrey's political coloration, which is socialist, radical, and left wing, if not precisely 'Red,' they will be wrong."[21] Defending the security precautions that prompted television references to "Fort Chicago," the newspaper stated, "To Chicago authorities the greatest danger was not from the new left agitators but the possibility that they might arouse violence by black power groups."[22] Two days later, the *Tribune* noted: "The Negroes, we are glad to say, refused to be sucked into the revolution. ... The entire city should be glad its black citizens were decent, responsible citizens in a time of crisis."[23] The newspaper regularly blamed "outsiders" for instigating most of the violence, though the vast majority of those arrested lived in the Chicago area.[24]

The street violence at the convention was carried live throughout the country to TV viewers, and in newspaper and magazine photos: fresh images of chaos from a year that claimed Martin Luther King Jr, Robert Kennedy, and more U.S. soldiers than any other year of the war. Society seemed to be out of control, and newspapers both reported and bemoaned conflicts that went beyond the Vietnam War. A *Tribune* editorial blamed the deaths of King and Kennedy on rising liberalism, including drugs, coed dormitories, immodest dress, free speech movements, and parental permissiveness—signs that "Moral values are at the lowest level since the decadence of Rome."[25]

The *Chicago Tribune's* concerns about "black power" reflected another of the most troubling issues—lingering battles over civil rights and race that began in the 1950s and exploded in the 1960s. One Gannett editor argued, "The racial problem is the biggest story since the Civil War."[26] Martin Luther King Jr. and other civil rights leaders learned quickly to alert the media before making a stand; after all, taking a beating with no cameras present did little or nothing to advance the goals of the movement. At one time in America, of course, race-based lynchings had sometimes become public spectacles, where those involved struck smiling poses with burned and mutilated corpses. Well before 1965, lynchings had become relatively rare, and less openly accepted, but many egregious problems remained, and news cameras brought some of the other visible atrocities of the struggle—forced segregation, fire hoses, police dogs, club-wielding cops on horseback, and jeering white faces—into the living rooms of the nation. Television and newspaper pictures also went overseas, where Soviet-bloc propagandists made cold war use of them, providing more impetus for the U.S. government to intervene in a situation that, from the Civil War until the 1960s, it largely ignored. Many credit television cameras with bringing about the landmark Civil Rights Act of 1964 and the Voting Rights Act of 1965.[27]

No doubt as a reaction to the civil rights movement, news media around the country began to pay more attention to race in a number of areas. One was the question of when a person's race served as an appropriate identifier in news stories. Some editors asked for continued racial identification in wire service stories: "Include us among the bigots, for the majority of our readers and the mores of our community want to know the race of those creating the news. Much of the heinous crime news is created by those who are just doing 'what comes naturally,'" one editor wrote. "When race is included in a UPI story, those equalitarian evangelists who don't want it have only to stroke a pencil."[28] A typical 1965 Associated Press story from New York matter-of-factly started with the sentence, "A Negro who raped two women last month was seized early today, police said." Similar stories prompted a New York City assemblyman to introduce a bill that would have forbidden racial or ethnic descriptions of accused criminals.[29]

Some newspapers still ignored most of the accomplishments of blacks, for example, generally only including African Americans who were accused of crimes or who were nationally known entertainers or athletes. Some of those same publications dutifully reported the activities of "civic associations," at least some of which existed almost solely to "protect" white neighborhoods from encroachment by African Americans.[30] Regardless of their policies, of course, newspapers had little choice but to recognize an accomplished African American in 1967, when Johnson appointed Thurgood Marshall to the Supreme Court.

Race became the main story for newspapers throughout the country with 1960s riots in several cities, most notably the Watts section of Los Angeles. Years later, many Los Angeles reporters called the rioting the most interesting, and the most frightening, story of their careers. Triggered by a traffic stop, the August 1965 rioting lasted for six days and left at least thirty-four people dead, more than 1,000 injured, nearly 4,000 arrested, and hundreds of buildings destroyed. Calling forth images of the ongoing Vietnam War, the front page of the *Los Angeles Times* proclaimed: "21,000 Troops, Police Wage Guerrilla War."[31]

Both newspapers and television tended to cover the riots (and those that came later) as spot-news crime stories, with little examination of why the riots took place. As with the war in Vietnam, television brought the most exciting pictures and drew the most criticism. "With its insatiable appetite for live drama, television turned the riots into some kind of Roman spectacle," wrote *New Republic* critic John Gregory Dunne. "Not only did television exacerbate an already inflammatory situation, but also, by turning the riots into a Happening, may also have helped prolong them. One channel went so far as to score its riot footage with movie 'chase' music."[32] In future years, television regularly would be criticized for helping prolong or inspire news events ranging from student demonstrations to international terrorism.[33]

Cultural and racial gaps also complicated coverage of racial issues. Most reporters and editors had no more understanding of blacks in Watts than they did of the enemy in Vietnam. American daily newspapers employed a total of *twelve* black editorial staffers in 1952, but in the 1960s they began seeking more minority reporters. Still, in 1968 fewer than 200 black men and women worked on the nation's 1,749 daily newspaper staffs as reporters, photographers, copyreaders, and feature writers. That figure represented well under 1 percent of the editorial staffers, and the percentages in the South were even more disproportionate.[34]

The urge to improve their coverage left newspapers with another problem. With a new demand for black reporters, there were not enough applicants to go around. Fewer than 2 percent of 1968 journalism majors were black—meaning there were more than seven U.S. daily newspapers for each black news-editorial or photojournalism student.[35]

Faced with the need to recruit reporters of color, in 1966 the Newspaper Guild published a booklet titled *Careers for Negroes on Newspapers*, and newspapers throughout the country began training programs for would-be African American reporters. Sigma Delta Chi addressed the issue at its 1969 national convention, proposing a journalism council that would work full time on the issue of minority recruiting. Journalism schools began to benefit from an influx of minority scholarships, funded by news organizations. By that year, an estimated 3.9 percent of U.S. journalists were black—unfortunately, the apparent high-water mark, slightly higher than the total twenty years later.[36]

Still, many minority journalists who were hired found themselves distrusted and lonely. "It was just a white establishment," black journalist Susan Watson recalled about her job at the *Detroit Free Press* in 1965. "People talked openly about 'cheap murders,' which was a black person killing a black person. It was hard, real hard, because folks didn't expect you to succeed. There were photographers who didn't want me to ride in their cars and editors who wouldn't give me assignments because they 'knew' I'd fuck them up."[37]

Many African American journalists worked for the black press, which then boasted more than 170 newspapers. At least two black dailies, the *Chicago Defender*, founded in 1905, and the *Atlanta Daily World*, founded in 1928, each served approximately 30,000 readers during the 1960s, while New York's weekly *Amsterdam News* had a weekly circulation of more than 70,000. Some white journalists turned to the black press to try to improve understanding of racial issues. Of course, most white Americans read only their local mainstream daily, so their understanding of those issues was much more limited.[38]

In the continuing struggle to broaden journalism beyond white males, employers and job prospects alike battled difficult and conflicting issues such as tokenism, proportionality, fairness, and preferential treatment. Nonwhites typically found themselves less likely to be promoted than whites and were more likely to consider leaving journalism because of job dissatisfaction. Minority women, the group most likely to express a desire for a career in management, were least likely to be given managerial responsibilities. "Editors profess to believe in some notion of equality, but in a variety of comments and actions—subtle and overt—question the competence of the minorities on their staffs," black journalist Ellis Cose wrote.[39] Later minority journalists voiced similar concerns, noting that they sometimes were held to a higher standard than were white journalists. "An error on my part is poor journalism," a black *Cincinnati Inquirer* reporter said. "An error on a white man's part is just a typo."[40]

Despite minority under-representation and some conflict in newsrooms, racial division remained an important topic for the press. Openly racist stories became much less common, though sometimes portrayals that reinforced stereotypes about minority criminals and "pushy" black leaders persisted. Washington, D.C., Mayor Marion Berry and some of his supporters claimed in 1990 that racism contributed to his arrest on drug charges and to negative media coverage about him and the incident.

The *Los Angeles Times, Dallas Morning News, Atlanta Journal and Constitution,* and *Boston Globe* all won Pulitzers in the 1980s for examining race issues. The *Globe* spent sixteen months studying discrimination, employment, and "livability" in Boston and in other major cities, producing numerous stories—finding that it, too, fell short. A couple of years later, the *Globe* noted that the number of blacks at the newspaper had increased (though not in management positions). The *New York Times'* Howell Raines collected a 1992 feature-writing Pulitzer for a first-hand story about his childhood relationship with his family's black housekeeper. Television also offered meaningful depictions of race issues. Of particular note was a widely heralded 1985 international story, ABC's *Nightline* broadcast from South Africa. The following year, Bill Moyers produced a CBS documentary titled *The Vanishing Family— Crisis in Black America.*[41]

Three important stories of the 1990s, however, called to mind the racial conflicts of decades earlier while incorporating new issues. They were the stories of three African American men: O.J. Simpson, one of the most-recognized men in America; Clarence Thomas, a nominee for the highest court in the nation; and Rodney King, of whom almost no one had ever heard. Because the Simpson and Thomas cases were more about celebrity and spectacle than about race, they are discussed in more detail in a later chapter. But the case of King took journalists and television viewers back to Watts in 1965.

As with Watts, the story began with a traffic stop of a black man by white police officers. What was new about the case was how it began—a bystander videotaped the severe beating of King by Los Angeles police officers. The television networks extensively played the most inflammatory piece of the tape, contributing to a climate in which riots erupted after a jury found four white police officers not guilty of any charges related to the beating. Rioting in Los Angeles resulted in more than fifty deaths, thousands of injuries, the destruction of hundreds of buildings, and more than a billion dollars in damage. Two of the officers later were convicted and imprisoned on federal charges for their involvement in the beating. King, who became widely recognized and quoted for asking, "Can't we all just get along?" went on to have several more scrapes with the law.

American journalism was not just a primarily white institution through the 1960s. It was a white male institution, and racial minorities were not the only ones who had trouble getting jobs. Though male editors may have been less frightened of white women than of black men, no gender equivalent of Watts helped bring attention to any lack of understanding of women's issues. With little perceived need to understand women, editors saw little need to hire them. Women's concerns, whatever they might be, typically were not considered news.[42]

"You've never seen this newspaper scene before," stated a 1965 advertisement with a photo of "The Evening and Sunday Bulletin's news desk ... a ceiling's-eye view of four editors working to keep well-informed families in Greater Philadelphia even better informed."[43] In one respect, though, it was a scene well-known to women—each of the four editors was a man. Trade journals boasted rows of photographs of white male faces, and columns of type devoted to the accomplishments of journalists with masculine names. Want ads sought more of the same. Editorial jobs typically were listed under HELP WANTED—MEN. A typical ad read: "Six-day, afternoon paper, not afraid to tackle real depth reporting, needs a *man* who wants to direct reporters who do more than skim the surface. Not a job for a faint-hearted news*man* afraid to use a copy pencil. Right salary for dedicated news*man*."[44] (emphases added.) An ad might ask for "a man in his early 30's of solid character," or a "young man in twenties with college education." Roughly 10 percent of the *New York Times'* 6,000 employees were female, almost none of them in management or editorial positions. Women were paid significantly less money than men for the same positions, even after more time on the job, at newspapers throughout the country.

Gloria Steinem founded *Ms.* Magazine, which quickly became the leading voice of the Women's Movement, in 1972—the same year that Theta Sigma Phi, a 63-year-old organization for female college journalism students, became Women in Communications, Inc., voted to admit men, and called for more female journalism professors. Unfair treatment prompted a group of *New York Times* women, calling themselves the Women's Caucus, to demand better treatment for female employees. Two years later, the Women's Caucus sued in the case that became known as *Boylan v. New York Times*. Black employees filed a similar discrimination suit against the *Times* at the same time. The same year, the Equal Employment Opportunity Commission declared that the *Washington Post* "restricts the opportunities of female employees to occupy its higher paying positions." Women at newspapers, broadcast networks, and television stations around the country began filing lawsuits.[45]

Though newspapers had complained about a lack of minority candidates, the same could not be said about women. By the mid-1960s one university journalism department chairman noted that close to half of the students in journalism programs were female, compared to "six or seven to one" just fifteen years earlier. "Journalism may be losing its manly spirit," he complained.[46] He predicted that the trend would continue. "They won't go away; they're women," he argued. "Any officer who has worked with women in uniform, regardless of rank, knows that most of them need a male colleague looking over their shoulders or available for such duty on short notice. Journeyman reporters who have covered a story with a woman know the pattern."[47]

With that kind of bias, it was no surprise when Sigma Delta Chi voted 96–47 against a 1966 proposal to admit women—despite the fact that just a few months earlier, a trade publication ran a front-page story lauding a female college newspaper editor's fight to protect her sources. That student editor failed to make Sigma Delta Chi's annual college awards list, restricted to "outstanding male journalism graduates." Three years later, the organization voted to admit women. In 1971 the National Press Club finally followed suit.[48]

Women journalists who found jobs commonly were saddled with producing so-called women's pages that targeted women primarily as stay-at-home consumers. The sections covered shopping tips, recipes, fashion, and society news. Editors assumed that women lacked interest in weightier issues, even though a third of housewives were in the workforce, women voted at about the same rate as men, and most of the soldiers fighting and dying in Vietnam had mothers at home.[49]

A typical trade publication ad seeking a "young woman, J-grad or experienced," established the prospective reporter's limited prospects up front, seeking someone "with imagination, resourcefulness and ability to write features and women's news." When Liz Trotta (later a longtime television journalist) joined the *Chicago Tribune* as a section reporter in the early 1960s, the main newsroom had two women reporters. One wrote features; the other produced stories about pets.[50]

Women commonly were noted at least as much for their appearance and other "feminine attributes" as for their activities. Typical examples included a full-page trade journal photo of a woman in fishing gear that asks, "This is a Philadelphia society editor?" before saying surf-casting editor and pheasant hunter Ruth Seltzer was "a handsome indefatigable woman...who manages to get to and report on everything from meetings of the Numismatic Society to Fernanda Wanamaker's latest party for her chimpanzees. Nobody knows how she does it."[51] An Alabama newspaper included photos of women in its classified advertising department, and readers were invited to vote for the favorite to become "Miss Advisor." A typical drawing in an *Editor & Publisher* ad showed an editor addressing a buxom "Miss Sharp," apparently a secretary. The same publication even described UPI war correspondent Betsy Halstead, who in 1965 had already been on combat missions, as "a perky five-foot-two-inch, 110-pound redhead" and "a brave girl [she was 23, older than many of the soldiers] ... doing a man's job."[52] The article also noted the date of her marriage, though it was two years earlier and irrelevant to the story.

In 1969, a woman sportswriter who "invaded" the "male domain" of covering sports admitted that after being insulted by a sportswriter for a Chicago newspaper, she "decided to go home and lose a few pounds."[53] An article about another sportswriter started out: "She's young. She's pretty. And she's an expert on pro football.... How does an attractive girl become an expert on pro football? By going out with boys, says Elinor."[54] That reporter, the first female member of the Pro Football

Writers Association of America, compared her efforts to enter the press box to a famous temperance campaign: "Carrie Nation set about her daily work carrying an axe. I carry a typewriter. So far Carrie has been much more successful."[55] She noted that her male colleagues discriminated against her more than her sources did. Even her male "supporters" called forth differences. After she was assigned her own separate row of seats, so the "press box technically remained inviolate," one male ally noted: "It was the type of ploy worthy of a female. I hate to see man winning a skirmish vs. woman by using female strategy."[56] It would be several more years before women reporters were allowed access into locker rooms.

Television stations and networks began to hire more women as reporters during the 1960s but treated women much the same as newspapers did, relegating them to "women's issues" and light features, and barring them from hard news or management. Many started their hiring of females with "weather girls"—cheerful, attractive young women who often wore short skirts while pointing at weather maps. Female reporters and anchorwomen followed the weather girls, though sometimes the hiring criteria did not change much. Physical appearance still mattered more for women than for men, a priority that existed for viewers as well as for managers. One female anchor said her male general manager described the job hunt that she won as a "Miss America search," while audiences "ask my co-anchor about the latest 'hot' story, and they ask me about my clothes!"[57]

One place, oddly, that women often did find themselves on more equal footing with men was in coverage of the war in Vietnam. In all, the U.S. military accredited 267 women as reporters. Because of the relatively uncensored nature of the war, "If one possessed a visa and a plane ticket, one could go," noted historian Carolyn Kitch. "Once there, getting accredited as a war correspondent was not difficult, either."[58]

Newspapers throughout the country were glad to get Vietnam news from wherever they could. One woman correspondent, who previously "had never written anything in my life," recalled: "I called up the government office in charge and found out what you needed for accreditation. They sent me a form. It was so incredibly easy. I found three news organizations willing to vouch that they would use my work and that I was a bona fide journalist. . . . With this, I became an accredited war correspondent."[59]

Even in Vietnam, female correspondents often were expected by editors and military officers to cover "softer" stories about orphans, refugees, and the lives of men in camp away from the fighting. In some cases, military officers were more hesitant to take female reporters along on an operation than they were men, and having the women along may have caused some consternation. "The men are there to fight a war and I get the feeling that they have to look out for me," said reporter Becky Halstead.[60] However, another strongly disagreed with the view that "chivalry will get to the point where they will be risking their lives," saying battle equalized things: "I cannot tell you how many bruises I have sustained from men pushing me out of the way, diving for foxholes, knocking me over. It's self-preservation. Basic human instinct. Fuck chivalry."[61]

Back in the United States, though kept off "hard news" pages at home, women's page editors did manage to use their sections to cover important issues overlooked elsewhere in their newspapers. Those issues included poverty, childcare, birth control, and the growing Women's Movement. The same topics also sometimes were covered by the growing alternative press, which many hoped would provide more journalistic jobs for women. Those hopes largely went unrealized. Alternative publications, like to their mainstream counterparts, were almost all controlled by men. In addition, the open sexual tone of the publications, some of which turned to overt pornography, objectified women at least as much as the mainstream media.

A few "women's liberation" publications began to pop up. *It Ain't Me Babe*, started in Berkeley in January 1970, was one of the first. It was followed quickly by *off our backs* in Washington, D.C., which would become the longest-surviving and perhaps the most respected newspaper of the Women's Movement. "We must strive to get off our backs, and with the help of our sisters to oppose and destroy that system which fortifies the supremacy of men while exploiting the mass for the profit of the few," stated the newspaper's mission statement. "Our position is not anti-men but pro-women."[62] Feminists also staged a 1970 "sit-in" at the offices of the *Ladies Home Journal*, which finally agreed to turn over eight pages of its August issue to the activists. Much of the press generally ignored or downplayed the Women's Movement, but as it continued to pick up steam, journalism—as with the issues of race and opposition to the war—would follow, though not wholeheartedly until pushed by lawsuits.[63]

Though not involved in any of the litigation, one woman did noticeably succeed—Barbara Walters. She left NBC's *Today* show in 1976 to join ABC as Harry Reasoner's co-anchor, becoming the first newscaster to make $1 million per year (half of which came from the news division for her co-host duties, half from the entertainment division for news specials). The experiment did not last long, and other news media widely criticized ABC for placing entertainment values over news values, despite the fact that Walters previously had covered significant news events that included President Richard Nixon's historic 1972 trip to China. Of course, ABC was in third place of the three networks in terms of ratings and therefore more likely to experiment. The only other time a woman has taken a regular seat at the hallowed anchor desk was during a two-year mid-1990s pairing of Connie Chung and Dan Rather at then-third-place CBS.

Rather was less critical of Walters than some, recognizing her as a gifted interviewer whom "no one outworks." He, too, questioned her salary, however, writing that "no one in this business is [worth $1 million], no matter what or how many shows they do, unless they find a cure for cancer on the side."[64] A few years later, Rather signed a $7 million, six-year contract to anchor *CBS Evening News*.[65]

Incidentally, as news organizations began to hire more women in the 1960s and 1970s, many were similar to Chung, Charlayne Hunter-Gault, and Carole Simpson—credible newswomen who also happened to be members of racial minorities. An organization could then cover two affirmative action bases, race and gender, with one new employee, while (in the view of management) perhaps also getting someone who understood "race issues." The hiring of such "two-fers" (as in two-for-one) sometimes caused tension in the newsroom. Simpson, who in 1965 was the first woman to broadcast hard news in Chicago, recalled: "I walk in there, black female, straight out of college, no commercial experience, and there was great resentment among these white male colleagues of mine. . . . They knew it was because I was black and because I was female and I was different."[66] Later critics also suggested that television viewers (at least in the view of TV executives) would be more accepting of a white man paired with a woman of color than vice versa. True or not, newspapers and television stations did hire increasing numbers of women, but the number of black male broadcasters actually began to decrease after the mid-1970s.[67]

National network news has stuck to the old anchor format. Middle-aged white men generally have manned the anchor desks, while female and minority anchors have been relegated to mornings, weekends, short-term substitutions, and magazine shows. Except for the Walters and Chung experiments, the only other exception before 2005—when Latina newswoman Elizabeth Vargas became one of two co-anchors to replace Peter Jennings at ABC—came in 1978 when ABC hired Max Robinson as one of three nightly co-anchors (a format used for about five years). The networks did hire a few on-air men and women of color in the early 1970s, including Simpson at NBC. CBS hired Chung, Bernard Shaw, and Ed Bradley, who just a few years before in 1968 had been the only black man on radio in New York and who in 1974 was wounded while covering the war in Cambodia. Off-camera, women made gains, but few minorities were hired at either the local or network level.[68]

The *New York Times* finally settled with the Women's Caucus in 1977 (NBC and *Reader's Digest* had previously agreed to settlements) and agreed to place women in one of every eight top corporate positions during a four-year period. The paper also agreed that women would fill

25 percent of the top news-editorial positions within five years. In 1983, the Associated Press also settled differences with women employees (and black reporters). Still, neither women nor racial minorities have ever held news positions in either newspapers or magazines, especially in editorial or management positions, in numbers comparable to their percentage of the American population.

The 1960s also brought increased attention and eventually more respect to another American minority group, a group much less difficult to identify and even more controversial than women or racial minorities—homosexuals. Though a gay subculture had existed in American cities for at least two decades and President Dwight D. Eisenhower issued a federal order banning homosexuals from holding government jobs, most Americans remained largely unaware of their existence. A few small-circulation publications discussed gay issues, but unlike with women or racial minorities, no one could begin to tell how many gays worked in the mainstream press. They likely would have been less welcome than women or African Americans in the workplace, and most gays stayed "in the closet." Family friendly mainstream newspapers generally ignored the issue of homosexuality, though some published the names of men who were arrested in raids of gay bars, destroying the careers and families of some of those who were rounded up. One such raid, however, became recognized as the beginning of an organized American "gay rights" movement.

In June 1969, New York police raided the Stonewall Inn to enforce a liquor license violation. Some patrons—many of them apparently "drag queens" dressed as women—resisted, taunting and attacking police officers. The conservative tabloid *New York Daily News* later bombastically reported: "Queen Power exploded with all the fury of a gay atomic bomb. Queens, princesses and ladies-in-waiting began hurling anything they could get their polished, manicured fingernails on. Bobby pins, compacts, curlers, lipstick tubes and other femme fatale missiles were flying in the direction of the cops. The war was on."[69]

Not surprisingly, the *New York Times* used less flamboyant language, reporting, "Hundreds of young men went on a rampage . . . after a force of plainclothesmen raided a bar that police said was wellknown [sic] for its homosexual clientele." The ten- paragraph, page 33 *Times* story listed items thrown at police as "bricks, bottles, garbage, pennies and a parking meter," while matter-of-factly reporting that street demonstrations continued for several days.[70]

With a more liberal perspective, an office in the same neighborhood as the Stonewall Inn, and two reporters on the scene, the alternative newspaper the *Village Voice* probably did the best job of reporting the incident. It also was the most prophetic of the newspapers: Despite still relying on stereotypical language and potentially offensive phrases such as "the forces of faggotry," the *Voice* concluded one of its first two Stonewall articles with: "Watch out. The liberation is under way."[71]

What became known as the "Stonewall riot" helped lead to the formation of several gay and lesbian organizations, some of which worked to become more visible in the press (and therefore presumably more accepted by society). Homosexual activists learned from, and sometimes acted with, other protest groups. Some began producing their own newspapers. In 1973, the American Psychological Association voted to declassify homosexuality as a mental illness, and many states decriminalized homosexual behavior. Fears and prejudices over the issue exploded again a few years later, however, when the first few cases of a frightening health crisis began appearing among gay men.

The first few U.S. cases of what became known as Acquired Immune Deficiency Syndrome appeared in homosexual men during the late 1970s. Even after Americans started becoming aware of the disease, no one yet understood it and many still tried to ignore it. Many considered AIDS a homosexual disease, and some went so far as to suggest that God was using the AIDS to punish gays for wicked acts. Most scientists were more cautious, though even some of them at first called the disease Gay-Related Immune Deficiency. The AIDS virus finally was identified in 1983, and actor Rock Hudson's death from the disease two years later demonstrated a consistent truth—the death of one celebrity could bring much more press attention to an issue than could the deaths of hundreds of less-known people.[72]

Many in the gay community criticized the press for ignoring or downplaying the AIDS crisis, though the *New York Times*, the *Philadelphia Inquirer*, *Newsweek*, and NBC covered the epidemic better than others. Awareness especially was increasing in San Francisco, a city with a large openly homosexual population where Randy Shilts worked for the *San Francisco Chronicle*. He spent years researching and reporting on the AIDS explosion for the *Chronicle*, eventually producing a groundbreaking book before dying of the disease himself in 1994.[73]

Throughout the crisis, most journalists generally avoided "scare coverage" or stereotyping gays, focusing primarily on providing information about the disease. Many newspapers may have given the issue less coverage than it warranted, but even President Ronald Reagan did not publicly address AIDS until a year after the first international conference on the disease had taken place in Atlanta. Right or wrong, many journalists ignored AIDS largely for the same reason they have always ignored some issues—because they thought the disease had little relevance and posed little risk to most of their readers. They were wrong, of course. By the end of 1988 the total number of U.S. AIDS deaths was about the same as the number of Americans killed in Vietnam, and it was growing rapidly. The number would surpass a half million by the end of 2002 and had hit virtually every sector of American society, homosexual and heterosexual.[74]

NOTES

1. William M. Hammond, *Reporting Vietnam: Media & Military at War* (Lawrence, Kan.: University Press of Kansas, 1998).
2. Michael D. Sherer, "Vietnam War Photos and Public Opinion," *Journalism Quarterly* 66 (Summer 1989): 391–394, 530; Oscar Patterson III, "Television's Living Room War in Print: Vietnam in the News Magazines," *Journalism Quarterly* 61 (Spring 1984) 35–39, 136.
3. Jurate Kazickas, quoted in Christine Martin, "War Stories: Women Correspondents Battle to Cover the Vietnam Conflict," paper presented at 1997 American Journalism Historians Association Conference.
4. Edward Jay Epstein, *News from Nowhere: Television and the News* (New York: Random House, 1973); Phillip Knightley, *The First Casualty: From the Crimea to Vietnam: The War Correspondent as Hero, Propagandist, and Myth Maker* (New York: Harvest Books, 1975).
5. Unnamed author, "U.S. Officials Hamper Reporters in Viet Nam," *Editor & Publisher*, March, 5, 1966.
6. "Anti-Viet Nam Rallies Go Off Front Page," *Editor & Publisher*, 26 February 1966. Also see Knightley, *The First Casualty*; Daniel C. Hallin, *The "Uncensored War": The Media and Vietnam*, paperback ed. (Berkeley: University of California Press, 1989); Dan B. Curtis, " Vietnam War Coverage," in Michael D. Murray, ed., *Encyclopedia of Television News* (Phoenix: Oryx Press, 1999).
7. Charles Mohr, quoted in "The New York Times Shot Back," *Editor & Publisher*, 5 March 1966, 47.
8. Ibid.
9. Ibid. Also see John Laurence, *The Cat from Hue: A Vietnam War Story* (New York: Public Affairs, 2002); Ruth Adler, ed., *The Working Press* (New York: Bantam, 1970).
10. Liz Trotta, *Fighting for Air: In the Trenches with Television News* (New York, Simon & Schuster, 1991). Also see James Landers, "Specter of Stalemate: Vietnam War Perspectives in *Newsweek, Time*, and *U.S. News & World Report*, 1965–1968," *Journalism History* 19 (Summer 2002): 13–38; Ray Erwin, "The Green Berets' Land on Comics Page," *Editor & Publisher*, February, 12, 1966. The same issue of the publication carried a two-page, green-headlined ad for the strip.
11. Harry D. Marsh and David R. Davies, "The Media in Transition, 1945–1974," in Wm. David Sloan, ed., *The Media in America: A History*, 5th ed. (Northport, Ala.: Vision Press, 2002).
12. Jerry LeBlanc, "A Newsman's Assignment: I Picketed with 'Peaceniks,' *The Quill*, March 1966, 24–26.
13. Associate Press Website, accessed at http://wire.ap.org/APpackages/history/history05/0504kentstateSTY.html. July, 14, 2002.
14. John Kifner, "4 Kent State Students Killed by Troops," *New York Times*, Late City Edition email May, 4, 1970.
15. John Boychuck, "Rough History of V.V.A.W.," *Helping Hand*, August 1972. According to the nameplate, the Mountain Home (Idaho) Air Base publication was "written, drawn, edited and published for and by Gs—with a little help from their friends"; also see undated first issue printed sometime in 1971.

16. Rodger Streitmatter, *Mightier than the Sword: How the News Media Have Shaped American History*. (Boulder, Colo.: Westview Press, 1997). Also see "The Massacre at Mylai," *Life*, December 5, 1969; Knightley, *The First Casualty*, 390.

17. For a comprehensive summary of the case, including public opinion polls regarding the verdict, see a web summary by the University of Missouri-Kansas City, http://www.law.umkc.edu/faculty/projects/ftrials/mylai.htm (accessed May 6, 2006).

18. Quoted in Winant Sidle, "Unfortunate Stupidity," *Media Studies Journal* 12, (Fall 1998): 13.

19. Streitmatter, *Mightier than the Sword*; Walter Cronkite, *A Reporter's Life* (New York: Alfred A. Knopf, 1996). Once or twice previously Cronkite had commented about the importance of the First Amendment.

20. Dick Gregory, quoted in "Dems Insure Nixon Victory, Gregory Says," *Chicago Tribune*, August, 29, 1968. Also see "City to Probe Police Beating of Newsmen: 24 File Protests," *Chicago Tribune*, August, 28, 1968.

21. Editorial, "Hubert Humphrey's Record," *Chicago Tribune*, August, 25, 1968. The nickname came from Humphrey's rosy complexion.

22. Editorial, " 'Fortress Chicago,' " *Chicago Tribune*, August, 29, 1968.

23. Editorial, "Responsible Citizens in a Crisis," *Chicago Tribune*, August, 29, 1968.

24. Editorial, "Name Persons Arrested in Disturbances," *Chicago Tribune*, August, 30, 1968.

25. Editorial, "Another Day of Mourning," *Chicago Tribune*, 6 June 1968.

26. Vincent S. Jones, "How Rochester Reacted," *Nieman Reports*, June 1965.

27. Streitmatter, *Mightier than the Sword*.

28. J. Raymond Long letter to *U.P.I. Reporter*, quoted in "At Issue: Name? Age? Address? Race?" *Columbia Journalism Review*, Spring 1965.

29. J.Raymond, "At Issue: Name? Age? Address? Race?"

30. Samuel H. Day, interview by author, August, 18, 1995.

31. "Negro Riots Rage On; Death Toll 25: 21,000 Troops, Police Wage Guerrilla War; 8 p.m. Curfew Invoked," *Los Angeles Times*, 15 August 1965. Also see oral histories of California journalists from the California State University, Fullerton, Oral History Program and the Southern California Journalism Oral History Project, California State University, Northridge.

32. John Gregory Dunne, "TV's Riot Squad," *The New Republic*, 11 September 1965, 26.

33. Carolyn Martindale, "Selected Newspaper Coverage of Causes of Black Protest," *Journalism Quarterly* 66 (Winter 1989): 920–923, 964; Earnest L. Perry, "Coverage of Crime," in W. David Sloan and Lisa Mullikin Parcell, eds., *American Journalism: History Principles, Practices* (Jefferson, N.C.: McFarland & Company, 2002), 189–197.

34. Andrew Jaffe, "Viewed Behind Guns," *Columbia Journalism Review*, Fall 1965; Armistead S. Pride, "Opening Doors for Minorities," *Quill*, November 1968.

35. Pride, "Opening Doors."

36. Edward J. Trayes, "Recruiting Black Journalists: They're Wanted, but Not Available," *Quill*, April 1969, 16; "Women are 'In'; SDX Name's the Same," *Quill*, December 1969; "Speaking Out About Crime," *Chicago Tribune*, 6 December 1971; David H. Weaver and G. Cleveland Wilhoit, *The American Journalist in the 1990s: U.S. News People at the End of an Era* (Mahwah, N.J.: Lawrence Erlbaum, 1996).

37. Susan Watson, quoted in Jill Nelson, "Integration When? A Tale of Three Cities," *Columbia Journalism Review*, January/February 1987.

38. Bernard Roshco, "What the Black Press Said Last Summer," *Columbia Journalism Review*, Fall 1967.

39. Ellis Cose, "Keeping the Faith," *Quill*, October 1985, 8–13.

40. Unnamed journalist quoted in Stephen J. Simurda, "Living With Diversity: Talking it Through in Three Newsrooms," *Columbia Journalism Review*, January/February 1992, 19–24.

41. Robert M. Entman, "Blacks in the News: Television, Modern Racism and Cultural Change," *Journalism Quarterly* 69, Summer 1992, 341–361; "Integrating Boston's Work Force," *Boston Globe*, 5 May 1983; Jonathan Kaufman and Ross Gelbspan, "More Blacks are at Globe, but None in Senior Ranks," *Boston Globe*, 12 November 1985; also see Carolyn Martindale, "Coverage of Black Americans in Four Major Newspapers," *Newspaper Research Journal* 11 (Summer 1990): 96–112.

42. Association of Women in Communications website, http://www.womcom.org.

43. Full-page advertisement for *Philadelphia Bulletin* in *Editor & Publisher*, 15 January 1965.

44. Classified advertising section, *Editor & Publisher*, 2 January 1965.

45. Maurine H. Beasley and Sheila J. Gibbons, *Taking Their Place: A Documentary History of Women and Journalism* (Washington, D.C.: American University Press, 1993), 239.

46. John B. Barron, "The Paper Dolls are Paper Tigers—but They're Crowding Journalism Schools," *Quill*, September 1965, 12–15.

47. Ibid.

48. "Convention Votes Down Admission of Women, Keeps Society Name," *Quill*, December 1966, 32; Ann Sullivan, "Annette Buchanan's Fight to Protect a Reporter's Sources," *Quill*, August 1966, 12–17; "Women are 'In.' "

49. Bureau of Labor Statistics website: http://www.bls.gov; Cynthia Harrison, "From the Home to the House: The Changing Role of Women in American Society," *Electronic Journal of the U.S. Information Agency*, June 1997: http://usinfo.state.gov/journals/itsv/0597/ijse/tocsv.htm.

50. Classified advertising section, *Editor & Publisher*, 2 January 1965.; Trotta, *Fighting for Air*, 21.

51. Advertisement for *Philadelphia Bulletin* in *Editor & Publisher*, 2 January 1965.

52. "Where a Brave Girl is Doing a Man's Job," *Editor & Publisher*, 25 December 1965. Also see advertisements in *Editor & Publisher*, 30 January 1965.

53. Lynda Morstadt, "She, too, Invaded Male Domain," *Quill*, December 1969, 11.

54. Untitled sidebar article, *Quill*, December 1969, 9.

55. Elinor Kaine, "A Woman's Right to Write and Sit with Men in Press Box," *Quill*, December 1969, 8–11.

56. Ibid., 10.

57. Quoted in Anthony J. Ferri and Jo E. Keller, "Perceived Career Barriers for Female Television News Anchors," *Journalism Quarterly* 63 (Autumn 1986): 463–467. Also see Marion Marzolf, *Up from the Footnote: A History of Women Journalists* (New York: Hastings House, 1977).

58. Carolyn Kitch, "Women in Journalism," in Sloan and Parcell, *American Journalism*, 87–96. Also see Beasley and Gibbons, *Taking Their Place*.

59. Kazickas, quoted in "War Stories," 22.

60. Betsy Halstead, quoted in "Where a Brave Girl is Doing a Man's Job."

61. Kazickas, quoted in "War Stories," 26.

62. Mission statement, *off our backs*, printed in first issue and on the web site of the newspaper, which survives: http://www.igc.org/oob/Mission.htm, 22 July 2002.

63. Laura Ashley and Beth Olson, "Constructing Reality: Print Media's Framing of the Women's Movement, 1966 to 1986," *Journalism & Mass Communication Quarterly* 75 (Summer 1998): 263–277.

64. Dan Rather, *The Camera Never Blinks: Adventures of a TV Journalist* (New York: William Morrow, 1977), 272.

65. Doug James, *Walter Cronkite: His Life and Times* (Brentwood, Tenn.: 1991).

66. Carole Simpson, interviewed by Donita Moorhus, 19 November 1992, Women in Journalism Oral History Project transcript, Washington Press Club Foundation, Washington, D.C.

67. Vernon A. Stone, "Trends in the Status of Minorities and Women in Broadcast News," *Journalism Quarterly* 65 (Summer 1988): 288–293.

68. Robert C. Maynard Institute for Journalism Education website, http://www.maynardije.org; Vernon A. Stone, "Changing Profiles of News Directors of Radio and TV Stations, 1972–1986," *Journalism Quarterly* 64 (Winter 1987): 745–749; J. Fred MacDonald, *Blacks and White TV: African Americans in Television Since 1948*, 2nd ed. (Chicago: Nelson-Hall, 1992).

69. Jerry Lisker, "Homo Nest Raided, Queen Bees are Stinging Mad," *New York Daily News*, 6 July 1969.

70. "Four Policemen Hurt in 'Village' Raid," *New York Times*, 29 June 1969.

71. Lucian Truscott IV, "View from Outside: Gay Power Comes to Sheridan Square," *Village Voice*, 3 July 1969; Howard Smith, "View from Inside: Full Moon Over the Stonewall," *Village Voice*, 3 July 1969.

72. Rodger Streitmatter, "AIDS: 'It's Just a Matter of Time,'" *Quill*, May 1984, 22–25, 27; Philip J. Hilts, "2 Mysterious Diseases Killing Homosexuals," *Washington Post*, 30 August 1981; David Durack, quoted in United Press International, "Homosexuals Found Particularly Liable to Common Viruses," *New York Times*, 10 December 1981.

73. "Covering the Epidemic: AIDS in the News Media, 1985–1996," *Columbia Journalism Review*, July/August 1996, supplement; Richard J. Meislin, "Jeffrey Schmalz: Fanning a Spark of Change at the *New York Times*," *Media Studies Journal* (Spring/Summer 2000): 102–105; Robin Marantz Henig, "AIDS: A New Disease's Deadly Odyssey," *New York Times*, 6 February 1983; Randy Shilts, *And the Band Played On: Politics, People and the AIDS Epidemic*, paperback ed. (New York: St. Martin's 1999).

74. Reagan addressed AIDS in 1987, calling it "public health enemy No. 1" and appointing a national AIDS commission, though he drew fire for at first excluding any known gays from the commission. By then, more than 20,000 Americans had died of the disease. Gerald M. Boyd, "Reagan Urges Abstinence for Young to Avoid AIDS," *New York Times*, 2 April 1987. About 58,000 Americans died in the Vietnam War. AIDS figures from the Centers for Disease Control and Prevention *HIV/AIDS Surveillance Report 2002*. Also see Larry Bush, "Journalists aren't Asking the Tough Questions," *Newspaper Research Journal* 11 (Summer 1990): 50–52.

CHAPTER 2

New Kinds of News Media

To the frequent chagrin of those in the print media, in the second half of the twentieth century, television news seemed to be everywhere—from the front lines of the Vietnam War and civil disturbances to outer space, when the 1969 Apollo 11 lunar landing became perhaps the most-watched event in history.

Print journalists were not always sure how to handle the threat of television news. Many essentially tried to ignore it, though some crossed the line and became TV reporters. Newspaper editors sometimes refused to run program schedules and even went so far as to black out station call letters on microphones that appeared in news photos. Television journalist Liz Trotta noted that on-the-scene sabotage included "pulling out plugs at news conferences, stepping in front of the lens at a critical point in a statement, even cutting cables."[1] Some newspapers pledged not to participate in multimedia news conferences, except in extreme cases: "The citizen deserves complete and comprehensive information, and he is unlikely to get the type he needs from meetings that take on the atmosphere of a stage," said *Utica Daily Press* editor Gilbert Smith.[2] "We are asked to argue that just because another business seeks the same dollars, it fills the same role. Can we believe that?" scoffed another editor. "In effect, we are asked to argue against our profession itself, against the uniqueness of the local, printed medium."[3]

Convinced of their own superior product, newspaper editors had trouble believing many people watched TV news, though at least one of their trade journals accepted full-page advertisements for new color televisions. Print journalists complained that television, by focusing on pictures and brief snippets of information, distorted events. "A picture may be worth a thousand words ... but at least *we* write those words," one newspaper reporter complained.[4] Newspaper people also regularly complained about a lack of depth with TV news and its alleged unwillingness to explore controversy—a claim that gained validity as network documentaries, still a staple of early 1960s network programming, began to disappear. In their place came TV newsmagazines, the most notable of which, *60 Minutes*, first appeared in 1968. In truth, television producers stayed away from controversy in part because of the Federal Communication Commission's "Fairness Doctrine." The doctrine, upheld by the Supreme Court in the 1969 *Red Lion* decision, required stations to notify and provide airtime for individuals who were personally attacked on air, or who were the subject of broadcast editorials. Newspapers never faced the same restriction.

Those in television recognized that print and broadcast news played different roles. "For one example, television can place before your eyes the experience of a Winston Churchill funeral in all its pageantry, but it will not tell you about the death of your neighbor," said NBC board chairman Walter Scott.[5] At the local level, those in both kinds of journalism knew television could not match the newspaper in chronicling the daily public business of the courts and local government offices. Not all broadcasters themselves were sure of what role they wanted to play in covering the news, and their views varied according to their interests. Some network affiliates elected to run movies rather than 1966 election coverage.[6]

Newspaper editors took delight in predicting the eventual demise of television as a news medium, and even some broadcasters expressed concerns about their future. Others worried about their effect. "Surveys indicate that many viewers and listeners tune in only to find out in the first 30 seconds of a news broadcast that the world has not yet come to an end," said venerable news anchor Walter Cronkite. "The problem is that we do such a good job, such a slick job in our presentation of the news that we have deluded the public into a belief that they are getting all they need to know from us."[7]

Traditional print journalism faced other competitive battles besides television and a few news magazines. All-news radio appeared in a few places, though it did not become a significant news factor until the mid-1970s or a political phenomenon until a decade later. Lacking the visual impact of television, its effect on newspapers was negligible.[8]

Free papers, which frequently consisted mostly of advertising, also began popping up to serve some communities, though by far the most interesting and pervasive news competitor of the period was the "alternative newspaper" of the so-called underground press. Though desktop publishing was still years in the future, offset printing and press-type (letters that could be rubbed off of a plastic sheet and "pressed" onto a page) made publishing much easier and cheaper than printing with hot lead type. The technology especially suited smaller publications. And, as evidenced by Berkeley's Free Speech Movement of 1964, political activists sought new outlets for expression. The 1960s and early 1970s saw the publication of perhaps thousands of alternative newspapers, some of which lasted only one issue. "Such papers are like wildflowers which spring up, bloom for a quick day, then wither away," wrote the editor of one.[9]

Many of the newspapers came from college campuses, where students wanted to be politically active and had the time to do so. They did not have much access to the mainstream news media, however, so they developed their own. The Vietnam War often served as a focal point, and almost all of the new publications were politically liberal in nature. Besides the war, stories focused on topics that included racial equality, socioeconomic issues, women's rights, the environment, sexual openness, drugs, gay rights, and labor issues. As journalist Jacob Brackman wrote about a New York paper, *The East Village Other*: "The *Other* doesn't separate fact from opinion. Its journalism is unabashedly, militantly interpretive: pro pot, peace, sex, psychedelics and subversion; anti most of what remains in switched-off American society."[10]

A dedication to single issues such as women's rights, gay rights, or the environment drove some of the alternative papers. Though publications dedicated to those issues were not new, the 1960s versions were more numerous, more strident, and more militant in their demands. In all, as noted by the *Seattle Post-Intelligencer*, they ranged "all the way from little sheets explaining how to make a Molotov cocktail to large publications that are so serious they are Dullsville."[11] One thing they tended to have in common was disdain for the "establishment" press. "Their charges run from 'bland' or 'ignorant' all the way to 'fascist,' 'hypocritical' and 'brainwashery,'" editorialized the P-I, quoting nationally syndicated underground columnist John Wilcox, who "insists that 'big-city dailies are a corrupt advertising medium; they've forfeited their right to be called newspapers.'"[12]

In most cases, "underground" was a more romantic than factual characterization. Despite their often-angry tone, few publications were threatened by anything more sinister than poor management or a lack of funding. Without the personnel or money to conduct meaningful research, many editors filled their newspapers with political opinion pieces, movie and music reviews, cartoons, and reports about political rallies and rock concerts. They regularly criticized the police, often simply referred to as "pigs," and the power structure, while frequently ignoring even violent criminal actions such as bombings and rioting by those they supported.

Oddly, many in the "peace movement" seemed fascinated by weapons and violence. The *Rat* in New York City offered an article about how to hijack an airplane, and pictures of guns were common in many of the publications. And while perhaps none of the editors joined in overt acts of violence, such as the bombings that became an increasingly common form of protest, they also failed to criticize that violence. The FBI kept an eye on the publications as part of its 1960s COINTELPRO program, intended to monitor the counter-culture movement.

Most of the publications drew attention more from their frank characterizations of the 1960s "big three"—sex, drugs, and rock 'n roll—than as a result of either violent action or political expose. Some editors were arrested on pornography charges, and many of the publications relied heavily on sexually oriented personal ads for financial survival. "It is ironic that the alternative press proved in many cases an instant success with its readers, even if economic success was elusive, by using the same devices that the established press at its worst exploited—sex, sensationalism, violence, highly colored viewpoints and a fascination with the lawless elements in society," a mainstream editor complained.[13]

Typically produced cheaply by volunteers or small, poorly paid staffs, their poor quality and obvious bias meant few of the publications provided more than a mild annoyance to either the mainstream press or the local power structure. Some alternative newspapers did achieve influence, however. A couple of the more notable, New York's *Village Voice* and the *Texas Observer*, actually arrived much earlier than most, during the 1950s, and still survive. The *Village Voice*, founded in part by Norman Mailer, was the best-known alternative publication and was noted for literary journalism and creative writing by writers that had included I.F. Stone, Ezra Pound, Henry Miller, Katherine Anne Porter, James Baldwin, E.E. Cummings, and Allen Ginsberg. By 2001, it called itself "the nation's first and largest alternative newsweekly," and had won three Pulitzer Prizes and a host of other awards. Notably, though it achieved national recognition from readers for the quality and tone of its writing in the 1960s and early 1970s, none of its more than 100 awards came in the turbulent years between 1966 and 1978. Since 1970, it has changed ownership several times.[14]

Some of the most-respected alternative papers tended to more closely resemble mainstream newspapers than did their cousins, though with a more literary writing style and a more obvious liberal bent than the dailies most Americans read. The *Texas Observer* covered Texas politics, much of which became national politics, especially after Lyndon Johnson's bid for the 1960 presidential election. One of its political writers, Molly Ivins, went on to become one of the nation's leading nationally syndicated liberal columnists, and the newspaper survived into the new century.

The Boise, Idaho, *Intermountain Observer* drew praise from *Time*, *Newsweek*, *Harper's*, *The New Yorker*, *Columbia Journalism Review*, Senator Frank

Church, and U.S. Supreme Court Justice William O. Douglas, despite a three-person staff and a circulation of fewer than 4,000 readers. It died in 1973 largely because of the political activism of its editor.[15]

The *Los Angeles Free Press*, founded in 1964 and considered by many to be the first of the underground papers, inspired similar publications around the country. It lasted ten years, and at one time boasted a circulation of 95,000 readers and a staff of more than 100 people. Even then, as a reflection of its counter-culture status, it still could not get a Los Angeles police press pass—perhaps not surprising, considering that it once published the names of all known narcotics officers from Los Angeles, San Francisco, Santa Ana, and San Diego.[16]

The *Berkeley Barb*, a student publication that eventually grew to a circulation of 85,000, provided the San Francisco area with a strong youthful voice before internal infighting gutted it. Cities often boasted two or more similar newspapers, and Berkeley alone had at least six. Less strident in tone, the *San Francisco Bay Guardian* became a significant part of the Bay-area scene, typical of post–1975 "alternative journalism": liberal, but well-respected and not so radical as to offend advertisers (though offending advertisers in San Francisco might have been more difficult than in most cities).

Boston After Dark became part of the *Boston Phoenix* and remained alive as part of a chain. Some alternative magazines of the period also survived, continuing to seek and publish stories missed or ignored by the Associated Press and national newsmagazines. During the height of social tension in America, the alternative publications often were able to cover issues or events that the mainstream press could not. For one thing, sometimes those involved in political activities, such as the take-over of buildings on college campuses, also worked for alternative newspapers. In addition, those in the counter-culture movement were less trusting of the mainstream press, which was viewed as part of the establishment—a view not helped by its regular support of government policies or by an ongoing series of newspaper labor problems.[17]

The underground press sometimes is wrongly credited with introducing a new "literary journalism" to American readers. In fact, the literary journalists of the 1960s and 1970s worked mostly for magazines, which paid better than newspapers. Several wrote books, such as Tom Wolfe's *The Kandy-Kolored Tangerine-Flake Streamline Baby* in 1965. Their work tended to have three things in common. First, it combined elements of fiction, such as plot, pacing, and long stretches of dialogue (sometimes recreated or imagined) into their writing. Second, though much of their work pointed out societal problems, the writers tended to focus more on individuals than on institutions. Third, writers immersed themselves in their stories. Some, though not all, used first-person. "Literary Journalists gamble with their time," Wolfe noted. "Their writerly impulses lead toward immersion, toward trying to learn all there is about a subject. The risks are high."[18] Leading literary journalism practitioners included Joan Didion, Norman Mailer, John McPhee, and Jane Kramer, some of whom still were contributing important works decades later.

Some classify the new literary journalism and the underground press together as "New Journalism." Both contributed to important changes in the mainstream press, which, thanks in part to television and in part to its own recognition that political leaders were not above lying, was seeking to define itself. Mainstream journalists used the alternative newspapers to keep track of counter-culture thought and events. Alternative journalists, aided by their willingness to irritate those in power, sometimes uncovered significant stories that mainstream publications had missed, but which larger news organizations then followed up.[19]

Some of the alternative publications, especially magazines and larger newspapers, helped prompt a new focus on investigative reporting. Some daily newspapers picked up the ball. Of course, a few dailies already were doing serious investigative work. For example, the *Chicago Tribune*, a politically conservative newspaper in a Democratic city, regularly uncovered abuses at City Hall in the early 1960s.[20]

Influenced by their new competitors, the writing style of even established dailies also began to change noticeably. Stories began to carry more literary elements, not only with features but with news stories. The "news feature," which focused on individuals affected by events, became more common. Though journalists still stressed objectivity, they also recognized the benefits for readers of interpretation. Some of the more influential newspapers now saw it as their duty to help guide public opinion, and in some cases did so. Interpretive pieces made it onto the front page, and news articles were more likely to include historical or political context, particularly in stories about politics.[21]

Not all journalists agreed with the shift from traditional efforts to be objective: "In time, we are sure, the activist press will do its part and get back to reporting the news instead of trying to make it," a *Chicago Tribune* editor wrote.[22] News analysis was in American newspaper stories to stay, however. Further analysis came from "op-ed" pages, which offered differing opinions from a variety of columnists. The *New York Times* version debuted in 1970.[23]

As more and more cities found themselves losing daily newspapers, suburban newspapers began taking up some of the slack. Though it started much earlier, the most notable of the suburban papers during the 1960s was the tabloid *Newsday*, which began serving New York's Long Island in 1940. It was published by Alicia Patterson, one of few women in positions of media power. Bill Moyers left his position as an aide to President Johnson to become *Newsday* publisher in late 1966, and the newspaper soon went from being a neighborhood paper to having a national voice—a sometimes schizophrenic voice, as the antiwar Moyers and *Newsday* president Harry Guggenheim disagreed publicly over Vietnam. The paper won two Pulitzer Prizes in 1970. Moyers left the same year, when control of the newspaper was sold to the Los Angeles *Times-Mirror* Company.[24]

Newspapers also began to look different. In terms of appearance, "perhaps the major contribution of the underground press to newspaper graphics has been psychedelic art," Robert J. Glessing wrote in his book about alternative publications.[25] "Some newspapers have made radical changes in format overnight," an *Editor & Publisher* editorial stated, suggesting that editors "pull out the bound volumes of 20 years ago and get a jolt at how 'old fashioned' those papers appear."[26]

In truth, most newspaper design remained predictably dull, especially compared to later standards. In 1965, *Columbia Journalism Review* offered the *Boston Herald-Traveler* and the *Sunday Herald* a "welcome to the twentieth century" for devoting the front page to news, "after years of cluttering their front pages with advertising."[27] Advertisers used more spot color as processing improved, but editorial sections remained black and white. Daily newspapers still used few photos, keeping them small, and presented stories in long gray columns of type.

Still, editors experimented with layout and design. Some headlines grew in both point-size (height) and column width. Many newspapers went from an eight-column (or nine, in some cases) to a more-readable six-column format, at least on the front pages of sections. That switch initially created problems for some newspapers that used wire service copy. Wire copy came off the wire machine in preformatted widths, and a publication using wider columns had to reformat, or retype, all of the wire copy it used. The increased use of computers, which had begun to find their way into newsrooms, simplified the process.[28]

The *Los Angeles Times* began running some front-page photos three columns wide, half the width of the page, something more common to tabloids and alternative newspapers. In 1966, the *Times* began devoting all of page 2 to news capsules that summarized stories found throughout the newspaper. The *Cleveland Press* and other newspapers began using varied column measures on a single page. Horizontal layouts increased, and "wrapping" of one story around part of another decreased. Even "the gray lady," the *New York Times*, made minor changes that proved noticeable enough to draw reader complaints.[29]

Coin-operated newspaper racks began showing up outside supermarkets and other businesses, prompting more dramatic changes. With the top half of the front page serving as a sales tool to capture the attention of passers-by, what appeared "above the fold" increased in importance. Without the newsboys of an earlier time yelling out the top stories, street sales depended heavily on what might grab the eye.

A 1966 *Editor & Publisher* photo shows four coin-operated racks outside of a California supermarket. The racks belonged to the Coin-Trolled Equipment Corporation, not to the newspapers. Of course, most newspapers soon realized the financial benefits of handling their own street sales, and vending boxes were less consistent in style, contributing to what some critics saw as clutter. Some communities would try, with varying success, to restrict the use and appearance of those boxes.[30]

Perhaps the most notable new design came with the publication of a Gannett paper started in 1966 on Florida's Atlantic Coast. In many respects, *Today*, subtitled "Florida's Space Age Newspaper," looked like an early model for the company's *USA Today*, which was still eighteen years away. A distinctive $7\frac{1}{2}$-column format permitted the use of conventional wire tape and 11-pica columns, which, with 6 picas in an inch, meant standard column widths still were less than 2 inches wide. But other elements looked more modern. No rules (vertical lines between columns) were used, leaving more attractive white space and a less-cluttered look. One wide column ran down the left side of the front page, telling readers what they could find inside. Photos were larger than those used by most newspapers. Page 1 mugshots were larger than a single column and focused on faces, even if that meant cutting off part of someone's head, an uncommon practice at the time. Headlines used modern sans-serif typefaces.[31]

Later the same year, a 42,000-circulation newspaper from America's heartland demonstrated even better what the future of newspaper design would hold. The *Dubuque* (Iowa) *Telegraph Herald* used large photos, abundant white space, and decorative feature headlines to take advantage of what it called "the first high-speed newspaper offset press in the world."[32] In a redesign exercise that would become common for newspapers around the country, editors consulted with design experts and readers. The editorial page became a reader's forum, some days entirely devoid of editorials. News and feature sections included large photos, sometimes eight or more sprawled across a two-page spread.

All of the previous visual changes would pale in comparison to those brought in 1982 by *USA Today* when Gannett, which owned a national news service, more than 100 newspapers, and a number of broadcast stations, began producing what it called "the Nation's Newspaper." *USA Today* looked unlike anything most readers had ever seen. Though presented in a traditional broadsheet format made up of logical subject-related sections, the pages used numerous large color photos. Stories were shorter than what most readers were used to, rarely jumping from one page to another. A front-page directory guided readers to the sections and pages that most interested them. And brightly colored graphics abounded, using art and graphs and charts to explain or highlight key story elements, so that readers did not have to dig those elements out of the text.

To better illustrate the differences: The *Washington Post*, for example, used only one multicolor illustration, five full-color front-page photographs, and a few artistic illustrations during one full week. During the same week, *USA Today* printed fifty-one full-color photographs and thirty-eight multicolor diagrams, charts, and pictographs, along with more spot color, artists' drawings, and screens. Indicating that the publication would also differ from most newspapers in terms of news judgment, the lead story of the first issue covered the death of former American actress Princess Grace of Monaco. Most newspapers considered more newsworthy the killing of Lebanese President-elect Bashir Gemayel.[33]

Newspapers and trade journals publicly criticized and dismissed what they called "McPaper," the journalistic equivalent of fast food. "I have seen the future and it is *USA Today*," *Washington Post* critic Jonathon Yardley wrote immediately after the newspaper appeared. "As a barometer to what America will be like 15 or 20 minutes from now it is doubtless at least as reliable as the copyrighted 'Accu-Weather' forecasts to which it devotes an entire color-coordinated page. It may also be a barometer to the future of American journalism, a prospect that I view with decidedly mixed emotions."[34]

Still, newspapers around the country took notice. As the *New York Times* noted a year later, *USA Today* was "loudly mocked and quietly mimicked."[35] Many newspapers soon adopted variations of the *USA Today* weather map and full-page color weather pages would eventually become a staple of newspapers around the country. Less than two years after it first appeared, a group of designers ranked *USA Today* as the third-best in the country in terms of design, and *Advertising Age* suggested that it probably was better than those available in most cities. By then most dailies were using more color and relying less on text for telling stories. Still, the *New York Times*, which remained among the grayest of newspapers, was ranked first in the survey. *USA Today* especially appealed to travelers and became a fixture at airports and in hotels.[36]

Satellite technology, which during the Vietnam War had energized television news, made the national newspaper possible. Complete pages could be composed in one location and then transmitted to printing plants around the country, making distribution of printed newspapers faster, easier, and more economical. *USA Today* began with printing sites in Washington, Atlanta, Minneapolis, and Pittsburgh, then, a year later, added ten more sites: Los Angeles, San Francisco, Seattle, Denver, Houston, Miami, Chicago, Detroit, New York, and Philadelphia.[37]

USA Today eventually would boast more than forty printing locations (including several outside of the United States). But it was not the first newspaper to take advantage of the new satellite possibilities. The *New York Times* had proceeded slowly with many innovations (for example, not going to a six-column page format until 1974, or switching to "cold type" printing until 1978) and would not begin using full-color photos until 1993. But it began producing its national edition in 1980, two years before the appearance of *USA Today*. Versions of the *Times* eventually were printed in New York, Chicago, Washington, Atlanta, Denver, Phoenix, California, Florida, Texas, New Jersey, Ohio, and Washington State.[38]

Readers of newspapers that made *USA Today*-style changes often found the newspapers more attractive and easier to read, with information easier to recall. Improved printing presses made color photos more attractive and easier to use, and newspapers were looking for ways to slow or halt declining readership. Not surprisingly, newspapers that were second or third in circulation in a market tended to use more of the new techniques. Though newspaper experimentation has sometimes been thought of as a response to television, competition among newspapers often was a more significant motivator. Afternoon papers, fighting a losing circulation battle, were more likely to experiment than were morning papers. Smaller papers tended to be more daring than large established papers.[39]

Where *USA Today* led, most newspapers eventually followed. Newspaper insiders long had recognized that the *New York Times* slogan "All the News That's Fit to Print" would more aptly be phrased for all news media as "all the news that fits." But even that adage no longer applied when page design became more important during the 1970s and 1980s. Page designers concentrated more on making pages attractive, not just on making things fit. Text and illustrations became complementary design elements. "Designers regard photographs and other illustrations as shapes and sizes, patterns of dark and light, large and small, as related to the shapes, sizes, and dark/light patterns of headlines and body type," noted a 1983 journal article.[40] Thanks in part to improved printing presses, large color photos became the norm (especially on the front pages of sections). Stories became shorter, laid out in modular (rectangular) formats, with fewer "jumps"—meaning, among other things, that front-page story counts dropped from thirteen in 1965 to just six by 1985. More prominent indexes, digests, briefs, and "teasers" (often above the front-page flag of the newspaper) made those stories easier to find. Newspapers hired artists and began using "infographics" to tell more of the story, and large colorful drawings were used in place of (or along with) bold headlines and photos to draw the reader's attention. "White space," which had improved as newspapers eliminated black lines between columns of type, became recognized as a valuable design element. Headlines increased in size, and most newspapers went to downstyle headlines in which only the first word of a headline and proper nouns were capitalized.[41]

In some respects, daily print news began to look more like that of the one-time enemy, television. Emphasizing the nature of its news presentation, early *USA Today* vending boxes looked much like television sets. The *USA Today* marketing emphasis on those vending machines, and the need for local newspapers to compete, also led to a significant increase in on-street machines (and a number of lawsuits, as communities sought to curb that increase). One researcher warned of potential dire consequences for newspapers wanting to appeal to young adult readers or fend off Gannett encroachment, if they failed to adopt *the USA Today* approach to news and marketing: "One good reason for taking the USA Today phenomenon to heart," John Hartman wrote, "is that the Gannett Co. has the resources and the will to come into any location and publish a quality product."[42]

While in most cities the number of dailies declined, another significant new newspaper appeared in the nation's capital in the same year as *USA Today* when the Rev. Sun Myung Moon, Korean billionaire founder of the Unification Church, started the conservative *Washington Times*. Moon, commonly viewed as a cult leader whose followers were known as "Moonies," had drawn considerable media attention through mass "marriages" involving thousands of couples and served a brief prison term after a 1982 conviction for tax fraud. The *Times* ignored suspicions about its founder, boldly calling itself "America's Newspaper." It provided Washington with a well-funded politically conservative newspaper less than a year after Time, Inc., had closed the failing *Washington Star* and made the nation's capital another city with one daily newspaper. Since the arrival of the *Times*, the nation's capital has provided a too-rare example of what once was common: a city with daily newspapers that compete ideologically and fiscally.[43]

Broadcast news, like its print counterpart, also was changing dramatically. One important change came from government action, when 1967 congressional legislation authorized the Corporation for Public Broadcasting, a private nonprofit corporation (not a governmental agency) that formed the Public Broadcasting Service and National Public Radio. Most of the stations already existed, typically operated by universities or community organizations, but the new corporate setup allowed for better news and public affairs programming that was more widely circulated. Throughout their history, PBS and NPR have been funded by a combination of businesses, charitable foundations, government subsidies, viewers, and listeners.

One of the first PBS shows to make a significant impact was *The Mac-Neil/Lehrer Report*, which, starting in 1976, devoted a daily half hour to coverage of a different single issue. Robert MacNeil and Jim Lehrer first had been paired during congressional hearings of the Watergate scandal. As *The MacNeil/Lehrer NewsHour* in 1983, the show became the first hour-long national nightly news broadcast. Charlayne Hunter-Gault—who in 1962 had been the first African American woman to graduate from the University of Georgia before going on to work as a reporter for the *New Yorker*, WRC-TV in Washington, and the *New York Times*—became its national correspondent. By the end of the decade, many recognized PBS as, in the words of an *Oregonian* editorial, an "indispensable tool for our people and our democracy."[44] Later PBS offerings such as *Frontline* would do what network documentaries once had, devoting longer time periods to issues of concern. PBS never drew as many viewers as did other networks, however, and sometimes was denigrated as a liberal bastion watched primarily by intellectual liberal elites.

Cable and satellites also made possible the Cable-Satellite Public Affairs Network (C-SPAN) created by the cable industry to cover the House of Representatives in 1979. Seven years later it expanded its coverage to the Senate and other public policy arenas. C-SPAN let viewers bypass traditional news outlets to see some of what was happening in Congress, though it has never boasted a large audience. At first, cameras focused only on speakers, letting some members of Congress grandstand with expansive late-night speeches to an empty House floor. Later, footage began including shots of the audience, giving a truer picture. Even so, Congress continued to control the cameras, though C-SPAN executives decided which committees, floor debates, etc., would be covered. In some cases the network also let reporters cover congressional speeches without actually being present for them and without having to rely on edited transcripts.

A cable/satellite innovation that drew a larger audience than C-SPAN was Ted Turner's WTCB, broadcast via satellite beginning in 1976 as the first "superstation." Three years later the name of the station was changed to WTBS. Though it provided little in terms of news, it set the stage for Turner Broadcasting's Cable News Network (CNN): the first 24-hour all-news network, which debuted in 1980. The arrival of CNN meant viewers, or at least viewers in some of the roughly 20 percent of American homes then connected to cable, could tune in to breaking news at any time, day or night.

Home Box Office and Turner's WTBS already had proven the viability of cable/satellite television aimed at subscribers, but the idea of an all-news network met with skepticism before it aired, and then with criticism after it was launched. *Washington Post* writer John F. Berry warned just before the first show that "the premiere will be greeted with almost universal skepticism both by the TV and financial communities alike."[45] After all, Turner, known nationally as a yachtsman, sports team owner, and businessman, had no news experience. Still, apparently he had been considering the idea at least since the mid-1970s. After the show, a *New York Times* critic Tony Schwartz stated, "For all the 'revolutionary' fervor, CNN, at least in its tentative first steps, too frequently emerges as something resembling all-news radio with photographs or, in television terms, talking heads with the latest headlines."[46]

CNN did change the look of broadcast news. African American anchor Bernard Shaw, a former ABC reporter, was the first face viewers saw when the network aired. CNN introduced the practice of putting the anchor desk in front of the working "open" newsroom, a format that pulled viewers into the process and made the anchor seem less remote from the up-to-the-minute breaking nature of news. Eventually all of the major networks and many local news operations would let viewers see behind the scenes in similar fashion.[47]

The serious and dignified treatment of national and international news on CNN made the network more difficult to dismiss. President Jimmy Carter, Turner's friend and a fellow Georgian, helped out by consenting to an interview about international affairs as part of the first day of broadcasting. The interview also provided the first example of a practice that later would become fairly common, especially with international news. Even leading newspapers sometimes ended up reporting what reporters and other Americans had watched on CNN.

From a news perspective, CNN debuted at a good time. The ongoing Iranian hostage crisis provided one guaranteed news topic. CNN also arrived in a presidential election year and separated itself from the other networks by providing airtime for independent candidate John Anderson after he was excluded from a debate between Jimmy Carter and Ronald Reagan. The network tape-delayed the debate, interspersing footage of Anderson responding to questions with statements made by the Democratic and Republican nominees. "We are setting our own ground rules," said CNN President Reese Schonfeld.[48]

With twenty-four hours of daily time to fill, much of what the network offered was less newsworthy than presidential politics, especially according to traditional news definitions. "If you're a TV junkie, you'll probably love the all-new, 24 hour Cable News Network (CNN)," noted *Christian Science Monitor* critic Robert M. Press a couple of weeks after the network debuted. "Just tune in, sit back, and get your fill of news, sports, fashions, gossip, financial and garden tips, and almost anything else you can think of."[49] More criticism greeted the perceived shallowness of CNN Headline News when it appeared a year after the CNN debut, giving updates of major news, financial, sports, and entertainment stories every half hour. In later years, the "Hollywood Minute" and sportscasters who mimicked the melodramatic delivery of famed ABC sportscaster Howard Cosell became "Headline News" staples, adding to the entertainment aspects of the presentation. Eventually actor

James Earl Jones would provide the tagline "This . . . is CNN," combining Edward R. Murrow's World War II phrasing and dramatic pause ("This . . . is London") with the behind-the-mask voice of *Star Wars* villain Darth Vader.[50]

Though some critics said the network had too many "talking heads," CNN was perhaps most criticized by those who hoped that twenty-four hours of news would allow much more contextual depth of coverage. Instead, CNN coverage did not vary significantly from that of the other networks. In the words of *Washington Post* critic Tom Shales: "Certainly keeping things brisk and brief had a higher priority than making them thorough or substantial. Often it seemed that, as with much of network TV news, the point of getting anything onto the screen was chiefly to get it off again and replace it with something else, lest viewers grow weary."[51] The network had enough airtime to cover events anywhere at any time, but not enough reporters or crew because its budget was considerably smaller than the news budgets of ABC, CBS or NBC. So stories often were repeated or given more weight than they deserved. The network was at its best with events such as natural disasters and wars, when news crews had time to get to the scene and could stay awhile. But it was criticized for devoting too much time covering camera-friendly events with little national impact, such as plane crashes and crime. In years to come, other news networks and local news also would discover and continue to appreciate the audience-drawing value of relatively innocuous "breaking news." CNN and other all-news cable networks became a news "habit" for some, siphoning viewers from the traditional network news offerings.[52]

The immediacy of twenty-four-hour news changed how political leaders would be expected to respond. Every move by the president had been followed since John F. Kennedy's assassination in 1963, in what has been termed the "body watch" or the "death watch." Still, politicians knew that except in rare cases no more than a few minutes of the evening news would be devoted to their actions. If a crisis occurred, the president or other officials could be briefed about it before speaking to the news media. The arrival of CNN meant that more than ever before sources would be pressured for answers before they had time to consider events or issues. With press-government conflicts of the 1970s still a vivid memory, sources who refused to speak quickly or completely faced the possibility of being made to appear stupid or corrupt—despite the fact that, thanks to CNN, a busy leader might know less about events than did television viewers.

Another supposed "CNN effect" was the hindering of overseas military or diplomatic operations because of the presence of news cameras. In fact, policymakers learned fairly quickly how to use the network to draw attention to desired activities. And because foreign leaders also watched

CNN, it gave American leaders another channel through which they could send messages. Perhaps the best example came with the Persian Gulf War of 1991, when the Bush administration had no other way of contacting Saddam Hussein but assumed the Iraqi leader would be following the war on CNN.[53]

Some argued that this "CNN effect" went further. With more time to devote to news (and mirroring Turner's own interests) much of the network's coverage was of international events. Some suggested that CNN now set much of the U.S. agenda overseas, by calling more attention to some areas than to others. Of course, the same complaint had been made in earlier years about newspapers, notably Joseph Pulitzer's *New York World* in the 1890s and the *New York Times* and *Washington Post* in later years. Still other critics pointed out that brief visual images, chosen for their news value, were bound to give Americans misleading impressions about other cultures, at a time when American newspapers were dramatically cutting back the attention given to overseas issues. Though some critics also claimed that troubling images on CNN "forced" government intervention in some crises while others were ignored, little supporting evidence exists for that claim. In fact, with more attention being paid to problems around the world, viewers sometimes became desensitized to those problems, suffering from what came to be known as "compassion fatigue."[54]

While the constant deadline cycle caused some problems for public officials, it also created problems for the news media. For better or worse, daily deadlines occurring at regular intervals let journalists slip into routines. Stress tends to increase at predictable times. News was competitive, but all of the nightly network programs aired at the same time, and the vast majority of newspapers appeared either in the morning or in the afternoon. With CNN, however, the pace of competition stepped up. With news a twenty-four-hour-a-day commodity, now deadlines also happened around the clock. The competition to be first made journalists more likely to be wrong, threatening their credibility. As CNN debuted, *U.S. News and World Report* warned that it "comes at a time when the accuracy, fairness and depth of TV news are being challenged as never before."[55]

Both print and broadcast journalism saw technological advances expand exponentially. A decade before the arrival of the personal computer in the 1980s, the video display terminal (VDT) changed the look of newsrooms forever. The *New York Times* employee magazine described the VDT, which came to the *Times* in 1974, as a "television screen attached to an electric typewriter keyboard."[56] It allowed reporters and editors to write, rearrange, save, and reuse text in new ways. As side benefits, VDTs also reduced spelling and typographical errors in the final product and sped up the copy-editing process. One editor later noted, "After about six years of using VDTs, I don't know anyone who would go back to hard copy!"[57] The machines did bring one drawback. As the number of video display terminals and then computers in newsrooms increased, they brought with them a sometimes crippling new keyboard-related ailment, repetitive strain injury, an ailment apparently unknown to old-time reporters pounding on keyboards.[58]

CBS, AT&T, and many newspapers experimented with videotext, a system that sent text via cable or phone lines to a television or computer screen. The early promise of the medium quickly faltered. One journal reported in 1987 that the number of newspapers planning to launch videotext systems had dropped from at least 125 to fewer than twenty. Though stories could be updated quickly, most readers quickly tired of the systems, reacting to videotext "as if it were a new toy or appliance rather than a replacement for a daily newspaper."[59] They might typically use the videotext system for a week or two and then drop it to go back to the simplicity of the daily newspaper or television. Reporters who were forced to write and constantly update short stories, ignoring the length and depth that could provide context—while perhaps typing in ads, as well—also disliked the systems.

Most of the technological advances of the period improved journalism and brought few complaints, however. By the early 1970s, the Associated Press and United Press International had begun to install computer terminals in their bureaus. Some newspapers put news databases available online even before the IBM personal computer, which quickly became the home PC standard, arrived in 1981. By the end of the century almost every daily newspaper, and many weeklies, had an online version. Of course, reporters also quickly made use of various commercial databases, not only for investigative work but also to prepare for interviews, check facts, make comparisons, or to identify story ideas, trends, or sources.

Time magazine named the computer as its "Man of the Year" for 1983. The following year, Apple introduced the Macintosh computer, with a graphics capacity superior to that of the IBM. Editors, designers, and artists quickly found new ways to use that capacity, changing the way in which newspapers were designed and produced. Previously, editors had drawn pencil-and-paper "dummies," diagrams that other newspaper employees would use to compose pages. Now the editors could lay out or "paginate" the pages themselves on a computer screen. That allowed them to see exactly how a page would look before it was ever printed, and the process reduced production time overall.

As has been common throughout American history, technological advances also brought losses. Many "back shop" workers such as Linotype operators and page composers suddenly faced unemployment because editors could do their jobs while sitting at their desks. Several newspapers were shut down by strikes as unions reacted to the lost jobs, just as the Linotype machine and other technical advances had prompted layoffs and strikes in earlier times. Their services no longer needed, the number of newspaper workers dwindled, and their unions became weaker.

The *New York Times* began the shift to pagination in 1978, and smaller newspapers had begun much earlier. Finally, in 1981 the *Pasadena Star-News* became the first paginated newspaper put together completely without any back shop employees other than those who ran the printing presses. The number of such newspapers probably surpassed 100 within five years. The arrival of the IBM PC and the Macintosh prompted computer companies to produce new layout and pagination software, perhaps most significantly QuarkXPress in 1987. By then at least 100 newspapers also had installed electronic libraries, making it easier for reporters to review clip files.[60]

Laptop computers also arrived in the 1980s, and use of the relatively new fax machine boomed (newspapers were among its first users)—sometimes causing problems when public relations professionals discovered how easy it was to fax news releases. Those machines and another new technological marvel, the cell phone, greatly increased the flexibility of reporters. Broadcast journalists found their range increased in other ways, too, first with smaller and lighter camera equipment, then with the 1984 arrival of the Satellite News Gathering (SNG) truck.[61]

Satellites and cable, which made possible the national newspapers, did even more for television news. The 1985 launch by RCA of a new type of communication satellite made it possible for local stations to transmit using smaller, cheaper equipment. Demonstrating the speedy progression of technology, that satellite came only about a decade after the introduction of practical videotape machines had reduced the amount of equipment needed. The news could now be presented more quickly and less expensively.

RCA gave satellite equipment to many local stations, making sure its satellite would be used. Local news could air live reports, and stations soon recognized that broadcasting from "on location" increased prestige and viewership. Reporters could travel far afield with "fly-away packs" of equipment that could be packed in a few suitcases, flown anywhere in the world, and assembled for broadcasting within minutes at the low cost of less than $20 a minute.

With more travel, television news staffs became larger—at the same time that some budget-minded newspapers were cutting editorial staffs—and producers took over some of the jobs formerly handled by reporters. Later deadlines and pressures to air as much "live" coverage as possible gave reporters less time to provide perspective and forced them to think on their feet more often. Producers controlled the new technology, increasing their editorial control over reporters' stories. The number of producers and the sometimes meaningless use of live coverage for stories that could just as easily have aired from the studio contributed to the growing concerns about style-versus-substance issues in TV news.[62]

NOTES

1. Liz Trotta, *Fighting for Air: In the Trenches with Television News* (New York: Simon & Schuster, 1991).

2. Gilbert P. Smith, editor of the *Utica (N.Y.) Daily Press*, letter to Paul Dunn, president/general manager of WTLB, January 16, 1974; records of the Associated Press Managing Editors Association, State Historical Society of Wisconsin, Madison.

3. Norman E. Isaacs, quoted in "Papers Quit All-Media News Parley," *Editor & Publisher*, January 1, 1966, 30. Also see Victor Jose, "Do Newspapermen Really Want Competition?" *Quill*, August 1965, 21.

4. Unnamed reporter quoted in Trotta, *Fighting for Air*, 25.

5. Walter D. Scott, "Today's Journalism: A Candid Appraisal," *Quill*, June 1965, 32.

6. Robert U. Brown, "Shop Talk at Thirty: Ratings and Circulation," *Editor & Publisher*, February 27, 1965; Alan Pritchard, "The Newspaper Responsibility," *Quill*, August 1966; ad for Zenith color television, *Quill*, June 1966, 31; Editorial, "Passing Comment," *Columbia Journalism Review*(Winter 1966–1967): 4.

7. Quoted in Charles R. Novitz, "The TV News Turn-off and What Can Be Done About It," *Quill*, December 1969, 14.

8. Eugene F. Shaw and Daniel Riffe, "NIS and Radio's All-News Predicament," *Journalism Monographs* 69 (August 1980).

9. Sam Day, "Desert Flowers that Bloom for a Day: The Comings and Goings of Idaho's Alternative Media," *Boise Intermountain Observer*, June 23, 1973. Also see Jose, "Do Newspapermen Really Want Competition?"; David R. Davies, *An Industry in Transition: Major Trends in American Daily Newspapers, 1945–1965*, doctoral dissertation, University of Alabama, 1997; Abe Peck, *Uncovering the Sixties: The Life and Times of the Underground Press* (New York: Citadel Underground, 1991); Robert J. Glessing, *The Underground Press in America* (Bloomington, Ind.: Midland, 1971); Michael L. Johnson, *The New Journalism: The Underground Press, the Artists of Nonfiction, and Changes in the Established Media* (Lawrence, Kan.: University Press of Kansas, 1971); Lauren Kessler, *The Press: Alternative Journalism in American History* (Beverly Hills, Calif.: Sage, 1984); Edwin Emery and Michael Emery, *The Press and America: An Interpretive History of the Mass Media*, 4th ed. (Englewood Cliffs, N.J.: Prentice-Hall, 1978).

10. Jacob Brackman, "The Underground Press," *Playboy* (August 1967): 83.

11. Editorial, "'Underground' Square?" *Seattle Post-Intelligencer*, January 28, 1971.

12. Ibid. Also see Rodger Streitmatter, "The Lesbian and Gay Press: Raising a Militant Voice in the 1960s," *American Journalism* 12 (Spring 1995): 142–161.

13. Editorial, "'Underground' Square?" *Seattle Post-Intelligencer*.

14. Village Voice Web site, http://www.villagevoice.com/aboutus/awds2.php. (accessed July 18, 2002); Kevin Michael McAuliffe, *The Great American Newspaper: The Rise and Fall of the Village Voice* (New York: Charles

Scribner's Sons, 1978). In 2000, the *Village Voice* was part of a chain that included several other large-city weeklies.

15. James B. McPherson, "Reasoned Protest and Personal Journalism: The Liberty and Death of *The Intermountain Observer*," presented at the 1996 American Journalism Historians National Convention, London, Ontario.

16. "Narcotics Agents Listed," *Los Angeles Free Press*, August 8–14, 1969.

17. Peck, *Uncovering the Sixties*; Glessing, *The Underground Press*.

18. Tom Wolfe, The *New Journalism* (New York: Harper & Row, 1973). Also see Norman Sims, ed., *The Literary Journalists* (New York: Ballantine, 1984); John C. Hartsock, *A History of American Literary Journalism: The Emergence of a Modern Narrative Form* (Amherst: University of Massachusetts, 2000).

19. James B. McPherson, "Government Watchdogs: How Four Newspapers Expressed Their First Amendment Responsibilities in Editorials," unpublished master's thesis, Washington State University, May 1993.

20. James AuCoin, "Investigative Journalism," in W. David Sloan and Lisa Mullikin Parcell, eds., *American Journalism: History Principles, Practices* (Jefferson, N.C.: McFarland & Company, 2002).

21. Bruce J. Evensen, "Objectivity," in Sloan and Parcell, *American Journalism*, 258–266; Bruce Evensen, "Surrogate State Department? *Times* Coverage of Palestine, 1948," *Journalism Quarterly* 67 (1990): 391–400.

22. Editorial, "Mohnihan on the Press," *Chicago Tribune*, March 31, 1971.

23. Timeline, *New York Times*, 150th anniversary edition, November 14, 2001.

24. "Newspapers: Lagging Downtown, New Life in Suburbs," *Business Week*, February 5, 1955; "Suburb and City," *Columbia Journalism Review* (Summer 1963): 13–14; Robert F. Keeler, *Newsday: A Candid History of the Respectable Tabloid* (New York: William Morrow, 1990).

25. Glessing, *The Underground Press*, inside front cover.

26. "Why Not Compare?" *Editor & Publisher*, March 5, 1966.

27. "Darts and Laurels," *Columbia Journalism Review*, Winter 1965.

28. Edmund C. Arnold, "6 Col. Swing Raises Wire Tape Problem," *Editor & Publisher*, March 12, 1966.

29. John B. Oakes, "The Times Goes 'Modern,'" *Masthead* 16 (Summer 1965): 22–25; Timeline, *New York Times*.

30. *Editor & Publisher*, 19 March 1966.

31. "Gannett to Start Daily for Florida Coast," *Editor & Publisher*, January 29, 1966, 9; Edmund C. Arnold, "Typography of Today Modern as the Rockets," *Quill*, June 1966, 29; H.G. (Buddy) Davis Jr., "Newspaper Collision Course in Orbit County," *Quill*, June 1966, 26–30.

32. James A. Galadas, "Let's Invent a Newspaper . . ." *Quill*, December 1966, 16–19.

33. Philip C. Geraci, "Comparison of Graphic Design and Illustration Use in Three Washington, D.C., Newspapers," *Newspaper Research Journal* 5 (Winter 1983): 29–39.

34. Jonathon Yardley, "A Paper for a U.S.A. On the Go," *Washington Post*, September 20, 1982.

35. Jonathon Friendly, "Questions Remain After *USA Today*'s First Year," *New York Times*, September 16, 1983.

36. Researchers have pointed out that many newspapers were in the redesign process when *USA Today* arrived, and that newspapers adopted many of the weather map features—including full color—more slowly than had been expected. Researchers disagree about how many newspapers "copied" *USA Today*. See Lois Romano, "Washington Goes Out to Launch; Reagan & Co. at

USA Today's First-Edition Fete," Washington Post, September 16, 1982; George Albert Gladney, "The McPaper Revolution? USA Today-style Innovation at Large U.S. Dailies," Newspaper Research Journal 13 (Winter/Spring 1992): 54–71; Mark Monmonier and Val Pipps, "Weather Maps and Newspaper Design: Response to USA Today?" Newspaper Research Journal 8 (Summer 1987): 31–42; Michael Emery, "New York Times Tops Designers' List," Advertising Age, November 19, 1984, 3, 36, 39; Bill Granger, "An In-Depth Look at USA Today," Advertising Age, January 30, 1984, M10–11, 16.

37. Monmonier and Pipps, "Weather Maps and Newspaper Design."

38. Ibid.

39. Sandra H. Utt and Steve Pasternack, "Front Pages of U.S. Daily Newspapers," Journalism Quarterly 61 (Winter 1984): 879–884; Jyotika Ramaprasad, "Information Graphics in Newspapers," Newspaper Research Journal 12 (Summer 1991): 92–103; Chic Bain and David H. Weaver, "Readers' Reactions to Newspaper Design," Newspaper Research Journal 1 (November 1979): 48–59; Keith Kenney and Stephen Lacy, "Economic Forces Behind Newspapers' Increasing Use of Color and Graphics," Newspaper Research Journal 8 (Spring 1987): 33–41; Sandra H. Utt and Steve Pasternack, "Use of Graphic Devices in a Competitive Situation: A Case Study of 10 Cities," Newspaper Research Journal 7 (Winter 1985): 7–16.

40. Geraci, "Comparison of Graphic Design."

41. Tim Harrower, The Newspaper Designer's Handbook, 5th ed. (Boston: McGraw-Hill, 2002); Associated Press Managing Editors study cited in Keith Kenney and Stephen Lacy, "Economic Forces Behind Newspapers' Increasing Use of Color and Graphics," Newspaper Research Journal 8 (Spring 1987): 33–41; Utt and Pasternack, "Front Pages of U.S. Daily Newspapers"; Sandra H. Utt and Steve Pasternack, "How They Look: An Updated Study of America's Newspaper Front Pages," Journalism Quarterly 66 (Autumn 1989): 621–627.

42. John K. Hartman, "USA Today and Young-Adult Readers: Can a New-Style Newspaper Win Them Back?" Newspaper Research Journal 8 (Winter 1987): 12. Also see George E. Stevens, "Newsracks and the First Amendment," Journalism Quarterly 66 (Winter 1989): 930–933, 973.

43. Ken McIntyre, "Surviving, and Thriving, as a First Source of News," Washington Times Web site, http://www.washtimes.com/ (accessed May 17, 2002); Lee Edwards, ed., Our Times: The Washington Times 1982–2002 (Washington, D.C.: Regnery Publishing, 2002).

44. Editorial, "Freeing Public TV," Oregonian, February 4, 1979; MacNeil retired in 1995, and "The MacNeil/Lehrer Newshour" became "The Newshour with Jim Lehrer."

45. John F. Berry, "Skepticism Greets Hype Surrounding Cable News Debut," Washington Post, June 1, 1980.

46. Tony Schwartz, "Cable News Network—In Search of an Identity," New York Times, June 29, 1980.

47. Hank Whittemore, CNN: The Inside Story (Boston: Little, Brown and Company, 1990).

48. "Anderson to Debate, too, Via Cable-TV Network," Christian Science Monitor, October 27, 1980. Also see John M. Goshko, "Allies Given A Warning On Mideast; Allies Warned on Backing Palestinian Resolution; Carter Would Veto U.N. Resolution on Palestian Rights," Washington Post, June 1, 1980.

49. Robert M. Press, "Nonstop News for TV Buffs Who Think They've Seen It All," Christian Science Monitor, June 16, 1980.

50. John J. O'Connor, "TV: The Early Days of 24-Hour News," *New York Times*, June 5, 1980.

51. Tom Shales, "Ted Turner's Nonstop Gamble: CNN Sets Sail; In Arlington, the Show," *Washington Post*, June 2, 1980.

52. Thomas F. Baldwin, Marianne Barrett, and Benjamin Bates, "Influence of Cable on Television News Audiences," *Journalism Quarterly* 69 (Fall 1992): 651–658.

53. Piers Robinson, *The CNN Effect: The Myth of News, Foreign Policy and Intervention* (London: Routledge, 2002).

54. Richard Davis, *The Press and American Politics: The New Mediator*, 2nd ed. (Upper Saddle River, N.J.: Prentice Hall, 1996); Bruce Evenson, "Surrogate State Department? Times Coverage of Palestine, 1948," *Journalism Quarterly* 67 (Autumn 1990): 391–400; Mehdi Semati, "Reflections on the Politics of the Global 'Rolling-News' Television Genre," *Transnational Broadcasting Archives* 6 (Spring/Summer 2001): available at http://www.tbsjournal.com (accessed March 5, 2006); Michael Emery, "An Endangered Species: The International Newshole," *Gannett Center Journal*, Fall 1989; Katherine N. Kinnick, Dean M. Krugman, and Glen T. Cameron, "Compassion Fatigue: Communication and Burnout Toward Social Problems," *Journalism & Mass Communication Quarterly* 73 (Autumn 1996): 687–707.

55. Alvin P. Sanoff, "TV News Growing Too Powerful?" *U.S. News and World Report*, June 9, 1980, 59. In 1982, morning circulation of daily newspapers surpassed evening circulation for the first time.

56. Timeline, *New York Times*, 150th anniversary edition, November 14, 2001.

57. Quoted in William R. Lindley, "From Hot Type to Video Screens: Editors Evaluate New Technology," *Journalism Quarterly* 65 (Summer 1988): 486–489. Also see James Aucoin, "The Re-emergence of American Investigative Journalism 1960–1975," *Journalism History* 21 (1995): 3–15; Starr D. Randall, "How Editing and Typesetting Technology Affects Typographical Error Rate," *Journalism Quarterly* 63 (Winter 1986): 763–770; "Then and Now," *Columbia Journalism Review*, November/December 1986, 47.

58. Diana Hembree and Sarah Henry, "A Newsroom Hazard Called RSI," *Columbia Journalism Review*, January/February 1987, 19–24.

59. Richard Bazanich, Suzanne Eckstrom, Wendy Pinchas, and Juliet Savage, "Videotext Jobs Can Frustrate Newsies," *Quill*, February 1985, 17–19. Also see Gary Stix, "What Zapped the Electronic Newspaper?" *Columbia Journalism Review*, May/June 1987, 45–48.

60. Jane B. Singer, "Changes and Consistencies: Newspaper Journalists Contemplate Online Future," *Newspaper Research Journal* 18 (Winter/Spring 1997): 2–18; Thomas L. Jacobson and John Ullman, "Commercial Databases and Reporting: Opinions of Newspaper Journalists and Librarians," *Newspaper Research Journal* 10 (Winter 1989): 15–25; John T. Russial, "Pagination and the Newsroom: A Question of Time," *Newspaper Research Journal* 15 (Winter 1994): 91–101; Doug Underwood, C. Anthony Giffard, and Keith Stamm, "Computers and Editing: Pagination's Impact on the Newsroom," *Newspaper Research Journal* 15 (Spring 1994): 116–127; Jean Ward, Kathleen A. Hansen, and Douglas M. McLeod, "Effects of the Electronic Library on News Reporting Protocols," *Journalism Quarterly* 65 (Winter 1988): 845–852.

61. Local TV stations still boast about when they acquired their first satellite trucks. WRAL-TV in Raleigh, North Carolina, claims to be "first on the East Coast to have a portable satellite truck for news [1984]": Capital Broadcasting Company

Website,   http://www.cbc-raleigh.com/who_we_are/profiles/ralprofile.htm (accessed May 6, 2006).

62. Lowell D. Frazier, "The Fax News Flood: Editors Grapple with Technology's Benefits, Burdens," *Newspaper Research Journal* 13 (Winter/Spring 1992): 100–111; Bill Adair, "Damming the Fax Flood," *Washington Journalism Review*, July/August 1989, 8; Stephen Lacy, Tony Atwater, and Angela Powers, "Use of Satellite Technology in Local Television News," *Journalism Quarterly* 65 (Winter 1988): 925–929, 966; Jeff Greenfield, "Making TV News Pay," *Gannett Center Journal* (Spring 1987): 21–39; Conrad Smith and Lee B. Becker, "Comparison of Journalistic Values of Television Reporters and Producers," *Journalism Quarterly* 66 (Winter 1989): 793.

CHAPTER 3

The Press Glory Years

By 1971 the Vietnam War was widely unpopular. President Richard Nixon, who had promised in 1969 to start withdrawing American troops, escalated the war the following year. The same year, student protestors were shot and killed at Kent State University and Jackson State University. One of the people becoming increasingly antiwar was historian Daniel Ellsberg, who as a defense department analyst had helped write a small portion of a forty-seven-volume report about American involvement in Vietnam for Secretary of Defense Robert McNamara. The report, which became known as the *Pentagon Papers*, showed that American leaders had consistently misled the public about the war. Ellsberg secretly copied most of the voluminous report and turned it over to the *New York Times*. The newspaper began running a series based on the report, complete with excerpts, in June 1971. Perhaps not coincidentally, the *Chicago Tribune* noted, publication began just days before the Senate was to vote on an amendment compelling American disengagement from the war by the end of the year. The *Tribune* later suggested it was "hardly coincidental that the documents were leaked to organs which are in the forefront of those calling for immediate withdrawal from Viet Nam."[1]

Claiming that publication of the report could harm national security, the Justice Department asked the newspaper to desist. Then, after publication of the third installment, it persuaded a court to grant a temporary restraining order that restricted further publication. It was the first time since World War II that a court had imposed a "prior restraint" on publication. After the *Washington Post* and other newspapers obtained copies of the *Pentagon Papers*, they, too, were prohibited from running articles. In a remarkably speedy case, the Supreme Court decided in favor of the newspapers fifteen days after the injunction was filed. The *Post* and the

Times both ran large front-page banner headlines announcing the 6–3 decision. If not for the hasty manner in which it was decided, the decision might have gone unanimously against the government. The articles began to run anew, winning the *New York Times* the Pulitzer Prize for Public Service.[2]

The *Times* and the *Washington Post* were not the only newspapers to recognize the significance of the court victory, though it was not yet clear how far the press would go in pursuing suspicions about government. Editorial writers throughout the country generally praised the court decision, but not all accepted the idea that the press and its allies could now declare open season on government. The Portland *Oregonian*, for example, termed publication of the report "a questionable act," later calling the decision one "for enlightenment, not license" while criticizing Ellsberg for releasing the papers.[3] "And who is to say what other secret or top secret documents may be in the same clandestine channels?" asked the newspaper. "Are the rest of the nation's critical documents—those classified for good cause—subject to the same willy-nilly distribution?"[4]

Even the conservative *Chicago Tribune* supported the Supreme Court decision, though it declared: "This doesn't mean that the Nixon administration wasn't justified in bringing action against the papers. The government could not have sat by and done nothing while documents which were officially labeled as top secret—rightly or wrongly—were being spread across the front pages of the country."[5] The paper also criticized the Nixon administration for attempting "to defend the indefensible efforts of prior administrations," those of Kennedy and Johnson.[6]

Other newspapers were even more open in their praise of the decision and their criticism of the government. After the Supreme Court decision, the *Seattle Post-Intelligencer's* lead Independence Day editorial declared that the Court had affirmed "that freedom of the nation's press is so vital that its preservation normally must take priority over all other considerations."[7]

The Pentagon took another significant hit from the news media four months before newspapers began publishing the *Pentagon Papers,* when CBS aired a documentary titled *The Selling of the Pentagon.* The show, which focused on the public relations efforts of the military, ran again just a month later. Some sources complained that selective editing had distorted the context of their comments, but the Federal Communications Commission refused to intervene. A congressional committee then recommended that CBS president Frank Stanton be held in contempt of Congress. Congress voted 226–181 against the recommendation, strengthening the argument that the First Amendment protected broadcast journalism just as it did print. Congress also rejected a bill (which likely would have been unconstitutional, anyway) that would have regulated how documentaries could be edited.

Though it came about more because of government action than by anything the newspapers did, the *Pentagon Papers* case helped the press reach perhaps its high point in terms of credibility and excitement during the 1970s. In part, it became more credible simply because government became less credible and Americans were looking for new sources of institutional authority. At the same time, empowered by new journalistic tools, journalists took on American institutions and engaged in unforeseen levels of investigative reporting. By the middle of the decade, Congress and every state had enacted open-meetings laws. Editorial writers reminded readers more regularly than they typically had about the role of the press, particularly in terms of its watchdog relationship with government. Philip Kerby of the *Los Angeles Times* won a Pulitzer Prize for his editorials against government secrecy and judicial censorship.[8]

As perhaps both a result and a reflection of the changing nature of that press/government relationship, the Supreme Court decided more key press cases during the 1970s than during any other decade in American history. Several of those conflicts came about because of an even more important court decision, *New York Times v. Sullivan* in 1964, which significantly changed the American press and its relationship with public officials. Stemming from an advertisement promoting the civil rights movement, the *Sullivan* ruling declared that public figures had little protection from media prying, even if the medium in question got the facts wrong. The press now had much more freedom to openly criticize public officials. Until *Sullivan*, printed personal attacks posed a much greater legal risk for newspapers. Though later journalists were quick to cite the case in defense of their actions, it is worth noting that the case, in which a Southern police commissioner claimed he had been libeled, resulted from an advertisement, not from a news article or editorial. It also was a case that even the mighty *New York Times*, then the most powerful newspaper in the country, pursued reluctantly out of fear it might lose.[9]

Sullivan and later clarifying decisions made libel extremely difficult to prove. Under the new guidelines, an aggrieved party generally had to prove that a story not only had been false and defamatory, but also that it had clearly identified the victim while causing demonstrable harm. The plaintiff also had to prove fault on the part of the publication, or at least a "reckless disregard" for the truth.

Sullivan helped change how the press covered political (and entertainment) figures. From a positive perspective, less fear of libel suits meant that journalists could be more fearless in their pursuit of the truth and could more easily call into question the acts of elected officials. From a more negative perspective, even the most untrue personal attacks gained legal protection. Personal problems also came to be considered more newsworthy, especially when coupled with increasing commentary by reporters and an increasing emphasis on personalities over policies.

Several other Supreme Court cases also helped define the freedom of the press. In *Miami Herald Publishing Co. v. Tornillo*, the Court ruled that broadcasting's "Fairness Doctrine" did not apply to print media. Florida electoral law required newspapers to provide a free "right to reply" to candidates who had been criticized in news reports or editorials, but the *Herald* refused to comply with the law. The plaintiff argued that most metropolitan newspapers had little competition—and therefore little chance of being corrected or contradicted by opposing reports—but the Court pointed out that requiring newspapers to print replies likely would have a chilling effect on future publication. As many broadcasters already did, editors would fear controversy and the increased expenses of providing replies and would limit their political coverage all together.

Besides learning more about what they could leave out, newspapers also learned more about what they could put in. *Cox Broadcasting Corp. v. Cohn* established a right to publish even the name of a juvenile rape/murder victim that was taken from open records or proceedings. The Supreme Court unanimously ruled in *Nebraska Press Association v. Stuart* that newspapers could not be prevented from writing about a case, even in an effort to reduce pretrial publicity and enhance a fair trial. A 7–2 decision in *Bigelow v. Virginia* upheld the right of a newspaper to run objectionable advertising about an issue of public interest (abortion, in this case).

The increasing number of First Amendment cases and concerns about the issue of confidential sources helped prompt the 1970 formation of the Reporters Committee for Freedom of the Press, an organization for working journalists who might find themselves in legal difficulty. The organization's steering committee included Barbara Walters and Howard K. Smith from ABC, Walter Cronkite and Lesley Stahl from CBS, Tom Brokaw from NBC, and representatives of the *New York Times, Washington Post, Los Angeles Times, Time,* and *Newsweek*. In 1977, the group began publishing the *News Media and the Law* six times per year (later quarterly) to discuss legal issues and cases. Several other press-related publications began to appear, as well. Prior to 1968, only three journalism reviews existed. About forty such reviews (including the *Washington Journalism Review*, later renamed the *American Journalism Review*) were started in the next nine years, though most quickly died out. The Newspaper Division of the Association for Education in Journalism also started a new publication devoted to newspaper-related research. *Newspaper Research Journal* debuted in November 1979, calling itself "the only publication that offers original research of practical value to the newspaper industry."[10]

Another organization, formed in 1975, began offering training for journalists and for teachers of future journalists. Nelson Poynter, publisher of the *St. Petersburg Times,* founded The Poynter Institute. He died in 1978 but willed the controlling stock of his newspaper to the nonprofit institute, helping guarantee its survival.[11]

Other factors also improved the technical aspects of newspapers. More journalists were graduating from journalism programs. In an effort to improve their own quality, at a time when newspapers were incorporating more literary elements into their news stories, some also began hiring "writing coaches."[12]

A new *Associated Press Stylebook and Libel Manuel* appeared in 1977 after two years of development and quickly became the style bible for most American newspapers (though not the *New York Times*, which maintained its own). AP executive editor Louis Boccardi wrote about the stylebook, "The orders were: Make clear and simple rules, permit few exceptions to the rules, and rely heavily on the chosen dictionary as the arbiter of conflicts."[13] Widespread adoption of the stylebook improved consistency among newspapers, while reducing the need to revise incoming wire copy (making that copy even easier to use).

The press made conscientious efforts to examine the behavior not just of other societal institutions, but also of itself. In 1973, news organizations and other corporations funded the National News Council to investigate complaints against the news media. It was modeled in part after the Minnesota News Council, founded a couple of years earlier, which still survives. Gannett and CBS strongly supported the national council, though others refused to go along.[14]

The *Louisville (Ky.) Times* and *Courier Journal* were among the biggest supporters of the National News Council—not surprising, as the *Courier Journal* previously had originated something else aimed at improving journalists' credibility: the news ombudsman. The typical role of the ombudsman (sometimes called by some other title, such as "reader representative" or "reader advocate") was to serve as a liaison between the newspaper and its readers, investigating reader complaints and then reporting in the newspaper itself what reporters or editors had done right or wrong. The *Washington Post, Chicago Tribune, Boston Globe*, and *Seattle Times* all added ombudsmen.

The *Los Angeles Times* went even further than most newspapers, naming reporter David Shaw as its media critic in 1974. Part of his job would be to investigate and write, sometimes in multipart stories, about the actions of the *Times* and other media. He continued to do so for more than twenty-five years, winning a 1991 Pulitzer Prize and making enemies as a result. "Various folks at the *Times*—including several high-ranking editors," he wrote, "have been so upset with my articles at various times that they've screamed at me or complained to the top editor or refused even to respond to my hallway 'hello.' "[15] He also wrote books and magazine articles related to the news media and became so well established that his own work frequently became a target for other newspapers' media critics until his death in 2005.

Better reporters, more self-examination, more legal freedoms, and stronger affiliations all made for better journalism and contributed to the increased emphasis on investigative reporting during the 1970s. Still, much of that increase came as a natural offshoot of the tumultuous times. Writer J. Herbert Altschull, noting that the optimism that had marked the 1960s disintegrated because of nationwide turmoil, said investigative journalists were among the "chief disseminators of cultural pessimism."[16] While alternative newspapers probably helped set the agenda for mainstream newspapers in some cases, investigative reporting provided a way to incorporate the activism of alternative publications into a format more palatable to mainstream journalists concerned with objectivity. As noted by one media history text, "Because the reporter stands aloof from the story, investigative reporting contrasts with another manifestation of the truth-behind-the-facts goal, the New Journalism of the 1960s and '70s."[17]

In some respects 1970s investigative journalism was simply a logical progression of what many publications had begun doing earlier, with the muckraking magazines and some of the so-called yellow journalism of the turn of the century perhaps providing the best examples. More recently, syndicated columnist Drew Pearson had been writing "Washington Merry-Go-Round" since the 1930s and was joined by Jack Anderson in 1947. The two men, who considered investigative journalism to be the most important part of their work, produced a book titled *The Case Against Congress* in 1968.[18]

Other journalistic teams helped prove that two or more reporters working together could achieve more than those working separately. *Newsday*'s Bob Greene, sometimes called "the father of investigative team reporting," set up a permanent investigations team at the newspaper in 1967. It won a Pulitzer Prize three years later and then a second in 1974. Donald Barlett and James Steele began a "temporary relationship" as a *Philadelphia Inquirer* investigative team in 1971. The partnership lasted more than thirty years, netting the duo Pulitzer Prizes in 1975 and 1989. As some newspapers began putting together investigative teams, the Associated Press established a Washington task force of top journalists to concentrate on special projects, mostly investigative stories.[19]

Investigation of the federal government became a bit easier, and perhaps more acceptable, with the 1966 passage of the Freedom of Information Act. The new law, modified the following year, instituted the Federal Public Records Law. Journalists had hoped for an even stronger bill, but they viewed the new law with cautious optimism. Many recognized that a change in the law did not necessarily change the attitudes of bureaucrats who tried to hold onto documents, and knew that legal battles would ensue to further define the boundaries. The first court ruling under the law went against the press, and government agencies were slow to make policy changes in regard to the release of information. Still, later journalists would regularly use Freedom of Information requests to pursue and uncover stories.[20]

At a time when bulky television cameras essentially precluded secretive recording, print journalists could do things that TV could not. Much of the information came from documents and secretive sources, neither of which was well suited for the visual nature of television, and print was much more conducive to the in-depth explanation needed for investigative stories. As electronic media acquired the ability to provide improved immediacy and impact, newspapers turned to things for which they were better suited—explanation and interpretation, both key factors in investigative reporting. Some investigative pieces began to appear on television, as well, though CBS correspondent Terry Drinkwater's 1972 suspension for "staging" news events helped demonstrate the disadvantages of broadcast media in dealing with investigative stories.[21]

Technological advances also improved reporting and contributed to the boom in investigation. The arrival of fully automated photocopy machines meant that by the 1960s reporters and their sources could soon begin easily duplicating documents. The cassette tape recorder appeared in the same decade, proving much more useful for reporters than bulky reel-to-reel machines. Microcomputers quickly became tools of the trade, as increasing numbers of reporters learned how to compile and analyze huge databases of information such as tax records, census data, criminal records, and legal decisions.

The use of computers became a central element of what was coming to be called "precision journalism," a brand of investigative journalism that relied heavily on statistics and social science research methods. Philip Meyer, one of the earliest and best proponents of the practice, argued that though computers improved journalism, the role of the journalist remained the same: "Find the facts, tell what they mean, and do it without wasting time. If there are new tools to enable us to perform this task with greater power, accuracy, and insight, then we should make the most of them."[22] While another author suggested that computers were good simply for math and "finding patterns," he noted, "It is, however, quite enough."[23] One of the first examples of how useful computers could be to compile related data came in 1968, when the *Miami Herald* produced a series detailing high crime rates, low arrest rates, and possible prosecutorial biases against blacks and the poor. Number-crunching precision journalism later let reporters in other states figure out which school bus drivers or teachers or day care workers had criminal records. In another example, Meyer shared a 1968 *Detroit Free Press* Pulitzer Prize for using survey data to better explain riots in Detroit. Among other surprising details, he found that college-educated people were as likely to riot as were high school dropouts. The rise in precision journalism, which some began to call "computer-assisted reporting," also meant that journalists had to become more comfortable with numbers or run the risk of misinterpreting data. "Computers make it possible to screw up on an even-larger scale," Meyer later warned.[24]

With or without computers—at a time when journalists had tired of being misled by the Kennedy and Johnson administrations, particularly in regard to Vietnam, leading to a more antagonistic press-government relationship—one of the most notable things about the rise in investigative reporting was how much of that investigation targeted government. Local investigative reporting became a Pulitzer Prize category in 1964. The point is that prizewinning investigative reporters before 1970 rarely targeted government, while prizewinning investigative reporters during the 1970s almost always targeted government. One likely reason is that government agencies kept better records than did private organizations. Because of new open meetings laws, open records laws, and computer databases, reporters also had more access to those records, though as reporters became more accustomed to seeking the information government officials also sometimes used computer record-keeping as a means of hiding information.[25]

National investigative reporting focused heavily on government, as well, though reporters also examined issues of public concern such as medicine, the environment, and unions. "It is sobering, maybe, to note that the Pulitzer Prizes in journalism are won by reporters who have bad news to report—usually scandals of some sort, government misdeeds, things that somebody would rather not have in print," editorialized the *Atlanta Constitution* in 1974.[26] In one major story of that year, Seymour Hersh, who as a freelancer had exposed the My Lai Massacre in Vietnam, reported in the *New York Times*: "The Central Intelligence Agency, directly violating its charter, conducted a massive, illegal domestic intelligence operation during the Nixon Administration against the antiwar movement and other dissident groups in the United States, according to well-placed Government sources." The agency maintained files "on at least 10,000 American citizens," Hersh reported.[27] The most important of the 1970s investigative stories came a bit earlier, however, and became known by a single word, a word that would be attached to numerous future scandals: Watergate.

"Five men, one of whom said he is a former employee of the Central Intelligence Agency, were arrested at 2:30 a.m. yesterday in what authorities described as an elaborate plot to bug the offices of the Democratic National Committee here," the *Washington Post* reported in a front-page story on June 18, 1972.[28] *Post* reporters Bob Woodward and Carl

Bernstein, both under 30 and paired for the first time, ran their first story about the case the following day, noting that one of the burglars "is the salaried security coordinator for President Nixon's reelection committee."[29]

Other news media gave the story considerably less attention. The *New York Times* carried the story on an inside page and some newspapers ignored it at first, a fact that CBS president Richard Salant later trumpeted while incorrectly recalling that CBS news "led the broadcast with the story—devoting over three minutes (15 percent of its news hole) to the story."[30] In fact, a plane hijacking led off the CBS report the Monday after the Saturday break-in, though all three networks devoted at least three minutes to the Watergate story.[31]

Six weeks later, the *Post* reported that one of the burglars had wound up with a $25,000 cashier's check designated for Nixon's campaign. Less than a month before Nixon's landslide win in the election, the *Post* reported, "FBI agents have established that the Watergate bugging incident stemmed from a massive campaign of political spying and sabotage conducted on behalf of President Nixon's re-election and directed by officials of the White House and the Committee for the Re-election of the President."[32] Watergate had become a full-time story for the two young reporters, but the American people, and most of the news media, had taken little notice. Other 1972 incidents drew much more media attention, enhancing the Republicans' chances of retaining the White House.

First, Nixon used his office to its full advantage by making historic trips to the Communist capitals of Beijing and Moscow. In February, his groundbreaking China visit allowed American television viewers to see sites previously hidden. Newspapers around the country used words and photos to carry scenes of Chinese life. *Chicago Tribune* reporter Hugh A. Mulligan noted that "spittoons are strewn about everywhere" and that China was "probably the only place left where you can get a good five-cent cigar."[33] The TV networks also were on the scene, though access for all reporters was limited. "Instead of opening a window on the world of the new China, TV gave us a peephole," *Los Angeles Times* TV critic Maury Green wrote, observing that for much of one 30-minute special, four reporters "sat around in a rather barren hotel room...talking about how little they knew."[34] Still, Americans saw scenes previously off limits, including Chinese schools, the Great Wall of China, and the use of acupuncture. In May, Nixon attended a weeklong summit with Soviet leader Leonid Brezhnev. The two men signed the Strategic Arms Limitation Treaty, and the American flag flew over the Kremlin for—as noted by reporters along for the trip—the first time in history. Along with Nixon's promise that he had a plan to end the war in Vietnam, the two trips made the world seem a safer place.[35]

Despite the positive imagery gained through activities on the world diplomatic stage, Nixon had a rocky relationship with the press, which he distrusted throughout his political career. "The truth is that President Nixon and some of his advisors have never really understood the role of the press in American life," the *Atlanta Constitution* editorialized during his first term. It then added prophetically: "They probably never will."[36] Like Lyndon Johnson before him, Nixon probably suffered to some degree simply because he was not John F. Kennedy, a press favorite (despite his sometimes-criticized efforts to manage or manipulate the news) who had excelled at live news conferences. Nixon's lack of charisma made him particularly vulnerable to journalists who were gaining more recognition of their own power. *Newsweek* magazine focused on the conflict with a 1973 cover story.[37]

Still, despite the fact that even Walter Cronkite had complained a year earlier that the Nixon administration might be engaging in "a grand conspiracy to destroy the credibility of the press," most newspapers endorsed him in 1968 and then even more convincingly in 1972.[38] Even some newspapers that endorsed Hubert Humphrey in 1968 climbed onto the Nixon bandwagon in 1972, endorsing him over Democrat George McGovern by a 14–1 margin. Working journalists covered the campaign in packs that followed the candidates, producing few surprises at a time when editors may have valued normalcy more than uncertainty or "scoops." Nixon easily won reelection, though not the hearts of the working press. In fact, the largest newspaper employees' union, the Newspaper Guild, endorsed McGovern in 1972, breaking a forty-year tradition of neutrality.[39]

By the 1970s, Nixon already had a long, mixed history with television. Suspected of campaign funding improprieties while a 1952 vice presidential nominee, he had used TV to appeal directly to the public. The appeal, which became known as the "Checkers" speech because of his reference to his dog, probably saved his place on the ticket. On the other hand, in the first 1960 Kennedy-Nixon debate, Kennedy's appearance may have overwhelmed Nixon's arguments. After he became president, a lack of respect between him and journalists became obvious. Nixon once responded to a tough question from CBS newsman Dan Rather with, "Are you running for something?" Rather replied: "No, Mr. President. Are you?" Through various approaches, the Nixon administration helped separate "the people" from "the media," then a relatively new term that since has been latched onto by a multitude of disgruntled politicians. Nixon generally tried not to openly antagonize the press, letting Vice President Spiro Agnew and Senator Robert Dole serve as the point men on the attack. Dole made veiled threats about not renewing the licenses of stations that criticized the administration, and Agnew once referred to journalists as liberal "nattering nabobs of negativism."[40] Those who offended the administration also sometimes found themselves left off of the press plane for future trips, and Cronkite and other journalists blamed the president. As he had in 1952, Nixon also continued to try to bypass reporters to talk directly to the American people through regular televised addresses.[41]

While many in the news media failed to recognize the significance of the Watergate break-in and later developments as they played out, giving the issue relatively little coverage, the *Washington Post* vigorously pursued the story from beginning to end. The *New York Times*, CBS, *Time*, and *Newsweek* eventually joined the *Post* in dogged pursuit of the story, and the resulting revelations led to two sets of congressional hearings that played out on national television. Nixon used several televised public appeals to address the case and defend himself, while noting in August 1973 that "the three major networks have devoted an average of over 22 hours of television time each week to this subject." Eight months later when the House Judiciary Committee subpoenaed White House audiotapes related to Watergate, Nixon used another public address to explain why he had withheld the tapes and then decided to release only edited transcripts. "In giving you these records—blemishes and all—I am placing my trust in the basic fairness of the American people," he said, while also predicting what journalists might do. "I realize that these transcripts will provide grist for many sensational stories in the press . . . certain parts of them will be seized upon by political and journalistic opponents." As Watergate revelations tumbled forth in the press and in public hearings, however, no public appeal could save Nixon. Viewers of the televised hearings watched the burglars and members of the administration admit wrongdoing, and it became clear that Nixon had been lying about his knowledge of the case. In August 1974 he resigned. Woodward and Bernstein won a Pulitzer Prize for their stories. In his final address to the nation, announcing his resignation, the 37th president began by noting, "This is the 37th time I have spoken to you from this office." For more than thirty years, journalists, government officials and others tried to guess the identity of the *Post's* leading anonymous source. In 2005, former FBI deputy director W. Mark Felt, who previously had denied it, admitted that he had been the source nicknamed "Deep Throat."[42]

Watergate sometimes is credited with increasing the number of college journalism majors, and a subsequent glut of journalism grads that held down salaries for beginning journalists for years to come. But crediting or blaming Watergate is to perpetuate a myth, or at best an exaggeration. The spurt began well before Watergate, with the number of U.S. journalism majors doubling between 1967 and 1972. The number more than doubled again over the next fifteen years. Factors such as overall population growth among college-age Americans and the number of students seeking a way to earn a "practical" degree or to find a field in which they could express an activist bent undoubtedly contributed to the growth in journalism's popularity. Improved recruiting of women and minorities also contributed. By the mid-1980s, women students outnumbered men 2–1 and the percentage of journalism degrees earned by minority students had also climbed.[43]

The increased visibility (and quality) of local television news, along with the general excitement of the era, also helped spur the increase. Many of the new students had at least as much interest in being "on television" as in being journalists, and much of the increase corresponded with a decrease in English and creative writing majors, suggesting that some students now recognized increased value in specific job-related skills training. The number of journalism majors who never sought jobs in the field also grew, indicating that at least some of the enrollment increases simply reflected a tendency for many unfocused degree-seeking students to gravitate toward journalism programs, or what were increasingly becoming known as communication programs. In addition, some young men attended college to avoid the military draft, and some of those students likely viewed journalism as a major that was either more socially conscious or less academically demanding than some of their other options.[44]

One development that helped enhance the credibility of investigative reporting, even among journalists, some of whom were uncomfortable with what might be perceived as attack journalism, was the 1975 formation of a national organization called Investigative Reporters and Editors (IRE). The Christian Church (Disciples of Christ), which had actively supported freedom of information, and a Lilly Endowment Grant both proved instrumental in helping a small group of journalists form IRE. Investigative reporters from around the country quickly joined. The organization drew national attention from outside of the industry a year later, when members descended upon Phoenix, Arizona, to investigate the death of one of their own. *Arizona Republic* reporter Don Bolles, an IRE founding member, died after a car bombing. That prompted dozens of IRE journalists from ten newspapers and television stations to spend five months investigating the political corruption that led to his death. Newspapers around the country published part or all of the resulting twenty-three-part series, which focused on organized crime in Arizona.[45]

Many newspapers, including the *New York Times* and the *Washington Post*, declined to participate in the massive "Arizona Project," in part out of a belief that journalists should not engage in personal crusades, and in part out of competitive concerns. "We shouldn't be getting together; if a story is worth investigating, we should do it ourselves," said *Times* editor A.M. Rosenthal.[46] *Post* editor Ben Bradlee said he did not believe in team journalism, at least if the team involved members from outside his own newsroom. The controversial project led to lawsuits, financial problems, and political differences within the organization but probably also helped guarantee IRE survival in the long run. Throughout most of its history, the organization has offered tips and training for investigative journalists and journalism educators, and it maintains a database of thousands of investigative stories. Bolles's killer was caught and sentenced to prison, but whoever funded the killing escaped.[47]

A 1970s highlight of television journalism came with the coverage of an event thousands of miles away when Iranian students took over the American embassy in Tehran, holding fifty-two Americans hostage for 444 days. ABC soon began a series of nightly updates about the crisis. As with virtually every ongoing crisis story that followed, the network came up with a bold title for the ongoing drama, *America Held Hostage*. The show, hosted by Ted Koppel, aired immediately after the nightly news, opposite the lighter fare offered by Johnny Carson on NBC and movies on CBS. On its 142nd day, the title of the program became *Nightline*. The constant coverage helped cripple the presidency of Jimmy Carter, who just a year earlier had overseen meetings that led to the historic Camp David Accords, a peace agreement between Egypt and Israel.

Nightline became an American late-night institution, winning over the critics and a dedicated audience with what the *Christian Science Monitor* called "the thinking man's alternative to late network viewing."[48] It won extra praise a few years later with two other international stories, a 1985 series from South Africa and a 1988 series from Israel. In each case, representatives from opposing sides spoke to Koppel on camera, helping viewers better understand the depth of the conflicts.

For the first half of what may have been American journalism's finest decade, Vietnam continued to be a top story. American troops pulled out in 1973, and one of the most memorable images of the decade came at the end of the war with the 1975 fall of Saigon. Newspapers around the country showed photos of U.S. Marine helicopters taking off from the roof of the American Embassy, carrying Americans and Vietnamese refugees. One Marine recalled: "We'd shove as many as 85 Vietnamese on one bird, designed to carry less than half that number of people. We made them leave the luggage behind. And then we finally decided to get the American journalists out of there because they were being such a pain in the ass."[49]

From the perspective of the reporter struggling to get out, the evacuation was frightening and perilous. For journalists, as for others, self-preservation took over. *Chicago Tribune* reporter Keyes Beech wrote:

> We had to fight off the Vietnamese. Ed Bradley of CBS, a giant of a man, was pushing, kicking, shoving, his face sad. I found myself pushing a middle-aged Vietnamese woman who had been sitting beside me on the bus and asked me to look after her because she

worked for the Americans and the Viet Cong would cut her throat ... Once we moved into that seething mass, we ceased to be correspondents. We were only men fighting for our lives, scratching, clawing, pushing ever closer to that wall. We were like animals.[50]

Da Nang, to the north of Saigon, had fallen the previous month. Paul Vogle's United Press International story began: "Only the fastest, the strongest, and the meanest of a huge mob got a ride on the last plane out of Da Nang Saturday. People died trying to get aboard and others died when they fell thousands of feet into the sea because even desperation could no longer keep their fingers welded to the undercarriage."[51] After the fall of Saigon, newspapers and television would carry numerous stories about desperate Vietnamese "boat people" escaping the country, but for American journalists the war was over. The press would experience fallout from the "last uncensored war" in years to come, however.

By the end of the turbulent 1970s, even members of the news media were uncertain about who or what comprised "the press," or what boundaries should exist in pursuit of the news. That point was made by the 1979 case of *United States v. the Progressive Magazine*, a case also worthy of mention because of how it compared and contrasted with the *Pentagon Papers* case early in the decade. A magazine that had been around since 1909, the *Progressive* was recognized as one of the leading alternative voices of the 1970s. In 1979, it produced an article titled, "The H-Bomb Secret: How We Got It; Why We're Telling It." For the second time in eight years, the U.S. government—expressing concerns that the article would help terrorists or enemy governments build a hydrogen bomb-went to court to impose a prior restraint, managing to suppress the article for six months. Of course, Justice Department officials knew about the article in advance only because a *Progressive* editor told them, hoping to prompt a reaction; the government took the bait.[52]

Despite the press-government antagonism that had helped characterize the decade, and despite the fact that no one outside of the magazine or the government knew the content of the article, many newspapers—including the *Washington Post*, the newspaper that had helped bring down a president five years earlier—immediately took the side of the government. Other large newspapers that opposed publication included the *Los Angeles Times, Boston Globe, Atlanta Constitution, Washington Star*, and *Christian Science Monitor*, the latter two of which maintained their opposition even after virtually everyone else recognized that the government had acted too quickly and too firmly. "Many of the mass media (though not all) proved themselves pathetically eager to support Government censorship," *Progressive* editor Erwin Knoll later wrote. "Their notion was that the First Amendment stopped where 'national security' began."[53] The *Atlanta Constitution* stated plainly: "The judge made the right choice. And the rest of us should thank him for it."[54]

A few newspapers did favor the magazine even from the beginning. The *Des Moines Register* called the ban "a failure of both law and courage," while the *Burlington* (Vt.) *Free Press* stated that the Justice Department had managed to convince the judge that "the First Amendment doesn't really mean what it says."[55] After some early waffling, the *New York Times* and the *Chicago Tribune* supported the *Progressive*. Other publications did so as the weakness of the government's case became increasingly clear, and eventually most major news organizations supported the magazine. Within a matter of months, the government dropped the case.[56]

But the case made clear that defining journalism was becoming increasingly complicated. "Rarely has the press been so reluctant to join an issue where its First Amendment protections are in danger," *Newsweek* noted about the H-Bomb case.[57] The *Atlanta Constitution* was more blunt, editorializing: "There are members of the journalistic profession who are more distinguished for stupidity than for anything else. The *Progressive* magazine is an example."[58]

Public criticism of the press in general began to sharpen. It seemed that with the *Pentagon Papers* and Watergate, the news media had reached a glorious summit of influence but then began to find themselves losing credibility—experiencing a decade-long rise and fall that would, in speedier form, face many public figures who came to owe both celebrity and humiliation to the media.

NOTES

1. Editorial, "Twice-Told Tales," *Chicago Tribune*, June 24, 1971. Also see editorial, "The Tangled Web," *Chicago Tribune*, June 16, 1971; *The Pentagon Papers* (New York: Bantam, 1971); David Halberstam, *The Powers that Be* (New York: Dell, 1979); Thomas Franck and Edward Weisband, eds., *Secrecy and Foreign Policy* (New York: Oxford University, 1974).

2. "Court Rules for Newspapers, 6–3," *Washington Post*, July 1, 1971; Hedrick Smith, "Supreme Court, 6–3, Upholds Newspapers on Publication of the Pentagon Report; *Times* Resumes Its Series, Halted 15 Days," *New York Times*, July 1, 1971; "Burger's Footnote," *Portland Oregonian*, July 8, 1971.

3. Editorial, "More than Meets Eye," *Portland Oregonian*, June 19, 1971; editorial "Court for Enlightenment, not License," *Portland Oregonian*, July 2, 1971.

4. Editorial, "Let's Get to Source," *Portland Oregonian*, June 23, 1971.

5. Editorial, "Censorship and Security," *Chicago Tribune*, June 17, 1971.

6. Editorial, "A Free Press Comes First," *Chicago Tribune*, July 1, 1971.

7. Editorial, "Historic Decision," *Seattle Post-Intelligencer*, July 4, 1971.

8. The Pentagon Papers series was not itself an example of investigative reporting, of course. Newspapers had the report dumped in their lap, after it was compiled by others. Sharon Hartin Iorio, "How State Open Meetings Laws Now Compare with Those of 1974," *Journalism Quarterly* 62 (Winter

1985): 741–749; James B. McPherson, "Government Watchdogs: How Four Newspapers Expressed their First Amendment Responsibilities in Editorials," unpublished master's thesis, Washington State University, May 1993; Pulitzer Prize Web site, http://www.pulitzer.org (accessed March 6, 2006).

9. Anthony Lewis, *Make No Law: The Sullivan Case and the First Amendment* (New York: Random House, 1991). The full-page ad, titled "Heed Their Rising Voices," was sponsored by a group called the Committee to Defend Martin Luther King and the Struggle for Freedom in the South. The ad listed the names of some prominent supporters, and sought contributions to help with the effort.

10. "We Were Wrong!" *Newspaper Research Journal* 1 (November 1979). Also see Michael Emery and Edwin Emery, *The Press and America: An Interpretive History of the Mass Media*, 6th ed. (Englewood Cliffs, N.J.: Prentice Hall, 1988).

11. Poynter Intitute Web site, http://poynter.org (accessed March 6, 2006).

12. Ray Laakaniemi, "An Analysis of Writing Coach Programs on Daily American Newspapers," *Journalism Quarterly* 64 (Summer-Autumn 1987): 569–575.

13. Louis B. Boccardi, "Forward," *The Associated Press Stylebook and Libel Manual* (New York: Associated Press, 1977).

14. Alex S. Jones, "News Watchdog Group to Vote on its Future," *New York Times*, March 21, 1984; Susan Buzenberg and Bill Buzenberg, eds., *Salant, CBS, and the Battle for the Soul of Broadcast Journalism: The Memoirs of Richard S. Salant* (Boulder, Colo.: Westview, 1999): 300; Jonathon Friendly, "National News Council Will Dissolve," *New York Times*, March 23, 1984.

15. David Shaw, "How I Got that Story: Full Disclosure," *Columbia Journalism Review*, March/April 2000, Web edition, http://www.cjr.org/year/00/2/shaw.asp (accessed July 26, 2003). Also, David Shaw, *Press Watch: A Provocative Look at How Newspapers Report the News* (New York: Macmillan, 1984).

16. J. Herbert Altschull, *From Milton to McLuhan: The Ideas Behind American Journalism* (New York: Longman, 1990).

17. Harry D. Marsh and David R. Davies, "The Media in Transition, 1945–1974," in Wm. David Sloan, ed., *The Media in America: A History*, 5th ed. (Northport, Ala.: Vision Press, 2002): 456. Also see Rainer Mathes and Barbara Pfetsch, "The Role of the Alternative Press in the Agenda-Building Process: Spill-Over Effects and Media Opinion Leadership," *European Journal of Communication* 6 (March 1991): 33–62.

18. Drew Pearson and Jack Anderson, *The Case Against Congress* (New York: Simon & Schuster, 1968).

19. John Ullmann, *Investigative Reporting: Advanced Methods and Techniques* (New York: St. Martin's, 1995); Robert F. Keeler, *Newsday: A Candid History of the Respectable Tabloid* (New York: William Morrow, 1990); Donald L. Barlett and James B. Steele, *America: What Went Wrong?* (Kansas City: Andrews and McMeel, 1992): vii.

20. "Year of the Lions and the Lingering Shadows," 1966–1967 report of the New Enterprise Committee of the Associated Press Managing Editors Association, records of the Associated Press Managing Editors Association, State Historical Society of Wisconsin, Madison. Also see James AuCoin, "Investigative Journalism," in W. David Sloan and Lisa Mullikin Parcell, eds., *American Journalism: History Principles, Practices* (Jefferson, N.C.: McFarland Paul E. Kostyu, "Nothing More, Nothing Less: Case Law Leading to the Freedom of Information Act," *American Journalism* 12 (Fall 1995): 462–476.

21. United Press International, "CBS Suspends Drinkwater in 'Staging' News," *Los Angeles Times*, May 19, 1972. Also see David Shaw, *Journalism Today*: A

Changing Press for a Changing America (New York: Harper's College, 1977); James B. McPherson, "From 'Military Propagandist' to The Progressive: The Editorial Evolution of H-Bomb Battler Samuel H. Day, Jr.," doctoral dissertation, Washington State University, August 1998.

22. Philip Meyer, *Precision Journalism* (Bloomington, Ind.: Indiana University Press, 1973): 15.

23. Ibid. Of course, computers actually did much more than recognize patterns and solve math problems for the newspaper industry, even though the Internet was still more than a decade away. For reporters and editors, computers did everything the VDT had done (see Chapter 2). In addition, in the new "cold type" environment, editors soon were setting their own type and laying out entire pages on computer screens.

24. Philip Meyer, quoted in Ullmann, *Investigative Reporting*. Also see Scott R. Maier, "The Digital Watchdog's First Byte: Journalism's First Computer Analysis of Public Records," *American Journalism* 17 (Fall 2000): 75–91; Margaret Sullivan, "Q&A: Reporting with Computers," *Columbia Journalism Review*, May/June 2001.

25. "Matthew D. Bunker, "Have it Your Way? Public Records Law and Computerized Government Information," *Journalism & Mass Communication Quarterly* 73 (Spring 1996): 90–101; Sigman L. Splichal and Bill F. Chamberlin, "The Fight for Access to Government Records Round Two: Enter the Computer," *Journalism Quarterly* 71 (Autumn 1994): 550–560.

26. Editorial, "The Pulitzers," *Atlanta Constitution*, May 8, 1974.

27. Seymour Hersh, "Huge C.I.A. Operation Reported in U.S. against Antiwar Forces, Other Dissidents in Nixon Years," New York Times, December 22, 1974.

28. Alfred E. Lewis, "5 Held in Plot to Bug Democrats' Offices Here," *Washington Post*, June 18, 1972.

29. Bob Woodward and Carl Bernstein, "GOP Security Aide Among Five Arrested in Bugging Affair," *Washington Post*, June 19, 1972. Also see Bob Woodward and Carl Bernstein, *The Final Days* (New York: Avon Books, 1976); Louis W. Liebovich, *Richard Nixon, Watergate, and the Press: A Historial Perspective* (Westport, Conn.: Praeger, 2003).

30. Buzenberg and Buzenberg, *Salant, CBS, and the Battle*, 117.

31. Vanderbilt Broadcast News Archives Web search, http://tvnews.vanderbilt.edu/ (accessed March 6, 2006).

32. Carl Bernstein and Bob Woodward, "FBI Finds Nixon Aides Sabotaged Democrats," *Washington Post*, October 10, 1972. Also see Carl Bernstein and Bob Woodward, "Bug Suspect Got Campaign Funds," Washington Post, August 1, 1972.

33. Hugh A. Mulligan, "Red China Has What the World Needs-A Good 5-Cent Cigar," Chicago Tribune, 2 February 24, 1972.

34. Maury Green, "Window on World More a Peephole," *Los Angeles Times*, February 25, 1972.

35. Theodore Shabad, "Kremlin Flies U.S. Flag—First Time in History," *Atlanta Constitution*, May 23, 1972.

36. Editorial, "Hang in There," *Atlanta Constitution*, May 25, 1971.

37. Russell Watson, "Nixon and the Media," *Newsweek*, January 15, 1973, 42–48. Also see "President and the Press," *Seattle Post—Intelligencer*, January 7, 1971; Harold W. Chase and Allen H. Lerman, eds., *Kennedy and the Press: The News Conferences* (New York: Thomas Y. Crowell, 1965); William Porter, *Assault on the Media: The Nixon Years* (Ann Arbor, Mich.: University of Michigan, 1976); Buzenberg and Buzenberg, *Salant, CBS, and the Battle*; James Keogh, *President Nixon and the Press* (New York: Funk & Wagnells, 1972).

38. Cronkite quoted in editorial, "Cronkite Talks Back," *Seattle Post-Intelligencer*, May 23, 1971.

39. Byron St. Dizier, "Republican Endorsements, Democratic Positions: An Editorial Page Contradiction," *Journalism Quarterly* 63 (Autumn 1986): 581–586; Haynes Johnson, "The Newspaper Guild's Identity Crisis," *Columbia Journalism Review*, November/December 1972, 44–48; Timothy Crouse, *The Boys on the Bus* (New York: Ballantine, 1972).

40. A few years later, the *Atlanta Journal and Constitution* reminded readers of Agnew's comments while discussing comments by Senator Herman Talmadge who also "descended to the level of alliteration" when he referred to the press as "pernicious paragons of perfidy"; editorial, "Fuss and Bluster," *Atlanta Journal and Constitution*, November 11, 1978.

41. "Cronkite Talks Back"; Michael Schudson, *The Power of News* (Cambridge, Mass.: Harvard University Press, 1995).

42. Ford had been appointed vice president the previous year when Agnew was forced to resign after pleading no contest on charges of evading income taxes.

43. David H. Weaver and G. Cleveland Wilhoit, *The American Journalist in the 1990s: U.S. News People at the End of an Era* (Mahwah, N.J.: Lawrence Erlbaum, 1996); Michael Schudson, "Watergate: A Study in Mythology," *Columbia Journalism Review*, May/June 1992, 28–33; Joseph A. Mirando, "Training and Education of Journalists," in Sloan and Parcell, *American Journalism*.

44. Maxwell E. McCombs, "Testing the Myths: A Statistical Review," *Gannett Center Journal* (Spring 1988): 101–108. In 1965 the journalism program at the University of Texas became part of perhaps the nation's first "school of communication"; "In 50 Years: From 'J' Shack to School of Communication," *Editor & Publisher*, January 23, 1965, 15, 56.

45. Investigative Reporters and Editors Web site, accessed at http://www.ire.org (accessed July 26, 2002).

46. Quoted in Maria B. Marron, "The Founding of Investigative Reporters and Editors, Inc. and the Arizona Project: The Most Significant Post—Watergate Development in U.S. Investigative Journalism," *American Journalism* 14 (Winter 1997): 54–75.

47. James L. Aucoin, "The Early Years of IRE: The Evolution of Modern Investigative Journalism," *American Journalism* 12 (Winter 1995): 425–443; Melvin Mencher, "The Arizona Project: An Appraisal," *Columbia Journalism Review*, November/December 1977, 39–45.

48. Arthur Unger, " 'Nightline'—A Thinking Man's Alternative to Late Network Viewing," *Christian Science Monitor*, November 13, 1980. Also see Ted Koppel and Kyle Gibson, *Nightline: History in the Making and the Making of Television* (New York: Times Books, 1996).

49. James Kean, quoted in Karen Jeffrey, "The Fall of Saigon," *Cape Cod (Massachusetts) Times* online edition, April 30, 2000.

50. Keyes Beech, *Chicago Tribune*, "We Clawed for Our Lives," reprinted in *Reporting Vietnam: American Journalism 1959–1975* (New York: Library of America, 1998): 742–743.

51. Paul Vogle, United Press International, "Flight into Hell," reprinted in *Reporting Vietnam*, 706.

52. Founded in by progressive Wisconsin Senator Robert La Follette, for the first twenty years the publication was called *La Follette's Weekly*; Howard Morland, "The H-Bomb Secret: How We Got It; Why We're Telling It," *Progressive* (November 1979): 14–23; Howard Morland, *The Secret that Exploded* (New York: Random House, 1981); A. DeVolpi and Others, *Born Secret: The*

H-Bomb, the Progressive Case, and National Security (New York: Pergamon, 1981); James B. McPherson, "From 'Military Propagandist' to The Progressive: The Editorial Evolution of H-Bomb Battler Samuel H. Day, Jr.," doctoral dissertation, Washington State University, August 1998."

53. Erwin Knoll, "Wrestling with Leviathan: The Progressive Knew It Would Win," *Progressive* (November 1979): 25.

54. "The Right Choice," *Atlanta Constitution*, March 29, 1979; *Editorials on File* 10, March 16–31, 1979.

55. Quoted in Bruce M. Swain, "The Progressive, the H-Bomb and the Papers," *Journalism Monographs* 76 (1982).

56. McPherson, "Government Watchdogs."

57. Arlie Schardt, Frank Maier, and Lucy Howard, "A Surfeit of H-Bomb Secrets," *Newsweek*, June 25, 1975, 62.

58. Editorial, "On Defending Stupidity," *Atlanta Constitution*, March 13, 1979.

CHAPTER 4

Backlash: The Press under Attack

Leaders of two newspapers found themselves under attack in an unusual way in February 1974, with what one editorial called "the first political kidnappings [sic] in [American] history."[1] *Atlanta Constitution* editor Reg Murphy was kidnapped and held for $700,000 ransom, which the kidnapper said would be used "to combat excessive liberalism of the press."[2] The kidnapper was quickly captured, and the newspaper thanked the *New York Times*, NBC, ABC, the wire services, and local television stations that cooperated in withholding the announcement until the FBI could get its men and equipment set up. The newspaper also noted that it had received letters from "nice little old ladies who wrote: 'I am glad you will have to pay the ransom. . . . The way you have persecuted the President has been awful. . . . God evens things out.' "[3]

A more notable kidnapping was that of Patricia Hearst, the 19-year-old daughter of *San Francisco Examiner* editor Randolph Hearst (and the granddaughter of the late William Randolph Hearst). A group calling itself the Symbionese Liberation Army demanded that millions of dollars be distributed to the poor, and then held the young woman for nineteen months. The Hearst newspapers and broadcast stations published political "communiqués" distributed by the kidnappers. At some point Patricia Hearst, who later maintained that she had been brainwashed, joined the group and participated in a bank robbery. She served almost two years in prison. The Murphy and Hearst kidnappings helped prompt a series of other American kidnappings during the mid-1970s, most conducted for ransom. But the kidnappings, while interesting, proved far less significant to the press as a whole than were other challenges that it began to face with increasing frequency.

As the news media gained influence, they also drew more criticism. The press had become a recognizable authoritative institution, and Americans had learned, largely from the news media, not to place too much trust in social institutions. Many of the complaints were justified, and the changing news values complicated things. Even the long-held notion of objectivity had faded with increased analysis. Journalists still claimed that they tried to be objective but were caught in the paradox noted by one writer that the "best" journalism—investigative reporting—"often seemed to be based upon outrage, indignation, advocacy, and calls for justice."[4] At the same time, the public became less enamored with even good investigative journalism, especially when it involved questionable methods.[5]

Regardless of the reasons, as the criticism increased, many in the press became less willing to subject themselves to scrutiny, or sometimes even to admit mistakes, because some worried that corrections could cause credibility problems. The ill-used and poorly promoted National News Council died in 1984 after eleven years of activity. Though a few news organizations strongly supported the national council, others refused to go along, and many hated to see their dirty laundry aired so publicly. The American Society of Newspaper Editors, *Chicago Tribune*, *Wall Street Journal*, and *New York Times* had refused to support it from the beginning, with the publisher of the *Times* arguing that the council "would divert attention from the actions of government officials that . . . were the real threat."[6] Richard S. Salant, the council's final president lamented, "Too much of the press was indifferent at best, hostile at worst."[7] In its eleven years, the council fielded 242 complaints, finding 82 of those complaints warranted, though the findings were nonbinding and carried no penalty. Of the complaints, seventy-eight were made against television networks, sixty-eight against newspapers, thirty against magazines, twenty-seven against news syndicates, nineteen against wire services, and twenty against a variety of print and electronic media.[8]

Some local news councils were established, but most of those also died, and a number of proposals for state councils went nowhere. Some newspapers began hiding their codes of ethics, afraid that the stated standards might be used against the press in legal actions. That was not an unreasonable fear. With libel suits increasing, some ombudsmen actually found themselves subpoenaed to testify against the newspapers that employed them. Enough newspapers added reader representatives during the 1970s to lead to the 1980 formation of the international Organization of News Ombudsmen, but perhaps fewer than 50 of the more than 1,500 daily newspapers in the United States have ever had an ombudsman (and many of those tried the experiment only briefly). Though the presence of ombudsmen typically had little effect on journalistic practices within newspapers, and even though most ombudsmen were themselves experienced editors, many journalists bristled at the idea of having an extra critic. Most newspapers were unwilling to pay a staff person to find and publicly point out their mistakes.[9]

Others outside journalism were more than happy to help point out those mistakes. New organizations arose during the 1980s to call attention to the faults of the news media. Unlike the largely academic publishers of journalism reviews that appeared in the previous decade, many of the new critics did not necessarily have the media's best interests at heart. Though they tended to call their activities "non-partisan," some were more obviously political than were the journalists they criticized. In 1986, the politically liberal Fairness and Accuracy in Reporting (FAIR) began providing an alternate voice to the politically conservative Accuracy in Media (AIM), which had been around since 1969. Both organizations found much to criticize, as both professed to be watching out for citizens by pointing out slanted and neglected stories. Each claimed that the mainstream media generally were politically biased, though the two disagreed on whether that bias was liberal or conservative. Two years after the arrival of FAIR came the conservative Media Research Center, with the slogan "Bringing Political Balance and Responsibility to the Media." In addition, less obvious in its political orientation but providing another regular critical voice was the research-oriented Center for Media and Public Affairs founded in 1985. As attacks increased, individuals and organizations found it increasingly easy to blame the news media for a host of problems.[10]

New legal decisions also complicated things for journalists. Though several 1970s Supreme Court cases favored the press, not all did. In *Branzburg v. Hayes* in 1972, the court narrowly ruled that reporters had no constitutional right to protect their sources and could be compelled to testify in court. That same year, *Los Angeles Herald Examiner* reporter William Farr went to jail for forty-six days after refusing to name a source. Six years later, *New York Times* reporter Myron Farber served forty days of a six-month contempt sentence, and both he and the newspaper were fined. Other reporters served less time, and judges occasionally continued to jail reporters or fine their employers.

In 1978, the Court ruled in *Zurcher v. Stanford Daily* that police could obtain warrants to search newspapers for evidence such as incriminating photos, even if no one at the newspaper was accused of a crime. That posed new concerns, though apparently fewer than thirty such searches were conducted before new federal laws restricted their use in 1981. *Gannett v. DePasquale* let judges exclude the press from pretrial hearings, and *Herbert v. Lando* established that a reporter's "state of mind" could be used to determine libel liability, leading to the possibility of more reporters being asked to identify sources or turn over interview notes and tapes. One newspaper complained: "The present Supreme Court has, with a series of recent decisions, amply demonstrated that it believes the press should be a lot less free than the press thinks it should be."[11] Though daily newspaper editors generally maintained that the *Lando* decision did not affect their decision-making, in fact many became more careful. Most daily newspapers carried libel insurance, for good reason. Two-thirds of newspapers in one survey reported being sued at least once between 1975 and 1981, another reflection of the contentious period. Though the news media almost always won, libel suits could be expensive to defend, and drew negative attention to journalists and their actions. A group of U.S. journalists created the Committee to Protect Journalists in 1981 to monitor and promote press freedom around the world. Perhaps they should have worried more about their freedom at home. They could expect even less help from the Supreme Court after President Ronald Reagan appointed William Rehnquist, the justice considered least friendly to the First Amendment, as chief justice in 1986. Antonin Scalia, also considered to be "anti-press," replaced the retired Warren Burger and a year later conservative Anthony M. Kennedy replaced Lewis Powell.[12]

Despite improved education of journalism students, increasing diversity among reporters, and more organizations and publications devoted to journalistic quality and ethics, the credibility of the news media proved to be a growing problem. Part of the problem stemmed from the success of the press during the previous decade; many Americans now viewed the news media as too powerful and biased in favor of powerful interests. For its part, the press consistently did a generally poor job of self-protection, failing to adequately explain its function to readers, or to justify its First Amendment protections. If they addressed the issue at all, editors tended to do so primarily as a defensive response to attacks, rather than as an ongoing process of citizenship education. The arrival of new cable news networks later worsened the situation for those who wanted the news to appear unbiased, as some used political bias to help carve out a market niche. Of the new networks, Fox News, with the perhaps-ironic slogan of "fair and balanced news," drew the most attention for its criticism of other media and its support of conservatives in government. Liberal activist organizations waged a 2004 Internet campaign to try to persuade the Federal Trade Commission to prohibit Fox from using the slogan, calling it misleading advertising.[13]

In fact, apart from questions of bias, many in the news media also became increasingly arrogant about their own power. National journalists in particular often came to view themselves as part of a special class, rather than as an extension of the people who made up their audience. That shift may be understandable, considering that the press as an institution had become more important during the 1970s and had, after all, helped topple a presidency. Still, those in the media found themselves as susceptible to the trappings of influence as did those in other institutions. "Inside the beltway" came to characterize the location and thinking of not just the politicians of Washington, D.C., but also of the journalists who worked there. By the mid-1980s, the distance that Richard Nixon had helped create between "the press" and "the people" had widened to a chasm. Meanwhile, the number of adults who said they read a daily newspaper dropped from more than 78 percent in 1970 to fewer than 64 percent by 1985.[14]

Most readers and viewers found fault with what were becoming increasingly popular journalism methods, such as the use of hidden cameras and unnamed sources; yet the news media seemed oblivious to the expressed concerns of the public—though perhaps "expressed" is the key word, since people often seemed most likely to watch and read what they most criticized. By the early 1980s, most network news stories and news-magazine stories, and a large percentage of stories carried by newspapers and wire services, contained anonymous attribution. Many journalists slipped into the now-common habit of using phrases such as "a White House official" or "Pentagon sources." Thoughtful news consumers were left to question for themselves whether the blind attribution was a conscientious effort to protect a source from political retribution or from simple embarrassment, an opportunity for a source to take political pot shots, simply lazy shorthand by the writer, or a way for the reporter to imply exclusivity while perhaps hiding the fact that the source was a low-ranking official or public relations person. What was gained in terms of exclusivity and perhaps drama may have been offset by questions about motives and credibility. *Newsweek* executive editor Maynard Parker warned that even though interviews might be easier and more productive if sources did not have to worry about being quoted, "we're also familiar with the price we pay for using blind quotes; each one leaves the reader less than fully informed and takes a small bite out of our credibility."[15]

Of the various aspects of investigative reporting, none was more controversial, than the use of deception or hidden cameras. In 1978, the *Chicago Sun-Times* bought and operated a bar (named the "Mirage") and then used hidden cameras to document the corruption of city employees seeking payoffs. The resulting series was a Pulitzer Prize finalist, but it lost after its use of deception drew criticism from some panelists, including those from the *New York Times* and the *Washington Post*. Most editors agreed with readers and viewers who said they opposed secretly recording sources. Still, neither journalists nor the courts agreed on hard-and-fast standards, and as hidden devices become smaller and cheaper their use continued to grow.[16]

Television newsmagazines later made the most dramatic use of the technology, typically using hidden surveillance equipment to track the behavior of dishonest auto mechanics, housekeepers, or salespeople.

More drama came when the alleged crooks were later confronted with the tape of their illicit activities. Yet while the resulting stories often proved entertaining, they also cheapened investigative journalism by using questionable investigative means to focus on small-scale corruption by individuals with little actual power, rather than on larger, institutional wrongdoing. A rare and costly exception came with what became known as the Food Lion case.

In 1992 after getting a tip about unsavory food handling practices, the ABC newsmagazine *PrimeTime Live* sent two producers undercover with hidden cameras to work for Food Lion supermarkets in North Carolina and South Carolina. The resulting stomach-turning images included unsanitary practices and the selling of old meat and spoiled food. The supermarket chain sued the show and ABC not for libel but for trespass and fraud because of the secretive taping and because the two "employees" had used phony résumés to get jobs with the company. A federal jury awarded Food Lion $5.5 million, maintaining that the press, for all its power and potential to serve the public good, had no special right that other Americans did not enjoy. The issue concerned news gathering rather than free speech, making the case that while the press has a First Amendment right to publish information, there is no corresponding "right to know" that justifies legal wrongdoing. Many inside and outside of journalism also questioned the ethical justification for engaging in illegal acts as anything other than a last resort, especially if such acts served primarily to improve the storytelling process rather than as a means of getting information unavailable in any other way.

Journalists contributed significantly to their image problem in other ways, as well. Viewers and readers expressed concerns about how well the news media separated fact from opinion, and the remnants of the novelistic free-wheeling style of some of the "new journalism" had made fact and fiction more difficult to differentiate. Still, some journalists went beyond any reasonable understanding of storytelling, engaging in outright lying. A 1980 story about an eight-year-old heroin addict won *Washington Post* reporter Janet Cooke a Pulitzer Prize, but then, as noted by *Columbia Journalism Review*, "became the gold standard by which all other acts of journalistic mendacity were measured."[17] The story (and much of Cooke's résumé) turned out to be fiction. Watergate reporter Bob Woodward was Cooke's editor, and she apparently told him that revealing the names of her sources would endanger her life. A positive result of the case was that it made editors around the country more likely to insist on knowing sources' names, reducing the likelihood of similar journalistic deception (though such incidents still arose in years to come).

One thing the Cooke case did not do was to discourage journalists from trying to win awards in hundreds of journalism competitions. Most newspapers encouraged journalists to compete for prizes. Though Cooke had not written her story to win a prize—in fact, the more attention her story got, the more she apparently worried about discovery—some critics wondered whether contests might prompt some journalists to take shortcuts, or encourage news organizations to pursue the kinds of stories that won prizes, while putting less emphasis on less journalistically "sexy" stories with more actual relevance to readers' lives.[18]

In another example of apparent journalistic falsehood, in 1985 CBS settled out of court with General William Westmoreland, who had served as commander of U.S. Military Forces in Vietnam. Westmoreland sued CBS over a 1982 broadcast titled *The Uncounted Enemy: A Vietnam Deception*, claiming the program distorted facts. A year later, *Time* magazine settled with Israeli government official Ariel Sharon, who said the magazine falsely implied that he encouraged a massacre in Lebanon. As part of the settlement, *Time* admitted that part of its report had been "erroneous." Ironically, *Time* had devoted a 1983 cover to "Accusing the Press: What are its Sins?"

With more people paying more attention to the press, those "sins" began to stack up. While problems with dishonesty probably were not becoming more common, they were becoming more noticed. Writers for several publications, including the *Cleveland Plain-Dealer, Missoulian, Pittsburgh Press, Chicago Tribune*, and *Philadelphia Enquirer*, were caught plagiarizing other publications or inventing supposed facts. Some of those incidents helped prompt the Society of Professional Journalists to adopt an amendment to its code of ethics that called plagiarism dishonest and unacceptable but that did not define plagiarism. Unfortunately, even editors disagreed in many cases about what constituted plagiarism.[19]

Other ethical problems also arose. Some print and television cameramen drew criticism for violating journalism ethics by staging photos and passing them off as reality. Editors for the *Minneapolis Star Tribune* and the *St. Paul Pioneer* revealed the name of a source, who had been promised confidentiality, prompting a breach-of-promise case eventually decided (against the newspapers) by the Supreme Court. The *Cincinnati Enquirer* later paid Chiquita Brands, Inc., a whopping $10 million and offered a front-page apology after a reporter broke into the company's voicemail system while working to document wrongdoing by the company. Each case prompted new doubts among readers and viewers and renewed hand wringing in trade journals.[20]

The press also drew fire at times when it acted honestly. Americans complained that journalists focused too much on bad news, and the more bad news people saw, the more they tended to blame the messenger. "Ambush interviews" of unwilling sources, made famous by *60 Minutes*, and brusque interviews of helpless victims (or victims' families) contributed to a view that journalists lacked sensitivity. On the heels of two 1983 military events, one *Chicago Tribune* letter writer stated: "Perhaps the most vulgar display was that of a television crew setting up its cameras on the front lawn of the home of a father awaiting news about his son who was missing in Lebanon. Or was it the 'Good Morning, America' host cheerfully interviewing the brother and sister of a young ranger killed in Grenada?"[21] Most Americans thought reporters prioritized getting good stories over the possible harm to individuals. Constant exposure may have aggravated the problem, making it more difficult for people to separate isolated incidents in the news from the possibility of harm in their own lives. Even as the crime rate dropped, for example, Americans became more fearful of crime.[22]

In 1981, the U.S. Supreme Court ruled that states could allow cameras in courtrooms. As the pictures came forth, people watched, enough that eventually an entire network would be devoted to trials. But old concerns about possible press influence on trials joined new questions about whether cameras threatened the decorum of courts or even the safety of witnesses. In one notable example, coverage of a trial that resulted from a barroom gang rape drew protests from women's groups who said the publicity might prevent other victims from coming forth, and from immigrant groups who said the news media overemphasized the rapists' ethnicity. Inaccurate early news reports about the initial incident apparently prompted increased media attention, as well, prompting one newspaper to editorialize that "the news media are victims of the information they get."[23]

Journalists did not help their faltering image when they sometimes seemed to focus on appearances and shy away from substance. Few newspapers added ombudsmen or reader's representatives, but many hired consultants and added artists and page designers. When costs were at issue and staff cuts had to be made, usually reporters and editors were the first ones cut. Others became timid. A tiny California weekly newspaper, the *Point Reyes Light*, won the top Pulitzer Prize (for Public Service) in 1979 for its dedicated investigation of Synanon, a religious cult. The case was noteworthy in part because many news media failed to pursue the story—especially after the cult began filing legal actions, including lawsuits against the Hearst Corporation and ABC (both of which settled out of court) and *Time*. Other suits, including half a dozen against the Point Reyes newspaper, were dismissed, but not before the media organizations involved expended a lot of money to fend them off.

Some critics expressed concerns about a shifting emphasis of priorities in covering political news, in which the media focused more on personalities than on processes, especially when conflict or scandal was involved. While a focus on personalities may have helped voters in determining issues of character they deemed important, the regular negative focus on them often turned off citizens. Two 1972 election coverage events helped illustrate the point, while simultaneously hurting the Democrats already-slight chances of regaining the White House. In the first, during the New Hampshire primary, the Democratic front-runner, Senator Edmund Muskie appeared to cry while responding to a newspaper article that questioned his wife's mental health. " 'What really got me was his editorial attacking my wife,' said Muskie, who became tearful at this point," the Associate Press reported.[24] Though he maintained that falling snow actually wet his cheeks, other newspapers throughout the country reported that he cried. United Press International called Muskie "visibly shaken and tearful."[25] Senator Bob Dole and others said Muskie's tears demonstrated "emotional instability," and Muskie's campaign faltered. He won the New Hampshire primary, but by less than had once been predicted.

The second 1972 example also involved the issue of mental health. Presidential candidate George McGovern selected U.S. Senator Thomas Eagleton as his running mate against Richard Nixon. Days later, the press discovered that Eagleton had been treated for nervous exhaustion years before. He admitted he had been hospitalized three times, twice receiving electric shock therapy. The press reacted strongly, to a degree that surprised Eagleton and McGovern, quickly calling for the candidate's withdrawal. McGovern first supported Eagleton, but after mounting pressure from the press and party leaders, Eagleton withdrew and was replaced by Sargent Shriver (after several others publicly refused). With less than three months to go before the election, *Time* magazine's cover photo showed McGovern standing beside Eagleton, whose head had clearly been cut out and replaced with Shriver's.[26]

The Muskie and Eagleton incidents reflected another new trend in the news media, what political scientist Thomas Patterson two decades later termed "gaffe-driven news." He wrote: "Never in history have blunders played the large role in election politics that they do today. The greater prominence of gaffes both parallels and results from the expansion of the press's large role in the campaign."[27] Incidentally, when it came to the 1972 national political conventions both parties learned from the Democrats' mistakes of four years earlier. The conventions were carefully scripted for television and, as with future conventions, produced little in the way of news.

Even those already in office found that press coverage of their activities would take on a new dimension: Private lives became newsworthy, if those lives were scandalous enough. Previously, alcohol use and the sexual peccadilloes of politicians had been considered off limits, even in the cases of presidents Kennedy and Johnson. But in October 1974, when Arkansas Congressman Wilbur Mills, chairman of the powerful House Ways and Means Committee, was arrested for drunken driving, a stripper ran from the car and had to be fished from Washington's Tidal Basin by police. The *New York Times* reported the incident, followed by the *Washington Post*. Mills was re-elected but lost his chairmanship and soon left office. Two years later, another Congressman would find himself in hot water after the *Post* reported: "For nearly two years, Rep. Wayne L. Hays (D-Ohio), powerful chairman of the House Administration Committee, has kept a woman on his staff who says she is paid $14,000 a year in public money to serve as his mistress. . . . 'I can't type, I can't file, I can't even answer the phone,' says Elizabeth Ray, 27, who began working for Hays in April 1974 as a clerk."[28]

In later years, several politicians would find themselves embarrassed by news coverage about their sex lives, and critics would find fault with the news media for ignoring weightier issues in favor of the scandalous. "The press and television gave something like saturation coverage in 1974 to Congressman Wilbur Mills' personal misfortunes; by contrast I do not recall reading anything in the press about the highly informative hearings on the Middle East, and another set on international terrorism," Former Senator William Fulbright wrote in 1975. "The crucial ingredient, it seems, is scandal—corporate, political, or personal. Where it is present, there is news, although the event may otherwise be inconsequential. Where it is lacking, the event may or not be news, depending in part, to be sure, on its intrinsic importance, but hardly less on competing events, the degree of controversy involved, and whether it involves something 'new'—new, that is, in the way of disclosure as distinguished from insight or perspective."[29]

Even when not tinged by scandal or revelations of apparent personal weakness, news coverage of political campaigns and candidates became more negative. For one thing, Americans in general became less trusting of those in authority. Journalists, skeptics by nature, joined in and helped promote that distrust. A focus on government-centered investigative stories generated some of the distrust, but some critics complained that another factor also came into play. In a rapid-paced competitive climate where the press could not hope to check all of the claims made by authorities, as a substitute for careful investigation journalists turned to politicians' political opponents to counter claims, leading to what Patterson called "news based on attack and counterattack." Soon the media skipped the middleman, regularly expressing "unsubstantiated and unattributed refutations" of their own.[30]

Another factor in the increasing negativity of coverage was the fact that those in the news media, tired of being lied to and perhaps becoming more cynical about the political process, began to change the tone of their stories. Though journalists had protested about "news management" by public officials and government repression of the media for years, they generally did little to combat it. But in the 1960s the "tone" setters of articles began to shift. Instead of letting partisan sources set the tone—whether the story was positive, negative, or neutral—the journalists determined the tone, and it increasingly was negative. For example, a candidate might have an event designed to generate positive publicity, and the available sources might all say good things about the candidate or event, while the resulting story focused on "problems" that might exist (or might not exist, for that matter, though that possibility was left unsaid). For television, "sound bites" (the parts of candidates' speeches that ran on the air) grew progressively and dramatically shorter, dropping from an average of more than half a minute in 1968 to about ten seconds twenty years later. Reporters and anchors claimed the space for their own description and analysis. As they took more control over what they reported, journalists looked much more confrontational, to the point of being viewed by some as antigovernment at best, anti-American at worst.[31]

Many stories for both print and broadcast media went from being primarily descriptive to primarily interpretive, a practice that spread beyond the coverage of politics to other public affairs reporting. In another example of the news media exerting their voice, most newspapers endorsed political candidates, though endorsements actually decreased in the years following 1975. Perhaps editors had more difficulty giving their seal of approval to anyone. Some publications generally had given presidential candidates more favorable than unfavorable coverage, but that shifted, until in 1980 the coverage became primarily about "bad news." For its part, television news focused on the positive for a bit longer, though it, too, would change.[32]

Election stories began focusing more on election strategy than on policy, while relying more on public opinion polls conducted by the news media themselves, two more trends that continue. Political journalists often were criticized, typically by trailing candidates, for their increasing reliance on polls and analysis. The increased reliance on polls changed the electoral process itself. For one thing, it created a cycle: Candidates who received the most media coverage tended to do well in polls, and then poll front-runners, viewed as the most credible candidates, received the most coverage. At the same time, coverage tended to be more negative for front-runners than for trailing candidates, a tendency that may in the long run have served to make races closer, and therefore more newsworthy in terms of drama. A heavier focus on polling provided plenty of ready-made news, created by the news media themselves, but probably also changed the electorate. "Americans used to read the newspaper to help them form their opinions," media scholar Leo Bogart noted. "Now newspapers and television tell them what their opinions are."[33] The presence of polls and increased commentary made many others, including even United Nations Secretary General Boutros Boutros-Ghali, worry that opinion was replacing law as the source of public authority.[34]

From a practical standpoint, polls also proved expensive, leading to some interesting pairings of broadcast and print news organizations. CBS started its own polling in 1967, combining polling efforts with the *New York Times* in 1975. Later pairings would include ABC and the *Washington Post*, NBC and the Associated Press, CNN and *USA Today*, and a multitude of local media organizations.

By then, politicians also were devoting much of their time and energy to polling. After he won the 1976 president election, Jimmy Carter's pollster "argued that politics and governing could not be separated. Thus was launched 'the permanent campaign,' with its armies of pollsters and political consultants."[35] Long before the election, Carter's campaign had recognized the value of getting attention early. The little-known former Georgia governor campaigned heavily in the New Hampshire primary, drawing 30 percent of the vote and, from then on, most of the attention, including cover photos in both *Time* and *Newsweek*. The news media declared Carter a winner after less than 5 percent of the primary delegates were selected.

The revolving-door nature of journalism and politics sometimes made it difficult to distinguish journalists and politicians. Bill Moyers went from the Johnson administration to *Newsday* and then to PBS. Former Nixon aide Diane Sawyer joined CBS. Ron Nessen left NBC to be Ford's press secretary. David Gergen worked for Nixon, Ford, and Reagan, became editor of *U.S. News and World Report*, joined the administration of Bill Clinton, then returned to journalism. Pat Buchanan served Nixon, Reagan, and CNN. Clinton advisor George Stephanopoulos joined ABC. Perhaps the most unfortunate example of the ties between politics and the press was less formal, when in 1983 it was revealed that three years earlier Pulitzer Prize-winning columnist George Will apparently saw a debate briefing book that had been stolen from the Carter camp, helped Reagan practice for the debate, and then, on *Nightline*, praised Reagan's debate performance. The incident caused few problems for Reagan or Will, though the *New York Daily News* dropped Will's column for violating journalist ethics. Will used his column to explain his actions, saying that columnists were not expected to be impartial like reporters but that he would not repeat his actions if given the opportunity.[36]

In an effort to broaden the perspectives being voiced, many newspapers increased the size of their letters-to-the-editor and opinion pages, but journalists still were viewed as caring more about competitive news values than about trying to improve democracy or the electoral process. It was an old complaint, but one that increased during the years after Vietnam and Watergate. Many Americans, including some politicians, accepted and promoted the argument that the news media had cost the nation victory in Vietnam. Other events also contributed to the view that journalists wanted to be involved in helping create news.

In 1985, television reporters ended up acting as intermediaries in the hijacking of a TWA airliner, and the next year NBC interviewed a terrorist after agreeing not to reveal his location. Those incidents raised new questions, previously prompted by the 1979–1980 Iranian hostage situation, about whether the actions of the news media encouraged terrorism.[37]

In 1980 and 1984, the television networks broke with tradition and told voters that Ronald Reagan had won each election before polls closed in some parts of the country, decreasing voter turnout in the West. Withholding information, NBC News President Reuven Frank said, was "inconsistent with traditional journalistic standards," though some newspaper editorial writers joined those who criticized the networks.[38] Of course, those writers were not faced with the option of projecting winners before polls closed, even if they wanted to do so. Some critics suggested modifying or ignoring the First Amendment or finding other means to restrict press power. At the very least, suggested some political scientists, the media would do more good by assuming a supportive role rather than an adversarial one, which they said undermined the credibility of American institutions.[39]

The news media continued to lose credibility, not only because of the reasons noted above but also because they succumbed to three other significant weakening influences that are discussed in the next two chapters: the growing importance of entertainment values, Ronald Reagan, and corporate business interests. Taken as a whole, perhaps it is no surprise that by the early 1990s journalism researchers David H. Weaver and G. Cleveland Wilhoit found some significant changes—and some significant nonchanges—among journalists. Though they tended to be slightly older, more experienced, more educated, and better paid than journalists of just ten years earlier they also were less happy with their jobs. Fewer journalists felt as if they controlled their professional lives, and more were planning future jobs outside of journalism.[40]

NOTES

1. Editorial, "Two Press Kidnapings," *Chicago Tribune*, February 22, 1974.
2. Editorial, "Left, Right Kidnapers," *Chicago Tribune*, February 26, 1974.
3. Editorial, "The Back-Patter," *Atlanta Constitution*, March 2, 1974.
4. Jack Lule, review of *Custodians of Conscience: Investigative Journalism and Public Virtue* in *Journalism and Mass Communication Quarterly* 75 (Autumn 1998): 662–663.
5. David Weaver and LeAnne Daniels, "Public Opinion on Investigative Reporting in the 1980s," *Journalism Quarterly* 69 (Spring 1992): 146–155.
6. Quoted in Alex S. Jones, "News Watchdog Group to Vote on its Future," *New York Times*, March 21, 1984. Also see Michael E. Cremedas, "Corrections Policy in Local Television News: A Survey," *Journalism Quarterly* 69 (Spring 1992): 166–172.

7. Susan Buzenberg and Bill Buzenberg, eds., *Salant, CBS, and the Battle for the Soul of Broadcast Journalism: The Memoirs of Richard S. Salant* (Boulder, Colo.: Westview, 1999): 300.

8. Jonathon Friendly, "National News Council Will Dissolve," *New York Times*, March 23, 1984.

9. Ronald Farrar, "News Councils and Libel Actions," *Journalism Quarterly* 63 (Autumn 1986): 509–516; David Pritchard, "The Impact of Newspaper Ombudsmen on Journalists' Attitudes," *Journalism Quarterly* 70 (Spring 1993): 77–86.

10. Accuracy in Media Web site, http://www.aim.org; Fairness and Accuracy in Reporting Web site, http://www.fair.org; Media Research Center Web site, http://www.mediaresearch.org; Center for Media and Public Affairs Web site, http://www.cmpa.com (all accessed March 6, 2006).

11. Editorial, "States of Mind," *Atlanta Constitution*, April 19, 1979.

12. Douglas A. Anderson and Marianne Murdock, "Effects of Communication Law Decisions on Daily Newspaper Editors," *Journalism Quarterly* 58 (Winter 1981): 525–528, 534; Donald M. Gillmor, Jerome A. Barron, Todd F. Simon, and Herbert A. Terry, *Mass Communication Law: Cases and Comment*, 5th ed. (St. Paul, Minn.: West Publishing, 1990); Editorial, "Editorial Processes are Opened," *News Media and the Law* (May/June 1979): 2.

13. Dorothy Bowles, "Missed Opportunity: Educating Newspaper Readers About First Amendment Values," *Newspaper Research Journal* 10 (Winter 1989): 39–53; James B. McPherson, "Crosses Before a Government Vampire: How Four Newspapers Addressed the First Amendment in Editorials, 1962–1991," *American Journalism* 13 (Summer 1996): 304–317.

14. Susan Miller, "America's Dailies and the Drive to Capture Lost Readers," *Gannett Center Journal* (Spring 1987):56–68.

15. Maynard Parker quoted in K. Tim Wulfemeyer, "How and Why Anonymous Attribution is Used by *Time* and *Newsweek*," *Journalism Quarterly* 62 (Spring 1985): 81–86, 126. Also see Weaver and Daniels, "Public Opinion on Investigative Reporting"; K. Tim Wulfemeyer and Lori L. McFadden, "Anonymous Attribution in Network News," *Journalism Quarterly* 63 (Autumn 1986): 468–473; Jane Delano Brown, Carl R. Bybee, Stanley T. Wearden, and Dulcie Murdock Straughan, "Invisible Power: Newspaper News Sources and the Limits of Diversity," *Journalism Quarterly* 64 (Spring 1987): 44–54; S. Shyam Sundar, "Effect of Source Attribution on Perception of Online News Stories," *Journalism & Mass Communication Quarterly* 75 (Spring 1998): 55–68.

16. Lois Wille, interviewed by Diane Gentry, April 1, 1992, Women in Journalism Oral History Project, Washington Press Club Foundation, Washington, D.C.; S. Elizabeth Bird, "Newspaper Editors' Attitudes Reflect Ethical Doubt on Surreptitious Reporting," *Journalism Quarterly* 62 (Summer 1985): 288; Robert L. Spellman, "Tort Liability of the News Media for Surreptitious Reporting," *Journalism Quarterly* 62 (Summer 1985): 289–295.

17. Author listed only as "R.P.," "The Big Lie," *Columbia Journalism Review* Web site, http://www.cjr.org/year/01/6/1981.asp (accessed August 10, 2002). Also see John Leo, "Oops: Bloopers of the Century," *Columbia Journalism Review*, January/February 1999, 38–40.

18. David C. Coulson, "Editors' Attitudes and Behavior Toward Journalism Awards," *Journalism Quarterly* 66 (Spring 1989): 143–147.

19. William A. Henry III, "Why Journalists Can't Wear White," *Media Studies Journal* (Fall 1992): 16–29; Tom Goldstein, *The News at Any Cost: How Journalists Compromise their Ethics to Shape the News* (New York: Simon & Schuster, 1985);

Marie Dunne White, "Plagiarism and the News Media," *Journal of Mass Media Ethics* 4 (1989): 265–280.

20. Elliot C. Rothenberg, *The Taming of the Press: Cohen v. Cowles Media Company* (Westport, Conn.: Praeger, 1999); Matthew D. Bunker and Sigman L. Splichal, "Legally Enforceable Reporter-Source Agreements: Chilling News Gathering at the Source?" *Journalism Quarterly* 70 (Winter 1993): 939–946.

21. Jack Latter, letter to the editor, *Chicago Tribune*, November 12, 1983.

22. Kristin McGrath and Cecilie Gaziano, "Dimensions of Media Credibility: Highlights of the 1985 ASNE Survey," *Newspaper Research Journal* 7 (Winter 1986): 57; Gerald Stone, Barbara Hartung and Dwight Jensen, "Local TV News and the Good-Bad Dyad," *Journalism Quarterly* 64 (Spring 1987): 37–44; Jack B. Haskins and M. Mark Miller, "The Effects of Bad News and Good News on a Newspaper's Image," *Journalism Quarterly* 61 (Spring 1984): 3–13, 65; Cecelie Gaziano, "How Credible is the Credibility Crisis?" *Journalism Quarterly* 65 (Summer 1988): 267–278, 375.

23. Editorial, "Barroom Rape's Ugly Lessons," *Seattle Post-Intelligencer*, March 24, 1984.

24. Associated Press story, "Muskie Shows Up at Paper, Calls Publisher Loeb 'Gutless Coward,'" *Los Angeles Times*, February 27, 1972.

25. United Press International story, "Muskie Calls Critic Liar, Gutless Coward," *Chicago Tribune*, February 27, 1972.

26. Donald S. Kreger, "Press Opinion in the Eagleton Affair," *Journalism Monographs* 35 (August 1974); "Democrats Try Again," *Time*, August 14, 1972, front cover.

27. Thomas E. Patterson, *Out of Order* (New York: Vintage Books, 1994).

28. Marion Clark and Rudy Maxa, "Closed Session Romance on the Hill," *Washington Post*, May 23, 1976. Because it involved possible drunken driving and personal scandal, the 1969 case of Senator Edward Kennedy and Chappaquiddick might be included among these, but it also included other aspects that made it notable under traditional definitions of news. Those aspects included the death of Kennedy's passenger, Mary Jo Kopechne, his failure to report the incident for several hours, previous driving offences, and the light sentence—two months in jail, suspended so that he served no time—that he drew after pleading guilty to leaving the scene of the accident.

29. J. William Fulbright, "Fulbright on the Press," *Columbia Journalism Review*, November/December 1975.

30. Thomas E. Patterson, "Legitimate Beef: The Presidency and a Carnivorous Press," *Media Studies Journal* (Spring 1994): 21–26.

31. Ernest C. Hynds, "Editors at Most U.S. Dailies See Vital Roles for Editorial Page," *Journalism Quarterly* 71 (Autumn 1994): 573–582; Erika G. King, "The Flawed Characters in the Campaign: Prestige Newspaper Assessments of the 1992 Presidential Candidates' Integrity and Competence," *Journalism & Mass Communication Quarterly* 72 (Spring 1995): 84–97; Patterson, *Out of Order*; Dennis T. Lowry and Jon A. Shidler, "The Sound Bites, the Biters, and the Bitten: An Analysis of Network News Bias in Campaign '92," *Journalism and Mass Communication Quarterly* 72 (Spring 1995): 33–44. The researchers report the results of three studies showing similar figures.

32. Richard Davis, *The Press and American Politics: The New Mediator*, 2nd ed. (Upper Saddle River, N.J.: Prentice Hall, 1996); Patterson, *Out of Order*; Doris A. Graber, *Mass Media and American Politics*, 4th ed. (Washington, D.C.: Congressional Quarterly Press, 1993).

33. Leo Bogart, "Media and Democracy," *Media Studies Journal* (Summer 1995): 9.

34. Boutros Boutros-Ghali, "Opinion—the New Authority," *Media Studies Journal* (Summer 1995): 20–24.

35. Quoted in Graber, *Mass Media and American Politics*. Also see Karlyn Bowman, "Knowing the Public Mind," *Wilson Quarterly* online edition, Autumn 2001, accessed at http://wwics.si.edu/OUTREACH/WQ/WQSELECT/BOWMAN.HTM (accessed August 2, 2002).

36. Richard Davis, *The Press and American Politics: The New Mediator*, 2nd ed. (Upper Saddle River, N.J.: Prentice Hall, 1996); Mary McGrory, "George Will Finds Being 'a Stablemate To Statesmen' Can Cost," *Washington Post*, July 12, 1983; George Will, "Backstage at the Presidential Debate," *Washington Post*, July 10, 1983, B7.

37. Ernest C. Hynds, "Editorials, Opinion Pages Still Have Vital Roles at Most Newspapers," *Journalism Quarterly* 61 (Autumn 1984): 634–639; Harry M. Clor, ed., *The Mass Media and Modern Democracy* (Chicago: Rand McNally, 1974); Richard W. Lee, ed., *Politics & the Press* (Washington, D.C.: Acropolis, 1970); Tony Atwater and Norma F. Green, "News Sources in Network Coverage of International Terrorism," *Journalism Quarterly* 65 (Winter 1988): 967–971.

38. Reuven Frank quoted in editorial, 'Staggered Voting to End Projections," *Seattle Post-Intelligencer*, July 24, 1983.

39. Samuel P. Huntington, *American Politics: The Promise of Disharmony* (Cambridge, Mass.: Belknap, 1981).

40. David H. Weaver and G. Cleveland Wilhoit, *The American Journalist in the 1990s: U.S. News People at the End of an Era* (Mahwah, N.J.: Lawrence Erlbaum, 1996).

CHAPTER 5

That's Entertainment

In 1977, fictional television character Lou Grant left a half-hour comedy set in a television station to become city editor of a Los Angeles newspaper in an hour-long drama. It is no surprise that CBS entertainment executives approved of the character's career change as a way of treating news seriously. After all, real television news shows were becoming more and more similar to the situation comedy Lou left behind, and the former "Tiffany Network" freely helped erase the line between news and entertainment. By the end of the 1980s, fictional CBS sit-com newswoman Murphy Brown had participated in fictional on-screen banter with Walter Cronkite and with most of the well-known members of various CBS newsmagazines, all "playing" themselves.

Even as they were finding news less credible, Americans found variations of "news" easier to access, or more difficult to escape, during the 1980s. News became more accessible, more visually appealing, more homogenous, more entertaining, and more desensitizing. At the same time, former actor Ronald Reagan used news cameras rather than movie cameras to play a lead role in helping Americans, tired of societal discord, feel better about themselves—and worse about the press.

The Iranian hostages were released in 1981 on the same day Reagan took the oath of office as president. Newspapers around the country faced the quandary of which event should lead the news as, in the words of one journalism history text, "the two stories produced an emotional outburst of headlines and color displays rarely seen in journalism."[1] Many newspapers opted for a banner head that summarized both events, before dividing the front page between the two. Other stories were pushed to later pages, as many publications responded to the newsworthiness of the two events by using larger-than-usual headlines and photos.

Perhaps oddly, though many newspapers and readers criticized tabloids as sensationalistic for their use of art and color, traditional newspapers looked more like tabloids as the news itself became more dramatic. Publishers typically adhered to the dictum of auto magnate Henry Ford, who had once offered the ultra-utilitarian Model T in any color buyers wanted, "as long as it's black," and newspapers stayed utilitarian and black far longer than the Model T. Front pages mixed small black-and-white photos with long columns of black text. Though photo sizes and headline font sizes edged upward, most newspapers still looked much as they had for years. Still, some newspapers began to experiment more with color and graphic elements even before the 1983 arrival of *USA Today*. The format changes reflected a trend toward entertainment, especially visual entertainment, in all sorts of news media. Entertainment values began to compete with functional elements in the news in numerous ways.[2]

Though newspapers were changing, broadcast news brought the obvious focus on entertainment. Even *Nightline*, the news show that arose from the hostage crisis, failed to impress everyone immediately. "It wasn't news, of course; it was the new news, neo-news, non-news, a sugary news substitute. Newsohol," *Washington Post* critic Tom Shales wrote about the premiere.[3] He criticized the fact that the program, like morning news programs and television newsmagazines to come, was produced like an entertainment show, "starting with its dizzy, busy, outer-spaced motif at the outset—a virtual duplicate of the outer-space motif used on the late-night 'Wide World of Entertainment' shows."[4] The complaints were the latest about what continued to be an ongoing trend with all types of news and pseudo-news: The news, especially on television, looked and sounded much like entertainment. At both the local and national levels, music, quick movie-style cuts, and flashing graphics (soon generated by computers) often did at least as much to generate a mood as to convey information. Eventually it would become possible to see half a dozen different elements on screen at the same time, most of them moving at various speeds and in different directions. Many critics worried about how the need to build audiences sometimes influenced the news product, emphasizing the dramatic and often the irrelevant at the expense of substance. That especially was true of television, the medium most Americans relied upon most heavily for their news.[5]

As well as television news had covered the civil rights movement, cameras did miss the murders of movement leaders Medgar Evers, Malcolm X, and Martin Luther King, demonstrating the biggest weakness of the visual nature that now characterized most of American news: Spontaneous, unexpected events, the kind of events that make up "spot news," rarely could be photographed. Not surprisingly, as Americans turned increasingly to television, news producers, and newsmakers would increasingly look for "news" that could appeal to cameras and for which cameras could be present. Because organized protests and war offered constant potential for sudden action, cameras were always ready. At home, activists concerned with a variety of issues became increasingly militant, increasing the possibilities for on-camera conflict.

The media—again, especially television—often were blamed for exacerbating volatile situations. They probably did so, though perhaps inadvertently. "The media have more commonly been acted upon than acted in their own right," argued one *Los Angeles Times* writer.[6] "Lacking any common agenda or the will to exercise power, the press and television have served mainly as a conduit for events and as potent instruments in the hands of others." *Life* magazine editor Robert Friedman suggested a less passive press role: "The press and protestors both got what they wanted: a chance to shape history."[7]

When the war wound down and protests mostly died, other less interesting pre-planned visual images took their place. Television faced the difficult reality that a lack of pictures made for dull television. Not surprisingly, much of what began to pass for TV news was made up of predictable events for which cameras could be set up in advance. Local TV reporters did not suddenly start showing up to cover every city council meeting. They were more likely to start filming petting zoos and mall grand openings.

The 1970s brought a rise in joking and friendly on-screen chatter between co-anchors or between an anchor and a weather reporter or sports reporter. The so-called happy talk probably was born in 1968 with two male co-anchors, Fahey Flynn and Joel Daley, of Chicago's WLS. With a 1970s rise in both female co-anchors and television news consultants, the phenomenon exploded, essentially eliminating the "straight news" format that preceded it. The tone of the news changed at the same time. On one hand, more positive local stories appeared, because those involved with community events actively sought coverage. Those stories were countered by stories, often not locally oriented, about fires (which almost always provide good video, regardless of their relevance to the lives of the audience) and about crime, which provided built-in drama. The slogan "If it bleeds, it leads" came into the vernacular.[8]

Political news and policy information decreased, as news directors tried to steer away from "talking heads." When interviewed news sources were heard, often their voices played over moving images that may or may not have been related to the story being told. Sometimes it was left up to the viewer to determine if the two might be related, and how, though in a society in which media literacy seldom was emphasized, few Americans had (or have) the skills for such analysis. Apparently it mattered little. What mattered was having something interesting on the screen. Just as radio producers had developed a mortal fear of "dead air," television producers found themselves working ever harder to develop ways to distract people from thinking about changing the channel.

Viewers now had more channels to consider, as expanding cable systems contributed to an explosion of independent stations. The new stations generally proved to be another lost opportunity for local television viewers seeking enhanced news coverage, however. Though the number of independents more than doubled between 1979 and 1984, most relied on syndicated programming such as talk shows and reruns of situation comedies, with relatively little local programming. Those that ran news did so primarily with either magazine shows or brief "rip-and-read" news briefs taken directly from wire services or in some cases from the daily newspaper. Some independents entered partnerships with network affiliates, so news crews suddenly found themselves doing double-duty providing stories for their network-affiliated employer and for an "extra" newscast on the independent station.[9]

Local stations brought in consultants for advice about building bigger audiences, resulting in both more entertainment and more consistency among various broadcasts. A viewer could expect a newscast in Twin Falls, Idaho, to look much like one in Greenville, North Carolina—or, despite a disparity in finances, much like one in Chicago or Los Angeles. *New York Times* critic Sally Bedell Smith decried the consulting "news doctors": "The results have given local news the feel of a fast-food franchise, with anchors dressed the same way and formats driven by pounding theme music and fast-paced reports heavy on crime and lachrymose human interest."[10] Advisors and news stations came to realize that more reporters meant more prestige and more viewers. "Eyewitness news," apparently nonexistent in America before the mid-1960s, soon became the favored format for stations everywhere. "News teams" dressed alike, with channel identification numbers as lapel pins and microphone labels. Reporters were filmed (later videotaped) "on location," even if the location added little to the telling of the story.[11]

Though the number of women in newsrooms was increasing, a 1981 incident highlighted the sometimes-shallow nature of television news. Christine Craft, a 37-year-old Kansas City anchorwoman who was paid less than half what her male co-anchor made, was demoted for, in the words of an executive, being "too old, too ugly and not deferential enough to men." She sued station owner Metromedia, Inc., twice winning judgments that were overturned. The Supreme Court refused to consider her appeal, in effect upholding the idea that television news was entertainment, dependent on attractive but disposable "talent." Justice Sandra Day O'Connor, the only woman on the court, cast the sole vote to hear the case. As unfair as the case may have been to Craft, it did illustrate an important aspect of TV news: Often people watched the news program they did in part because of the personalities who provided information, not just because of the quality of the information.[12]

Appearances mattered nationally as well as locally. A year after Reagan took office, longtime newsman Dan Rather, who had covered civil rights and the Vietnam War before joining *60 Minutes,* replaced the venerable Walter Cronkite as CBS anchor. The news set changed, as well, with a modern new blue-gray background that better complemented the color of Rather's skin, wrote a Cronkite biographer. "CBS News temporarily worked out of its Washington studios while the entire New York set was transformed from Cronkite's slightly worn-looking newsroom to Captain Kirk's bridge aboard the starship Enterprise."[13] Just two years later, Peter Jennings became sole anchor for ABC and Tom Brokaw did the same with NBC, completing a "big three" of anchors who would man the anchor desks for more than twenty years. Like local stations, entertainment-motivated network executives brought music and colorful graphics to the news. The networks also were increasing the amount of soft feature-oriented news stories that emphasized human interest over fact-based hard news, a trend that became even more pronounced after large conglomerates bought each of the "big three" networks in 1986 (becoming part of a trend discussed in the next chapter).[14]

Networks later began training programs developed in part to identify and promote qualified minority reporters, but also intended to find those with the most "star power." Characteristics such as perceived warmth and attractiveness figured into the equation. Intelligence mattered, but "before anything else you have to be attractive and charismatic," said former CBS executive Jeff Gremillion.[15] Male prospects generally could be older and "quirkier" than women, and standards sometimes shifted as desired racial or other physical characteristics became perceived as more popular at a given time.

Shifting perceptions of news complicated credibility issues for television viewers. Alternative newspapers of the 1960s and 1970s had made it more difficult to define who was a print journalist, and in the 1980s it became much tougher to determine who qualified as a broadcast journalist. A proliferation of tabloid-style pseudo-news shows such as *Entertainment Tonight* and *A Current Affair* freely mixed elements of news, entertainment, and often sensationalism. Those shows often aired immediately before or after local news programs and had "anchors" of their own, typically converted actors or models. In addition, cable brought new types of networks such as the all-sports ESPN and the originally all-music MTV. The newcomers ran their own "news" segments, hosted by people whose primary qualification was the ability to draw an audience.

Scholars and others warned that the proliferation of attractive newsreaders with no journalism training "may create the illusion of competence, decrease the tolerance for less attractive if more capable television newscasters and erode the appetite for serious news and analysis."[16] The networks also contributed to the problem by producing a host of new newsmagazines, all visually flashier "infotainment" than the original newsmagazine standard, *60 Minutes.* "They're like Hugh Hefner's rabbits: by turns fluffy, then aggressive, then sexy, but always profitable—and multiplying," wrote industry critic Russ Baker, noting that the number of network newsmagazines climbed from one (*60 Minutes*) in 1969 to at least seven by the early 1990s.[17] Later the networks learned to capitalize on their strongest titles, reducing the number of names for newsmagazines but not the overall number. CBS's *60 Minutes* and ABC's *20/20* each began appearing twice a week. NBC's *Dateline* might show up four times in the course of a week. While the network versions tended to focus less on crime and sensationalism than did their syndicated tabloid counterparts (though *Dateline* later began devoting entire shows to individual criminal cases), the differences often were unclear—a point illustrated when *Dateline* used a planted incendiary device to trigger an explosion in a pickup truck for a 1992 "expose." The tabloids also frequently uncovered stories that later drew more attention because more respected news media followed them up.[18]

Outside of television, even movies contributed to the confusion between news fact and entertainment fiction, with "docudramas" such as 1984's *Silkwood* appearing in theaters and on television. Many of those films combined fact and fiction, or filled in unknown events with guesswork. A far more important medium than movies in terms of making news and entertainment virtually indistinguishable, however, was one that newspapers and television news people largely had dismissed years before: radio.

A product of a shift toward highly segmented audiences that began in the 1960s, "talk radio" exploded on the media scene in the 1980s mostly because of one man who became synonymous for the talk phenomenon. Rush Limbaugh, a struggling radio newsman, found a large audience with a bombastically conservative message. A frequently witty personality who boasted regularly that he was dispensing wisdom through "talent on loan from God," he called himself a news "commentator" but freely mixed in elements of news. His show became a leading source of news for some regular listeners, many of whom proudly referred to themselves as "Dittoheads" because they agreed so completely with Limbaugh.[19]

Despite taking on the slogan "Excellence in Broadcasting," Limbaugh freely exaggerated or distorted facts to better support his arguments while attacking liberal politicians. His critics accused him of being racist and sexist, while his supporters praised his lack of "political correctness." He remained popular for years, becoming even more successful after Bill

Clinton's election as president. His success spawned numerous imitators of both genders, almost all of whom had the same political perspective as Limbaugh. He also briefly hosted a television show. It failed, but other politically slanted pseudo-news programs later succeeded, especially on cable networks. Most of those shows also had a conservative slant, though some political liberals also hosted programs. One thing the shows tended to share was more discussion of the people and policy they opposed than of the ideas they supported. A few shows, such as CNN's *Crossfire*, pitted liberals and conservatives against one another in short political debates that often degenerated into shouting matches.[20]

Though newspaper editors often criticized television for focusing on the trivial, newspapers also contributed to the problem, and not everyone blamed TV for Americans' declining attention to news of substance. "It's not the fault of television that the public is so easily satisfied," noted a 1971 *Seattle Post-Intelligencer* editorial.[21] As American social strife settled down, increasing numbers of newspapers began adding and standardizing their own new kind of "news"—the leisure section, containing restaurant and night club reviews, entertainment listings, travel features, and features on the arts. Most leisure sections arrived in the 1970s, and though they became a feature of most dailies, not all journalists were convinced of their value. Some reporters worried about having leisure stories added to their workloads or taking away time they could have been using to work on more serious stories. One committee report complained to the Associated Press Managing Editors Association that the sections devoted often too much space "to counter-culture and radical chic and other irrelevant nonsense."[22] Other critics were even harsher, with two journalism scholars claiming by 1980 that most newspapers catered to superficial audience whims and that most print journalism had become "splashy, superficial, thoughtless, and tenuous," while offering "no thoughtful selection, assessment of editorial matter, meaning or interpretation."[23] Of course, analysis was common, though as with many goods the overall quality of that analysis tended to decrease as the quantity increased. Also, with both circulations and competition from other newspapers declining, newspapers logically tried to appeal to the widest possible audience. Investigative stories still appeared in most newspapers, though they competed with features, puzzles, expanded comics sections, and lottery results.

The shift toward simplicity and entertainment was demonstrated in many ways. Though some members of the alternative press still offered occasional investigative depth, most of the few that survived hung on by focusing heavily on entertainment: They were filled primarily with such things as movie and concert schedules and reviews, cynically humorous opinion columns, and quirky personals ads. "Hard news" in most media turned increasingly away from news about political and social institutions to short-term coverage of crime, accidents, and disasters. Much of the loss, of course, came in explanatory journalism of all sorts. Both print and broadcast news media, afraid to risk "boring" their readers, strove for short, snappier, more sensational, more celebrity-driven stories. Sex and violence became journalistic staples, regardless of relevance to readers' or viewers' lives. Complexity became an enemy. Perhaps oddly, the addition of more entertainment values may have hurt the credibility of newspapers more than it did television journalism. Though more sensationalistic by virtually any measure, television still drew higher credibility ratings than print media, apparently at least in part because audiences judged credibility differently for the two media: For TV news, credibility was linked to popularity, not to substance or technical quality.[24]

Perhaps no entertainment value proved more important for the news media than that of celebrity. Local and national television news people were now becoming celebrities in their own right, and movie stars and professional athletes generally had replaced government officials and business leaders as heroes in the 1920s. The year 1980 brought the perfect president for an entertainment age, and for a citizenry tired of conflict. With President Ronald Reagan in the White House, the news media and citizens got less information about government and politics and seemed to care less about being misinformed. Perhaps tired of the social upheaval of the 1970s, or maybe mindful of the criticism it seemed to be receiving from all fronts, the press backed away from much of its former antigovernment pose. That was especially true in the case of the president, who like the media sometimes was criticized for preferring style over substance.[25]

Reagan received the most gentle press treatment of any president after Kennedy, in part because of factors beyond media control. In any popularity contest between Reagan and the press, officials knew whom the American people liked more. Journalists regularly complained that the administration encouraged popular disgruntlement with the news media and simply ignored legitimate requests for information. Some journalists justifiably feared political or legal threats, as the Reporters Committee for Freedom of the Press listed seventy-five moves against press freedoms, "ranging from efforts to eviscerate the Freedom of Information Act to ... threats to prosecute news organizations."[26]

Still, while the *Washington Post, New York Times,* and a few other newspapers regularly criticized Reagan, most journalists liked the president, who regularly was referred to as "the Great Communicator." In fact, especially in the early years of his presidency, the press apparently liked Reagan more than voters did and probably did more to improve his image than to harm it. That may have been even truer after Reagan survived being shot by a would-be assassin just weeks after taking office.

In the aftermath of the incident, Reagan displayed courage, humor, and concern for others. The news media and the American public ate it up. Journalists seemed to view the president as a positive, amiable man, steadfast in his convictions, and a contrast to an indecisive, detail-oriented Jimmy Carter, a somewhat bumbling Gerald Ford, and a sneaky, corrupt Nixon. Even if some of them thought he lacked intelligence. "So it is with Ronald Reagan; he doesn't tax our intellect," journalist Philip Geyelin wrote in the *Washington Post*. "So we—and I am talking here about my own profession as well as the president's political opponents—tend not to challenge his."[27] Several of Reagan's aides encountered legal or ethical problems, but generally those problems were not ascribed to the president, especially during his first term. In fact, Reagan picked up a widely used nickname because problems did not stick to him: After Democratic Representative Patricia Schroeder referred in a 1984 speech to what she called the "Teflon-coated presidency," press critics and others continued to refer to Reagan as the "Teflon President." Most notable of the problems Reagan faced became known as the Iran-Contra Affair, discussed in more detail in the next chapter. Reagan's wife, Nancy, sometimes drew more fire for her designer dresses and for ordering new White House china than the president did for his policies.[28]

A former movie actor, TV host, and radio broadcaster, Reagan showed an ability to be theatrical when it mattered, such as when a debate moderator tried to quiet him before the 1980 New Hampshire primary. "I'm paying for this microphone," Reagan barked, presenting newscasters with that evening's best sound bite and giving himself an immediate boost in the polls. Reagan's key staffers, especially aide Michael Deaver, were masters at presenting presidential politics through the media, with their techniques adopted by every successful candidate and president since. Reagan and his people tried to adhere to a "theme of the day," and the press mostly went along. Reagan demonstrated mastery of what became known as the "pseudo-event" and the "photo op"—staged events that attracted news photographers, who were directed where to stand as if they were playing a part in a film. Though staged events had made their way into the news at least since Calvin Coolidge dressed up as a cowboy for newsreel photographers in 1927, Reagan may have perfected the practice. Like his predecessors, he regularly posed with foreign dignitaries and other public figures. But he also regularly "made news" by posing with American heroes and ordinary citizens, and he let photographers follow him on vacation, where he could be seen pursuing such rugged activities as riding horses and chopping wood.[29]

Reagan avoided press questions better than had previous presidents. He held fewer news conferences than any predecessor since Calvin Coolidge (about the same number as Richard Nixon), in part because he often performed awkwardly without a script. At one mini-news conference about troubling unemployment figures, Nancy Reagan lightened the mood by walking in with a birthday cake for her husband, and correspondents joined in singing "Happy Birthday" to the president. Reagan also announced during his first term that he would no longer answer questions during photo opportunities, prompting one journalism scholar to note that the change turned the White House "photo op" into "nothing short of press agentry, no different from the Hollywood publicity stunt that Reagan mastered so many years before."[30] Reporters sometimes were reduced to shouting questions at Reagan as he made his way to a helicopter, off to engage in some other visually engaging presidential activity. He would cup his ear and smile but tended to hear only questions for which he had a ready quip.

Reagan, whose World War II service had consisted of making military training films, excelled at patriotic appeals. The fact that he could be seen at the center of three massive patriotism-invoking events also helped his popularity with the press and the American people. One of those events was the 1984 Olympics, staged on America's home turf in Los Angeles. The Soviet Union and other nations boycotted the event in retaliation for a U.S. boycott of the 1980 Moscow Olympics, and the lack of Soviet-bloc athletes meant Americans would claim more gold medals than any other country. Ringing chants of "U-S-A, U-S-A . . ." became one of the most distinctive memories of the games. A second patriotic event came in 1986, with the Statue of Liberty centennial celebration. It was highlighted by the July 4 unveiling of the newly refurbished statue, a made-for-TV extravaganza carried by all of the major networks. Still, throughout history the event best at stirring patriotism has been war. Though the United States avoided anything resembling previous military efforts in Europe, Korea, or Vietnam during the Reagan years, in 1983 it did find itself in a much closer, impossible-to-lose war—in the tiny island nation of Grenada.[31]

The first significant U.S. military action under Reagan actually began the previous year in Lebanon. He sent 1,800 Marines to Beirut as peacekeepers between warring Christians and Muslims, but the action came under increasing criticism as the military role seemed unclear, and even the secretary of defense urged withdrawal of the troops. Then, on October 23, 1983, a suicide bomber drove a truck into a U.S. Marine barracks in Beirut, killing 241 Marines. What could have been a low point for American morale turned around quickly, however, when just two days later, in what *U.S. News & World Report* called "the most dramatic move of [Reagan's] presidency," American troops invaded the smallest independent nation in the Western Hemisphere to overthrow a new communist government and rescue American medical students.[32]

The invasion of Grenada was titled "Operation Urgent Fury," a clear sign that the news media were not the only ones who appreciated catchy labels such as the "America Held Hostage" that ABC used during the Iranian hostage crisis. In a mass-media age, government officials also recognized the value of slogans, and several later military actions carried names (almost always quickly adopted by the news media) that were intended to convey power and justice. Recent presidential administrations in particular have named their military efforts. Under George H.W. Bush, the 1989 invasion of Panama and arrest of leader Manuel Noriega was titled "Operation Just Cause," while "Operation Desert Storm" was the official name of the Persian Gulf War two years later. After the 2001 destruction of the World Trade Center in New York, America's ensuing war against terrorism in Afghanistan under George W. Bush was titled "Operation Enduring Freedom." Commemorative T-Shirts sold through the White House gift shop at that time also reflected one of the senior Bush slogans, carrying the words, "Our Cause is Just."[33]

The timing and need for the 1983 Grenada invasion were later questioned in political circles, but the action demonstrated the military and public relations advantages of a speedy display of force. Reagan reiterated that lesson three years later, ordering the bombing of Libya after accusing it of sponsoring the terrorist bombing of a German disco frequented by American servicemen. Of more interest to the news media was the lesson the government apparently had learned from Vietnam: When waging war, keep the press out.[34]

Reagan ordered a complete press blackout of the invasion of Grenada. Journalists were kept off the island until the third day of fighting, after the American military had things well under control. Those who managed to reach Grenada on their own were placed under house arrest by the marines and removed from the island. As a result, "hundreds of newspaper reporters spent Thursday interviewing each other . . . a global stone's throw from the Grenadian invasion they had come to cover."[35] Viewers saw no scenes of Americans killing or dying, but two weeks later many did see a staged photo of Reagan saluting a marine who had participated in the conflict. The photo ran on the front page of the *Los Angeles Times* and in newspapers throughout the country. In the meantime, American officials exaggerated the size of the enemy threat from Grenadian and Cuban fighters, and lied about civilian casualties. "On the same day, the controlled news media in Cuba . . . accurately reported that the Cuban contingent numbered 750 and that there had been civilian casualties," *Washington Post* columnist Lou Cannon later wrote. "It is another irony of this anticommunist administration that Oct. 27 was one of the few times in history when citizens of a communist country knew more about what was going on than Americans did."[36] A Reagan press aide resigned over the incident, and even pro-Reagan news media complained vociferously about the administration's "private war." As a result, members of the press and the administration worked out details for a media

pool, in which a few pool members would be taken along to future conflicts, with their stories and photos shared by all media outlets. The
arrangement restricted competitive activities among reporters. It also
meant that pool reporters would be exposed to sources and scenes chosen
by the government, and only established mainstream journalists would
be chosen.[37]

Though editors complained that the Reagan administration had shown
contempt for the public as well as disdain for the press, few complaints
about media restrictions came from the public. Instead, the news blackout
and the ensuing complaints let some members of the press, and perhaps
the government, know just how low the media had fallen in the eyes of
the readers and viewers. "Reagan & Co. believe that they won a pair of
glorious victories on the beaches of Grenada two weeks ago," Cannon
complained. "The first was the defeat of the ragtag Grenadian army and a
band of armed Cuban laborers. The second was the rout of the U.S.
media. Reagan's advisers are convinced that the media are virtually
devoid of public support in their protests of both the news blackout of
the invasion and the misleading statements made about it."[38]

Apparently those advisors were right, as confidence in the press
dropped dramatically, "a jolting revelation to many people in the
news media," noted the *Chicago Tribune*.[39] Despite the presence of earlier
signs and their own culpability for the antagonism directed against the
press, many journalists found themselves shaken about their roll being so
misunderstood. Much of the anti-media feedback cited unsurprising concerns for military safety and effectiveness, but many critics went much
further, saying the press should be censored, in effect, because it
was...the press. A typical complaint condemned "the would-be
opinion-makers of the press," calling journalists themselves the worst
censors, "except that they refer to it as 'editing'."[40] The news media
proved to be seriously out of sync with their viewers' interests in
terms of news content. Of course, their unwillingness to hire ombudsmen
or to participate in news councils, and their failure to educate the public
about the democratic watchdog function of the press—or even to consistently perform that democratic function—made journalists less likely
to understand or to be appreciated by their audience. The fact that many
in the press apparently cared little about public perceptions, except those
perceptions that might affect their own work, also decreased the likelihood that the press-public relationship would improve.[41]

Aside from war, too much of that journalistic conduct continued to
focus on the trivial, on personalities and on conflict. One obvious area in
which the tendency to shy away from depth held true was with religious
coverage, a one-time mainstay of American journalism. In most cases
religion had been relegated to the one or two pages in the Saturday
edition that carried the advertisements for churches. The media granted

occasional exceptions for conflict-oriented Supreme Court stories about issues such as prayer in schools or for discussions of a presidential candidate's faith and how it might help or hurt him with the electorate. Avowedly "born-again" candidate Jimmy Carter's faith drew the most attention, especially after he granted an interview to *Playboy*. Other religious stories tended to be about those considered to be religious "extremists" such as Islamic militants or Baptist television evangelist Jerry Falwell's conservative Moral Majority, often credited with helping elect Ronald Reagan president.[42]

In most cases when it came to religion, the news media simply ignored it. In response, similar to those involved with various groups who had started alternative newspapers and magazines of the 1970s, some Christians and others produced their own publications. Religious radio and television stations and networks also sprang up, perhaps reaching their apex in the mid-1980s. The Christian Broadcasting Network, founded by Pat Robertson in 1960, grew dramatically, bolstered by its *700 Club*, a magazine-style show that offered viewers daily news and commentary from an increasingly conservative Christian perspective. Other news programs followed on the network, which, after a series of sales and mergers, eventually wound up being owned by the Disney Company (which by then also owned ABC). Encouraged by the popularity of the *700 Club*, Robertson ran for the U.S. presidency in 1988. Another prominent television ministry, though less news-oriented, was that of the *PTL* ("Praise the Lord" or "People that Love") *Club*, founded in the mid-1970s by Jim and Tammy Bakker. By the mid-1980s PTL called itself the largest television ministry in the world. Thanks to the Federal Communications Commission and a North Carolina newspaper, however, that soon would change.[43]

The combination of sexual scandal and celebrity long has enticed the media and their users, and adding religion to the mix made it all the more irresistible. In 1988 American Christians suddenly found themselves seemingly surrounded by leaders with feet of clay. Jim Bakker was convicted of defrauding his PTL followers of more than $150 million and he ended up serving five years in prison. The *Charlotte* (N.C.) *Observer* won that year's Pulitzer Prize for Public Service for reporting the financial wrongdoing, based originally on FCC records.[44]

Despite the financial magnitude of the case and the number of people affected by the television ministry, many of the media outside of Charlotte predictably focused heavily on the couple's excesses, such as gold-plated bathroom fixtures and an air-conditioned doghouse, and on Jim Bakker's sexual activities with another man and with a young female PTL worker who later posed for *Playboy*. In part because of the media focus, Bakker's followers may have been more offended by his sexual activities than by the couple's financial misdealings. Bakker was succeeded as PTL president by Falwell, whom Bakker later accused of stealing his ministry.[45]

At the time, Falwell was getting plenty of attention, anyway, suing *Hustler* magazine for an offensive parody advertisement. The Supreme Court ruled against Falwell in February 1988, in a case that has become a standard in journalism law texts. Just three days before that case was decided, popular television evangelist, Jimmy Swaggert—who had openly criticized Bakker for his moral lapses and then was himself photographed in the company of a prostitute—tearfully announced that he had sinned and resigned from his ministry. A year earlier, noted evangelist Oral Roberts also had drawn widespread ridicule after telling followers that God had told him he would die unless he raised $8 million to save his failing medical center within a year. Roberts later said the money had been raised, but the facility soon closed.[46]

The fallen leaders drew criticism and ridicule, much of it from the new pseudo-news produced by print and broadcast tabloids. Still, despite the claims of some religious conservatives, few of the news media were antagonistic toward religious belief. After all, many journalists also engaged in various spiritual practices, and from a practical standpoint publishers and network executives tried to avoid antagonizing a huge part of the potential audience. With religion as with elsewhere, however, the news media demonstrated not hostility to Christianity as much as a typical inability to adequately cover social institutions. News judgments based on conflict and immediacy, combined especially with the new focus on entertainment and personalities, joined with space limitations that ended up dictating "quotas" for various types of news. Journalists typically downplayed or ignored the everyday religious aspects of American life, along with other "less important" types of news such as international coverage. Meanwhile, more dramatic but therefore inherently distorted depictions of religion drew media attention. At the same time, religious conservatives often did a far better job of using the media, both mainstream news media and their own media sources, to promote their own agendas than did less conservative (and perhaps more typical) Christians.[47]

Sex and scandal proved irresistible to journalists and others in important arenas outside of religion. For the first time, in the 1988 presidential race the sexual indiscretions of a candidate drew widespread media attention and helped drive the Democratic frontrunner from the race. Colorado Senator Gary Hart dropped out after the *Miami Herald* posted reporters outside of his Washington townhouse, reporting that a young woman spent the night. Later the tabloid *National Enquirer* ran photos of Hart on a boat named *Monkey Business*, with a woman sitting on his lap. The story may have been at least as much about Hart's arrogance as about his infidelity, since when a reporter first asked if he was faithful to his wife (a question that once reporters would not have imagined asking), Hart challenged the press to follow him.

Some credit the Hart incident with helping Bill Clinton overcome his own sex scandal when he became a presidential candidate four years later. A woman claiming to have had a long-term affair with Clinton sold her story to a supermarket tabloid. Other news media then picked up the story. Clinton admitted "wrongdoing" but refused to address specifics when he and his wife, Hillary, appeared together on *60 Minutes*. He criticized the press for engaging in a "game of gotcha," and Hillary Clinton voiced strong support for her husband. Many in and out of the press raised new questions about the relevance of a candidate's sex life. The story faded, and Clinton became president, later finding himself embroiled in other scandals discussed in a later chapter.[48]

Clinton's 1992 problems came just a year after scandal and celebrity, along with race and gender, also proved to be central themes in Senate confirmation hearings of Supreme Court nominee Clarence Thomas. He was accused of sexually harassing a co-worker a decade earlier. National Public Radio and *Newsday* broke the story on the same day, after the allegations were leaked to the news media. The three main networks, which had not previously provided live coverage of the confirmation hearings, began airing the testimony of Thomas and his accuser—demonstrating the effect that controversy involving alleged sexual misconduct could have on ratings and on news decisions. "Even those who voiced disgust kept watching," a *Columbia Journalism Review* critic noted, pointing out that the graphic subject matter of the televised hearings probably contributed to the fact that a post-confirmation poll ranked the media performance lower than that of Democrats, Republicans, Congress, or the president.[49] Thomas, who termed the televised hearings "a high-tech lynching," was confirmed 52–48 by the Senate. The hearings led to widespread discussion in the news media about race relations, gender issues, and due process but prompted little true long-term consternation among the news media.

The low point in terms of sensationalistic, personality-driven entertainment-based coverage came three years later when famed black former football star, actor, and sportscaster O.J. Simpson was accused of brutally murdering his white ex-wife and another man. Occurring in the media capital of Los Angeles, the case became the most-covered crime story of all time. The case included a "low-speed chase" through Los Angeles of a white Ford Bronco in which Simpson was riding, a live broadcast of his preliminary hearing, and then daily live coverage of the longest jury trial in California history. "We Went Berserk," stated the headline for a *Columbia Journalism Review* article that noted that NBC, ABC, and CBS combined to air 874 Simpson stories in 1995 alone.[50] CNN devoted almost 400 hours of coverage to the case by the time it went to the jury. *Nightline* did fifty-three shows about it. More than 1,000 journalists received press credentials to cover the trial, and a third of American newspapers published special editions to announce the verdict. The tabloid TV show *Hard Copy* put at least thirty reporters on the case.[51]

The Simpson case turned the judge, attorneys, and some witnesses into celebrities and brought journalism ethics texts another issue to consider besides the sheer scope and frenzy of the coverage. *Time* and *Newsweek* both ran cover photos of Simpson's mug shot after he was arrested. Seeing the two side by side on newsstands made it easy to see that *Time* had darkened the photo, making Simpson look more sinister. A jury found Simpson "not guilty," prompting widespread amazement. The news media continued to pay in terms of credibility for their own crimes, however.[52]

NOTES

1. Michael Emery and Edwin Emery, *The Press and America: An Interpretive History of the Mass Media*, 6th ed. (Englewood Cliffs, N.J.: Prentice Hall, 1988): 527.

2. Al Neuharth, *Confessions of an S.O.B.* (New York: Ubleday, 1989).

3. Tom Shales, "Late-Night Newsohol on ABC's Diluted Report," *Washington Post*, March 26, 1980.

4. Ibid.

5. Joseph R. Dominick, Alan Wurtzel, and Guy Lometti, "Television Journalism vs. Show Business: A Content Analysis of Eyewitness News," *Journalism Quarterly* 52 (Summer 1975): 213–218.

6. Robert Shogan, "Enemas for Elephants," *Media Studies Journal* 12, Fall 1998.

7. Robert Friedman, "A Generational Divide at Columbia," *Media Studies Journal* 12 (Fall 1998): 84.

8. Though Flynn and Daley usually are credited with being the first happy talk duo, some sources credit teams in Minneapolis or San Francisco, or an earlier effort in Chicago.

9. Raymond C. Carroll, "Content Values in TV News Programs in Small and Large Markets," *Journalism Quarterly* 62 (Winter 1985): 877–882, 938; Gary A. Hale and Richard C. Vincent, "Locally Produced Programming on Independent Television Stations," *Journalism Quarterly* 63 (Autumn 1986): 562–567, 599.

10. Sally Bedell Smith, "News vs. Entertainment," *New York Times*, August 11, 1983.

11. Michael W. Singletary and Chris Lamb, "News Values in Award-Winning Photos," *Journalism Quarterly* 61 (Spring 1984): 104–108, 233; Gerald Stone and Elinor Grusin, "Network TV as the Bad News Bearer," *Journalism Quarterly* 61 (Autumn 1984): 517–523, 592; Jeff Greenfield, "Making TV News Pay," *Gannett Center Journal*, Spring 1987.

12. Carolyn A. Lin, "Audience Selectivity of Local Television Newscasts," *Journalism Quarterly* 69 (Summer 1992): 373–382; Erika Engstrom and Anthony J. Ferri, "From Barriers to Challenges: Career Perceptions of Women TV News Anchors," *Journalism & Mass Communication Quarterly* 75 (Winter 1998): 789–802.

13. Doug James, *Walter Cronkite: His Life and Times* (Brentwood, Tenn.: JM Press, 1991): 233.

14. For a brief period, Brokaw co-anchored with Roger Mudd. Jennings had also served as ABC's anchor during the mid-1960s. Also see David K. Scott and Robert H. Gobetz, "Hard News/Soft News Content of the National Broadcast Networks, 1972–1987," *Journalism Quarterly* 69 (Summer 1992): 406–412.

15. Jeff Gremillion, "Star School: On the Fast Track to Network News," *Columbia Journalism Review*, January/February 1995, accessed at http://www.cjr.org/archives.asp?url=/95/1/star.asp (accessed March 6, 2006).

16. Churchill L. Roberts and Sandra H. Dickson, "Assessing Quality in Local TV News," *Journalism Quarterly* 61 (Summer 1984): 392–398.

17. Russ W. Baker, "Truth, Lies, and Videotape," *Columbia Journalism Review*, July/August 1993.

18. William C. Spragens, *Electronic Magazines: Soft News Programs on Network Television* (Westport, Conn.: Praeger, 1995); Maria Elizabeth Grabe, "Tabloid and Traditional News Magazine Crime Stories: Crime Lessons and Reaffirmation of Social Class Distinctions," *Journalism & Mass Communication Quarterly* 73 (Winter 1996): 926–946.

19. Rodger Streitmatter, *Mightier than the Sword: How the News Media Have Shaped American History* (Boulder, Colo.: Westview Press, 1997); Gary W. Larson, "Radio Journalism," in W. David Sloan and Lisa Mullikin Parcell, eds, *American Journalism: History Principles, Practices* (Jefferson, N.C.: McFarland & Company, 2002): 277–285.

20. Howard Kurtz, *Hot Air: All Talk All the Time: An Inside Look at the Performers and the Pundits* (New York: Times Books, 1996).

21. Editorial, "Conclusion Jumpers," *Seattle Post-Intelligencer*, May 9, 1971.

22. Don Hatfield, "Leisure Sections: Are They Worth the Expense?" September 1978 report of the Modern Living Committee of the Associated Press Managing Editors Association, records of the Associated Press Managing Editors Association, State Historical Society of Wisconsin, Madison; Also see Walter D. Scott, "Today's Journalism: A Candid Appraisal," *Quill*, June 1965, 32.

23. John C. Merrill and Harold A. Fisher, *The World's Great Dailies: Profiles of Fifty Newspapers* (New York: Hastings House, 1980).

24. Kim Walsh-Childers, Jean Chance, and Kristie Alley Swain, "Daily Newspaper Coverage of the Organization, Delivery and Financing of Health Care," *Newspaper Research Journal* 20 (Spring 1999): 2–22; William R. Davie and Jung-Sook Lee, "Sex, Violence, and Consonance/Differentiation: An Analysis of Local TV News Values," *Journalism & Mass Communication Quarterly* 72 (Spring 1995): 128–138; Churchill L. Roberts and Sandra H. Dickson, "Assessing Quality in Local TV News," *Journalism Quarterly* 61 (Summer 1984): 392–398.

25. Douglas A. Anderson, Joe W. Milner, and Mary-Lou Galician, "How Editors View Legal Issues and the Rehnquist Court," *Journalism Quarterly* 65 (Summer 1988): 294–298; Deckle McLean, "Press May Find Justice Scalia Frequent Foe but Impressive Adversary," *Journalism Quarterly* 65 (Spring 1988): 152–156.

26. Reported in Eve Pell, *The Big Chill: How the Reagan Administration, Corporate America, and Religious Conservatives Are Subverting Free Speech and the Public's Right to Know* (Boston: Beacon Press, 1984). Also see Mark Hertsgaard, *On Bended Knee: The Press and the Reagan Presidency* (New York: Farrar Straus Giroux, 1988); Haynes Johnson, *Sleepwalking Through History: America in the Reagan Years* (New York: Anchor, 1991); Eleanor Randolph, "White House Cuts Flow of Information; News Media Treated As an Alien Force," *Washington Post*, June 10, 1985; Richard Curry and others, *Freedom at*

Risk: Secrecy, Censorship, and Repression in the 1980s (Philadelphia: Temple University, 1988).

27. Philip Geyelin, "What He Doesn't Know," *Washington Post*, August 17, 1984. Also see William J. Hughes, "The 'Not-So-Genial' Conspiracy: The *New York Times* and Six Presidential 'Honeymoons,' 1953–1993," *Journalism & Mass Communication Quarterly* 72 (Winter 1995): 841–850; Colman McCarthy, "Reagan & the Lie of the Land," *Washington Post*, December 7, 1986; Elliot King and Michael Schudson, "The Myth of the Great Communicator," *Columbia Journalism Review*, November/December 1987, 37–39; John Tebbel and Sarah Miles Watts, *The Press and the Presidency: From George Washington to Ronald Reagan* (New York: Oxford University Press, 1985): 538.

28. "Political Notes: What'sername?" *Washington Post*, May 5, 1984.

29. W. Lance Bennett, *News: The Politics of Illusion*, 2nd ed. (New York: Longman, 1988).

30. Rodger Streitmatter, "The Rise and Triumph of the White House Photo Opportunity," *Journalism Quarterly* 65 (Winter 1988): 981–985. Also see Richard Davis, *The Press and American Politics: The New Mediator*, 2nd ed. (Upper Saddle River, N.J.: Prentice Hall, 1996); Hertsgaard, *On Bended Knee;* Michael D. Murray, "The Contemporary Media, 1974–Present," in Wm. David Sloan, ed., *The Media in America: A History*, 5th ed. (Northport, Ala.: Vision Press, 2002).

31. Carter chose to boycott the 1980 Olympics because the Soviets invaded Afghanistan during that country's civil war. The boycott brought Carter considerable criticism during an election year in which he could ill afford it. D.W. Rajecki, Cheryl Halter, Andrew Everts, and Chris Feghali, "Documentation of Media Reflections of the Patriotic Revival in the United States in the 1980s," *The Journal of Social Psychology* 131 (June 1991): 401–411.

32. Dennis Mullen, "Why the Surprise Move in Grenada—And What Next?" *U.S. News & World Report*, November 7, 1983, 31.

33. Conservative radio personalities, who reached the peak of their influence during the late 1980s and early 1990s, later adopted "American Held Hostage" as a slogan to characterize the years of the Bill Clinton presidency.

34. In fact, the administration had become increasingly concerned about Grenada in the days before the Beirut bombing, and some of Grenada's neighbors had sought assurances of U.S. protection. In addition, some sources suggest that the Beirut bombing might have made Reagan less—not more—willing to risk American military lives elsewhere.

35. Jeff Nesmith, "Reporters Spend the Day Interviewing Each Other," *Atlanta Constitution*, October 28, 1983.

36. Lou Cannon, "President's Deeds Reveal His Real Opinion of Press Freedom," *Washington Post*, November 28, 1983.

37. Peter Braestrup, *Battle Lines: Report of the Twentieth Century Fund Task Force on the Military and the Media* (New York: Priority Press, 1985); Streitmatter, "The Rise and Triumph of the White House Photo Opportunity"; editorial, "Hiding a War," *Portland Oregonian*, October 28, 1983.

38. Lou Cannon, "Media Chose Wrong Targets in Hitting Subordinates for Blackout," *Washington Post*, November 7, 1983. Also see editorial, "When is an Invasion Not an Invasion?" *Atlanta Constitution*, November 5, 1983; editorial, "Public and Press: 'Us' vs. 'Them'?" *Seattle Post-Intelligencer*, December 22, 1983.

39. Editorial, "The Press Gets a Bad Press," *Chicago Tribune*, December 11, 1983. Also see editorial, "Press Needs Public Support," *Portland Oregonian*, December 2, 1983.

40. Walter Kelly, letter to the editor, *Chicago Tribune*, November 12, 1983.

41. K. Tim Wulfemeyer, "Perceptions of Viewer Interests by Local TV Journalists," *Journalism Quarterly* 61 (Autumn 1984): 432–435; David Cassady, "Press Councils—Why Journalists Won't Participate," *Newspaper Research Journal 5* (Summer 1984): 25.

42. Peter A. Kerr and Patricia Moy, "Newspaper Coverage of Fundamentalist Christians, 1980–2000," *Journalism & Mass Communication Quarterly* 79 (Spring 2002): 54–72; Wm. David Sloan, ed., *Media and Religion in American History* (Northport, Ala.: Vision Press, 2000). Falwell started the Moral Majority in 1979, disbanding it a decade later. Among other things, the organization supported conservative candidates and school prayer, and opposed gay rights and the Equal Rights Amendment.

43. Robert Abelman, "News on The 700 Club: The Cycle of Religious Activism," *Journalism Quarterly* 71 (Winter 1994): 887–892. The *National Courier* was one print experiment during the 1970s, but like other such publications it failed to establish a substantial audience and lasted less than two years: John D. Keeler, J. Douglas Tarpley, and Michael R. Smith, "The *National Courier*, News, and Religious Ideology," in Sloan, *Media and Religion*, 275–290.

44. Charles E. Shepard, "Bakker Misled PTL Viewers, FCC Records Show," *Charlotte Observer*, January 26, 1986.

45. Grant Wacker, "Jim Bakker and the Internal Revenue Service," review of Charles E. Shepard, *Forgiven: The Rise and Fall of Jim Bakker and the PTL Ministry* in *Christian Century* (New York: Atlantic Monthly Press, 1989), November 15, 1994, 1053.

46. *Hustler Magazine and Jerry C. Flynt vs. Jerry Falwell*, 485 U.S. 46 (1988).

47. Doug Underwood, *From Yahweh to Yahoo! The Religious Roots of the Secular Press* (Champaign, Ill.: University of Illinois Press, 2002); Doug Underwood and Keith Stamm, "Are Journalists Really Irreligious? A Multidimensional Analysis," *Journalism & Mass Communication Quarterly* 78 (Winter 2001): 771–786.

48. Doris Kearns Goodwin, "Every Four Years," Newseum Web essay, http://www.newseum.org/everyfouryears/essay.htm#17.

49. Christopher Hanson as William Boot, "The Clarence Thomas Hearings," *Columbia Journalism Review*, January/February 1992, 27. Also see Timothy M. Phelps, "Ex-Aide Says Thomas Sexually Harassed Her," *Newsday*, October 6, 1991.

50. "We Went Berserk," *Columbia Journalism Review*, November/December 2001, 118.

51. Elizabeth Blanks Hindman, "'Lynch-Mob Journalism' vs. 'Compelling Human Drama': Editorial Responses to Coverage of the Pretrial Phase of the O.J. Simpson Case," *Journalism & Mass Communication Quarterly* 76 (Autumn 1999): 499–515; Paul Thaler, *The Spectacle: Media and the Making of the O.J. Simpson Story* (Westport, Conn.: Praeger, 1997); Howard Kurtz, *Hot Air: All Talk All the Time: An Inside Look at the Performers and the Pundits* (New York: Times Books, 1996); Matthew G. Ehrlich, "The Journalism of Outrageousness: Tabloid Television News vs. Investigative News," *Journalism & Mass Communication Monographs* 155 (February 1996).

52. *Time*, front cover, June 27, 1994.

CHAPTER 6

Business

During the 1980s, the "hostile takeover" became a term related more to business than to war. "Corporate raiders" took over hundreds of companies, often through the use of the leveraged buyout (LBO). In an LBO the buyer offered high prices to stockholders and then typically financed the deal by borrowing money through the sale of high-risk "junk bonds" to banks and other investors. After the sale, the company often paid off the debt (and sometimes further enriched corporate officers) by selling off company assets, slashing the work force through layoffs, and cutting research and development.

In 1987, New York developer Donald Trump—one of whose prominent traits was a tendency to name most of what he owned after himself—produced a book titled *The Art of the Deal*. It quickly became a bestseller, and Trump's activities as a self-promoting businessman made him a media celebrity and what one critic called "a poster child for the 'greed is good' 1980s."[1] The attention paid to the opinions and activities of an egotistical billionaire typified what happened in, and to, the news media during the mid-1980s. Perhaps numbed by hits taken during the early Reagan years, the press became relatively passive during the last half of the 1980s. The investigative spirit of a mere decade earlier had faded, and business became much more important, both as an external subject and as an internal concern. By the early 1990s, Trump would be on the verge of bankruptcy, the largest banking scandal in American history would cost taxpayers an estimated half a trillion dollars, and two Pulitzer Prize-winning *Philadelphia Inquirer* reporters would write a book of their own, chronicling the problems of the middle class, titled *America: What Went Wrong?*[2]

Part of what went wrong was that Congress deregulated the savings-and-loan industry in the early 1980s. Within a few years, the *New York Times* reported nearly a third of the nation's savings and loan institutions were "insolvent or nearly so," primarily because of deregulation.[3] A combination of high interest rates, bad investments, greed, and fraud by S&L managers then led to the collapse of several banks and the seizure of others by government regulators. An ensuing government-approved bailout cost taxpayers billions of dollars. At the end of the decade, Sonoma State University's "Project Censored," which publishes a noted annual list of under-reported stories, listed three S&L or banking stories on its ten-item list for 1990, and regulators complained that most of the news media paid attention to what was happening too late to stop the financial disaster. Not everyone had ignored the crisis, however. As early as 1984, the *New York Times* warned that risky lending practices threatened the nation's 3,400 savings and loan institutions and nearly 500 saving banks. A year later, the *Washington Post* warned that 431 S&L institutions were insolvent, and that the cost of shutting them down would be "well over twice the $6 billion in the federal S&L deposit insurance fund."[4]

The savings and loan crisis was the biggest financial news of the decade, but far from the only financial concern for the news media and others. After the largest one-day stock market crash in American history, October 19, 1987, became known as "Black Monday." Journalists stressed human aspects of the crash with stories describing the hardships of overworked brokers, the financial damage suffered by some investors, and some of the implications of the crash for readers and viewers. The *Wall Street Journal* won a Pulitzer Prize for its coverage. A week later came the second-biggest drop in history, and some Americans worried about economic recession, or even a depression. By the end of the year, however, journalists joined economists in suggesting that the stock market decline might help the economy, in the long run, by bringing more attention to financial problems. "If it doesn't cause a recession, it will surely prevent one," said an analyst quoted by the *Los Angeles Times*.[5] For a time some newspapers continued to address rising concerns about Wall Street, with Pulitzers for explanatory journalism going to the *Washington Post* in 1990 for an analysis of the Securities and Exchange Commission, and to Susan Faludi of the *Wall Street Journal* in 1991 for a story about the leveraged buyout of Safeway Stores. Because the crash prompted financial services to buy more advertising, the media benefited from it in the short run.[6]

Of course, LBO's and stock market trading were not the only available forms of gambling, and big companies were not the only gamblers: The 1980s saw a surge in the number of states that began sponsoring their own lotteries. Of the more than two-thirds of states that have lotteries, more than half approved them between 1982 and 1992. Some newspapers favored legalized gambling, and some opposed it, but virtually all dailies and many local television newscasts in lottery states began carrying winning numbers.[7]

By then, financial news of all sorts was a hot topic for much of the press. Big business and Wall Street were providing plenty of the kind of intrigue and power struggles that generally make news, whether in government or crime stories. Some of the financial news involved both government and crime.

Charles Keating was convicted on state and federal charges that included racketeering and fraud for looting a failed California S&L and for bilking elderly investors out of their life savings. Bringing the case more attention was the involvement of five U.S. senators who became known as "the Keating Five." The Senate ethics committee investigated charges that the five tried to influence an investigation of Keating, who had contributed heavily to their campaigns. The Senate reprimanded Senator Alan Cranston and the ethics committee less severely reprimanded the others—a judgment the St. Louis Post-Dispatch called "nearly as infamous as the behavior it investigated," and which the Seattle Times said "condoned business as usual."[8]

Misdeeds by prominent business people prompted media coverage, some of it in depth. The Akron Beacon Journal won a 1987 Pulitzer Prize for its coverage of European investor/corporate raider Sir James Goldsmith's attempt to take over the Akron-based Goodyear Tire and Rubber Co. Though the bid failed, Goldsmith made millions of dollars when the company was forced to pay what was known as "greenmail" to buy back the stock he already owned. Other cases that drew considerable media attention and that helped illustrate the press fascination with rich business celebrities were those of Ivan Boesky, Michael Milken, and Leona Helmsley. Boeskey was arrested in 1986 on charges of insider trading and sentenced to three years in prison. He paid $100 million in fines and restitution. Newspaper reports put his personal wealth in excess of $250 million. Hotel owner Helmsley, whom newspapers nicknamed "Queen of Mean," was convicted in 1989 of tax fraud. Milken, commonly referred to by the news media as the "junk bond king" for his bond trading, pleaded guilty in 1990 to fraud, market manipulation, and other charges. Despite the royal titles newspapers gave Helmsley and Milken, both were sentenced to prison and ordered to pay millions of dollars in fines.[9]

Another "trading" story that had more impact, leading to a congressional investigation and the criminal indictments of half a dozen government officials, became known as the Iran-Contra Affair. In 1981, Reagan had authorized the CIA to help Nicaraguan rebels, or "contras," but Congress prohibited the use of government funds to aid any effort to overthrow the Nicaraguan government. Marine Major Oliver North then helped with a plan to sell American weapons to Iran illegally and divert the money to the Contras. Reagan eventually fired North, who had lied to Congress about his activities. He and National Security Advisor John Poindexter were convicted of various charges, though the convictions were overturned on appeal. Reagan was called to testify in congressional hearings, which failed to determine whether the president had approved of the plan. *Washington Post* television critic Tom Shales later wrote: "Reagan's frequent memory lapses during the testimony were embarrassing to watch—either in full on C-SPAN or in excerpts on other networks—but he did look like a man with nothing to hide. Or at least like a man who has forgotten if he has anything to hide."[10]

Though the *Miami Herald* won a Pulitzer Prize for its coverage of the issue, critics suggested that Congress was more interested than most of the press in investigating Reagan's Iran-Contra role and that the media should have dug deeper. Vice President George Bush's involvement, like many of the details of the plan itself, also drew relatively little attention from the press. Dan Rather broached the issue during a live interview in 1988, but Bush was ready. He dodged the issue and attacked Rather's professionalism, bringing up the fact that the anchor, miffed when a tennis match ran long, had walked off the news set for six minutes a few months earlier. What *Time* called "the ambush that failed" actually helped Bush combat a wimpy image, despite the fact that he "was not delivering a message, but beating up the messenger."[11] Shortly after he became president in 1989, Bush pardoned former Defense Secretary Caspar Weinberger and five others involved in the Iran-Contra scandal. Demonstrating the nature of fame in America, North later became a congressional candidate, a popular conservative radio talk show host (like Watergate conspirator G. Gordon Liddy, who spent almost five years in prison), and then host of a Fox News television program.

Corporate affairs provided a meaningful source for news in the 1980s, but business was much more than simply a topic for the press. Mergers and new ventures by the news media themselves increasingly became news. "The business of news, usually just an internal industry concern, looms large on the public agenda," the first issue of a new Gannett journal proclaimed in 1987.[12] That first issue focused entirely on business issues related to the production of news.

A year earlier, *New York Times* reporter Alex Jones had won a Pulitzer Prize for reporting about conflicts within a powerful Louisville, Kentucky, newspaper family. The saga led to the sale of two newspapers, a television station, and radio stations and became the focus of at least four books. A much more important series of sales had occurred earlier, however.

By 1985, Australian media magnate Rupert Murdoch had bought the *New York Post*, *Boston Herald*, and *Chicago Sun Times*, and he also owned newspapers and television holdings in Australia and England (and later in Asia and Latin America). He frequently was criticized for making publications more sensationalistic after he bought them, promoting the "tabloidization" of news. In 1985 he bought six American television stations, with plans to buy more, and sought FCC approval to add a fourth network to the existing lineup of ABC, CBS, and NBC. (Along with those three were a number of cable networks. The FCC, however, defined a TV network as an entity "that offers an interconnected program service on a regular basis for 15 or more hours a week to at least 25 affiliated television licensees in 10 or more states."). Murdoch won approval, with the stipulation that he become a U.S. citizen and agree to sell his Chicago and New York newspapers within two years. Under a rule adopted a decade before, the FCC generally did not permit ownership of a newspaper and a television station serving the same market, though exceptions were granted. The new Fox Network, headed by former ABC executive Barry Diller, established no significant news presence but laid the cornerstone for networks to come, most notably UPN and WB (which later joined together to form the CW network) in terms of entertainment, and the Fox News Channel.[13]

In granting Murdoch's application, the FCC cited a desire for increased competition among media. And though the number of networks continued to increase, in most respects competition did not. Ben Bagdikian's famous 1983 book *The Media Monopoly* expressed concerns about the fact that by the beginning of the decade, fifty corporations controlled most major American media. Bagdikian's concerns included potential conflicts of interest and diminishing perspectives that might result from increasing corporate consolidation. In fact, in some respects the trend was still in its infancy. At the same time that the FCC approved the start of Murdoch's network, it also approved Capital Cities Communications' $3.5 billion purchase of ABC. The sale went through in 1986, the same year in which General Electric bought NBC (as part of its purchase of RCA) and noted investor Laurence Tisch's Leows Corporation purchased CBS. The CBS sale came after the network fended off a takeover bid by Ted Turner—whose own network was saved from bankruptcy a year later by a merger with Time Warner and TCI. Networks suddenly were hot properties, though not necessarily for their news divisions. Those divisions found themselves increasingly answering to executives who specialized in entertainment and who expected each corporate division to contribute to the company's bottom line.[14]

The new management arrangement and new mergers let the various divisions help one another, resulting in numerous instances in which supposed news shows covered entertainment figures or shows that appeared on the same network, or that were produced by other divisions of the same corporation. For example, when a new Disney movie was about to hit theaters, ABC aired a thirty-minute entertainment program about the "making of" the movie. Then *20/20*, the network's newsmagazine, might feature one of the actors or offer a segment explaining the movie's special effects. *Dateline* often ran stories that capitalized on the resources of two shared media outlets. It typically called such a segment a *"Dateline-People* magazine exclusive" or a *"Dateline-National Geographic* exclusive," and a related story would appear in the magazine a day or so later. The practice also raised the question of whether a story could be "exclusive" to two media.

News organizations also drew criticism for potential conflicts of interest when they began letting advertisers attach their names to news segments, such as a drug company sponsoring a health segment. "It seems unlikely that Bristol-Myers would be particularly happy to see CNN do a hard-hitting investigation of the drug industry," suggested the *Washington Post*. "And with so much at stake, it also seems unlikely that CNN would undertake such an endeavor."[15] Other networks faced similar criticism, both for their sponsors and for their ownership by corporations not otherwise associated with news. In most respects, of course, those networks simply faced the same potential conflicts that newspapers always had with corporate owners and heavy advertisers, though in the case of direct segment sponsorship the ties perhaps were more obvious. Another complicating factor in terms of the news-sponsor barrier came from the increasing use of "advertorials," advertisements intentionally designed to look like editorial copy, especially in magazines.[16]

Bagdikian's warnings about potential conflicts of interest occasionally were borne out in more serious ways when journalists appeared to shade the truth in favor of company owners. For example, the *Today* show drew criticism after a 1990 segment about consumer boycotts failed to mention that NBC parent company General Electric was the focus of the country's largest boycott. Those who opposed war pointed out that GE made more money from defense contracts than it did from NBC. Critics slammed ABC, owned by Disney, when one of its newsmagazines apparently stopped pursuing a potentially negative story about Disney World. In a case that eventually formed the basis for a popular movie (*The Insider*), *60 Minutes* interviewed a tobacco company executive who revealed that company executives hid the truth about the harmful effects of their product. Apparently fearing a potential lawsuit, CBS refused to run the story until after details of it were leaked, embarrassing the company. The fact that CBS was for sale at the time (Westinghouse soon bought it) also apparently influenced the initial decision to kill the story because a lawsuit likely would have decreased the value of CBS.

With the possible exception of PBS, probably none of the corporate broadcast media gave one major issue—the Telecommunications Act of 1996—the attention it deserved. Media industries lobbied heavily for the legislation and benefited immensely from it. The new law produced huge changes in the structure of news and entertainment media by allowing corporations to own more media outlets and more types of media. Telephone companies could now own cable services, and vice versa, and one company could control an almost unlimited number of radio stations. Within six years, Clear Channel went from owning 43 radio stations to owning almost 1,700, controlling 20 percent of the nation's radio revenues. The act also significantly relaxed other ownership rules (which the FCC later eased even further), touching off a flurry of new media mergers that left far fewer but much larger companies in control of most American media. Viacom bought CBS (which previously had been purchased by Westinghouse). After Time Warner bought CNN owner Turner Broadcasting (keeping the Time Warner name), it then merged with America Online.[17]

Despite the massive mergers, perhaps the most controversial part of the new law involved the allocation of what was called the "digital spectrum," the means through which high definition television would be broadcast. Though a few senators and public watchdog organizations maintained that the spectrum was public property and worth tens of billions of dollars, Congress voted to award any future spectrum licenses to the existing broadcasters, free of charge. The ownership and consolidation provisions of the act received little coverage from the television networks, and newspapers did not do much better. Most of the coverage that did appear focused on sex and violence: the implementation of a new TV program rating system similar to that used for movies shown in theaters, and the so-called V-chip that would be added to all new televisions so that parents could—assuming they were more technologically advanced than their children—block out objectionable content.[18]

Of course, increasing consolidation was not an entirely new phenomenon even among the news media. Though print journalists felt threatened by the increasing influence of television at least as early as the 1960s, many newspaper owners did not—because they also had a financial stake in television. The *New York Times*, the *Los Angeles Times*, and other newspapers were among the early applicants for television licenses, and companies involved with television actively sought newspaper partnerships. "Publishers who own stations can tell you about profit," complained one editor at the beginning of the boom. "They enjoy 100 per cent (and up) return on their electronic capital investment as compared to 5 to 10 per cent from their newspapers."[19] Many cities already were down to one daily newspaper before the mid-1960s, a fact that did not trouble all journalists. "There is room for one [daily] in every town, but not two," argued one editor.[20] Others expressed more concern, including the NBC board chairman who said newspapers must provide the depth that television could not, but, "To accomplish this, the newspaper must find a way to check the decline of big city dailies."[21] Some argued that the only hope of competition in the newspaper business came from free papers such as weekly "shoppers" and the remnants of the alternative press that lingered in most major cities.

The number of American dailies, which peaked in 1952 before falling, had increased from 1958 until the mid-1960s, but then declined (other than a brief surge a decade later) for the rest of the century. The fact that in 1962 both the *Los Angeles Evening Mirror* and the *Los Angeles Examiner* had gone out of business meant that by 1965 the *Los Angeles Times* could lead the nation in advertising and volume of editorial matter. A dozen American cities saw new joint operating agreements (JOAs), in which two newspapers essentially merged all except editorial functions, in the 1950s and 1960s. The *San Francisco Chronicle* and the *San Francisco Examiner* joined in September 1965, the same year the *Arizona Daily Star* and the *Tucson Citizen* tried to renew a JOA.[22]

Concerned by the number of similar agreements, the Justice Department legally challenged the Tucson JOA, calling it an infringement on free trade. The Justice Department won in court in 1969, but in 1970 Congress officially sanctioned JOAs with the Newspaper Preservation Act, intended to help "save" second dailies. Publishers first proposed the law as the "Failing Newspaper Act" in 1966, but it gained little congressional support until the more positive name change. Despite its new name, the act did little to save newspapers, and critics argued that it actually hastened the deaths of some publications. "While JOAs probably have 'preserved' some papers, it's likely that they kill more competition, and more papers, than they save," one law professor argued. "Further, it's increasingly clear that JOAs perversely produce the single-paper monopolies they are supposed to prevent."[23]

Publishers found that shutting down newspapers made economic sense, in part because even if customers became angry the vast majority of them stayed with the new joint publication. Reporters thought a lack of competition hurt news quality, but Joint Operating Agreements continued to flourish even as newspapers involved in them continued to die. Nine JOA newspapers folded between 1970 (the year the Newspaper Preservation Act was enacted) and 1994, and the number of American cities with competing dailies fell to nine. The 1992 closure of the *Pittsburgh Press*, which had won reporting Pulitzers in 1986 and 1987, especially drew fire from labor leaders and others concerned about competition. In the middle of an eight-month strike against Pittsburgh's two dailies, the *Press* was sold to the *Post-Gazette*, supposedly the weaker of the two papers. Two weeks after the sale took effect, the strike ended and the *Post-Gazette* again hit the streets—without daily competition, as the new owners closed the *Press*. From 1983 to 1992, JOA newspapers also closed (or were absorbed by their partners) in St. Louis, Miami, and Tulsa and in

Franklin, Pennsylvania, and Shreveport, Louisiana. Another, the *Knoxville Journal*, went from daily to weekly publication.[24]

On a positive note, and perhaps surprisingly, most reporters apparently thought JOAs, which combined business operations, had little negative effect on editorial competition between newspapers. Though journalists might disagree, some critics even argued that increasing consolidation actually improved journalistic quality, because newspapers freed from competitive concerns could worry less about profits while focusing more on quality and on making staff members happy (though chains might restrict the autonomy of editors and publishers).[25]

There were two other somewhat positive notes for competitive journalism: The number of suburban newspapers continued to grow, and broadcast news was given the latitude to become more fearless in its pursuit of truth when the FCC killed the Fairness Doctrine in 1987. Broadcasters now had the same protection as print journalists, not being forced to air dissenting views. Always mindful of audience concerns, of course, most broadcasters did little to take advantage of their new freedom and continued to shy away from politically controversial stories.[26]

Newspapers also found other ways to become more like non-media businesses. By the 1970s, several newspaper organizations turned to the stock market, offering public shares of the companies and creating new economic pressures. Most daily newspapers belonged to chains or other corporate entities, further reducing editorial diversity. In a *Columbia Journalism Review* article, Ben Bagdikian had warned a few years earlier that large, diversified corporations were turning journalism into a "byproduct" of their other business activities.[27]

Newspaper chains were far from new, as more than 100 chains existed even before 1960, but by 1986 chains controlled 75 percent of American newspaper circulation. The number of chains had climbed to 127 by 1986, up from 109 in 1960. Far more dramatic, however, was the increase in the number of newspapers controlled by chains: 1,158 in 1986, more than double the 560 chain newspapers of 1960. The average number of dailies per chain jumped from 5.1 to 9.1. The number of independent newspapers plunged from 1,203 to 499, or in other words from more than two-thirds of newspapers to fewer than a third. That year the American Society of Newspaper Editors addressed the "mergers and acquisitions frenzy" with a panel at its annual convention, asking, "Where will it end?"[28]

The question remained (and remains) unanswered, though a securities analyst on the ASNE panel noted trends in other industries and expressed surprise that anyone would expect otherwise from newspapers: "I am only surprised that it has taken so long or that it shocks anybody, if it still does, because it has been happening everywhere."[29] A Gannett journal noted the following year: "The news has always been a commodity in

America, and its behavior has followed the dictates of business and technology. One of the central ideas of capitalism is that commodities work most efficiently when produced, bought and sold in bulk and mass."[30] Along with readers who were troubled by a potential loss of competitive voices, however, other business people—those who advertised in the news media—also had reason for concern. Despite the cost savings possible through economics of scale, large chains often took advantage of their power to demand significantly higher advertising rates.[31]

On the broadcast side of the news business, the FCC relaxed station ownership rules twelve years before the 1996 Telecommunications Act, increasing the number of TV stations a company could hold from 7 to 12 (fourteen, if at least two were minority-controlled). Many companies quickly took advantage of the opportunity to expand their holdings. The FCC kept a 1943 rule that generally prevented ownership of more than one TV station in a community and a 1975 rule prohibiting the formation of new newspaper-TV combinations within a community. Still, although the number of such single-community cross-media combinations declined significantly in the 1980s, the number of TV stations affiliated with newspapers from outside their own markets increased by even more. Several large media chains, including Gannett, Times-Mirror, Scripps-Howard, and ABC/Capital Communications, contributed to that growth. The leveraged buyout used in other industries also was used to buy media companies, which some observers noted were "perfectly suited for LBOs. They had little outstanding debt, assets with strong breakup values, and profit margins that were the envy of corporate America."[32]

In 1987, the number of American homes with cable passed the 50-percent mark, despite rising rates that resulted from deregulation of the cable industry. (Cable rates were again regulated in 1992, and then deregulated again with the Telecommunications Act four years later.) As with other media, concentration of ownership accelerated in the cable industry, though one researcher optimistically suggested, "As long as competitive independence and restrictive cross-media regulations prevail, the likelihood of adverse consequences to society appear to be minimal."[33] As noted, however, the FCC later relaxed those cross-media regulations thanks largely to heavy lobbying by media companies.

As the number of cable stations increased and financial considerations became more important, broadcast companies improved their use of market research to determine who was watching and at what times and how news might be tailored to better appeal to potential viewers. For example, when research found that working women were out of the home so that early newscasts "were watched mainly by 'the bedpan and walker set,'" noted one former station manager, "it didn't take long for one station,

WLS-TV in Chicago, to hire elderly reporters to cover this audience segment."[34]

Newspaper consumer research and marketing also became increasingly precise. Newspapers began tailoring stories to significant segments of their readership or to readers whom they especially wanted to reach. As a result, some traditional sources of news, ranging from international news wires to poor neighborhoods within individual cities, received less attention. Some news managers saw no reason to cover stories in neighborhoods where readership was low, especially if those neighborhoods offered relatively few potential customers for the newspapers' advertisers. That did not mean that reporters bought into the market approach. Many disliked the perceived effects of the business orientation of their own publications, and by 1991 a national survey found inept managers to be among the leading forces driving many journalists from the field. Not surprisingly, journalists were "happier when they are about the business of journalism—rather than the business of business."[35]

News organizations consistently sought and found new ways to bolster profits, eventually prompting some to warn about problems that occurred "when MBA's rule the newsroom," and efforts to appease readers and advertisers became more important than news values.[36] A decreasing number of newspapers, paired with an increasing number of journalism graduates, meant more competition for jobs and lower pay for new journalists. The influx prompted many newspapers to begin skills testing of applicants, a practice that continues. Taking a cue from other industries, the Knight-Ridder chain even began psychological testing of journalists. "Nowadays, if you want to become a reporter for the respected Knight-Ridder chain, you must take a test that measures—among other things—your masculinity and feminity," noted one writer. "And if you happen to be a woman, your prospects are better if you score high on the masculinity scale."[37] Though longtime journalists still engaged in the ever-popular activity of bemoaning the lost glory of earlier times, the skills testing did allow newspapers to hire better, more-educated writers and editors—for less money, because of the increased competition for jobs and the fact that at the same time newspaper labor unions were losing power. Membership in the Newspaper Guild climbed slightly in the 25 years from 1961 to 1986, but the number of newspapers with Guild contracts dropped from 180 to 144 during the same span.[38]

Many local TV stations began to succumb to increased influence from advertisers, such as sponsored news segments, and to the airing of advertising as news through use of the video news release (VNR). The VNR, a television version of a print press release, existed in limited form before the 1980s, but the rise of overnight mail services and especially satellite transmission of the releases helped the phenomenon explode. Medialink, founded in 1986, proved to be the most important company to start producing and distributing VNRs, which would come to be used by virtually every local station and national network. Several of the company's executives had roots in the news business, and the releases often were indistinguishable from segments aired by journalists. Some of the releases included voice-over by a narrator, while others included a script that could be read by a local newsperson, making the "coverage" seem even more like local news. The use of VNRs continued to spread, with the administration of President George W. Bush criticized years later for using disguised video segments, complete with a phony "reporter," to promote its policies.[39]

One telling complaint that arose was that media companies often seemed to have more trouble staying in journalism than they had staying in business. Publicly held newspapers had higher profits and tended to pay better, but they also relied on smaller staffs. Fewer people did more work, sometimes leaving less time for in-depth stories and fact-checking. In the 1990s media companies increasingly began trading properties with one another, so that each could achieve geographical prominence in a region. That permitted some to reduce staffs further, while limiting editorial diversity even further.[40]

As profits became increasingly important and local news expanded from an hour per day to two or more hours, the VNR became an increasingly important filler of local broadcast airtime. Other such fillers came via network feeds of footage from around the country, through which a viewer in Fargo, North Dakota, could see coverage of a nonfatal but visually appealing fire in Mobile, Alabama. Weather coverage expanded, dramatically, while the number of reporters needed for both television and the ever-consolidating newspaper business sometimes dropped. In recessionary times more reporters and editors lost their jobs, though, importantly, most cuts came to increase profit margins, not to prevent or forestall losses. Over all, newspaper newsroom employment stayed fairly consistent after 1986.[41]

Sometimes broadcasters also let their viewers provide the news footage. As home video cameras became more common, non-reporters often encountered news and sold or gave their tapes to stations. Many local stations encouraged viewers to submit newsworthy footage, recognizing it as a way to expand their coverage, though some worried about amateur journalists putting themselves in harm's way as they pursued stories. Regardless, some of the footage made gripping news. One journalist noted in 1991: "Some of the pictures can already be replayed in the nation's collective mind: a car falling through a hole in the Oakland Bay Bridge after the San Francisco earthquake, airplanes crashing into each other at air shows, huge tornadoes bearing down on small towns from Colorado to Ohio, and, of course, a group of Los Angeles police officers beating Rodney King." (The case is discussed in more detail in Chapter 1.)[42]

At the national level, profit-focused media managers slashed news personnel budgets. CBS made the deepest cuts, letting go about 75 news staffers in 1985, 86 more a year later, and more than 200 the next year—the biggest reduction ever made in any network news division— for a total loss of more than 350 people in less than three years. ABC and NBC also laid off news people during the same period. Alarmed by the trend, several prominent CBS news executives (including anchor Dan Rather) offered to take pay cuts while complaining publicly that the news would invariably suffer. Not everyone was sympathetic, however. Some critics pointed out that the network's news staff and spending had been ballooning for years and that the division was suffering in part because a dozen of its people made more than $1 million per year.[43]

One area in which the networks cut people was in their overseas bureaus. They began to rely increasingly on freelance journalists and on "pooling," with networks sharing the pictures taken by one camera. Later networks also agreed to share their own national feeds with each other's affiliates. Easier travel and better computers and satellites also made it easier for a person to cover more ground. A reporter based in one country, for example, could more easily fly into another nation on the same continent to air a story. "But physical mobility is not matched by the psychic mobility that would allow reporters to feel at home in more countries," noted one media scholar. "Nor is it accompanied by sudden spurts in knowledge that would permit such 'parachute' reporters to cover a new area with insight."[44] Further complicating the issue were old, ongoing problems. Some areas tended to be ignored because they were seen to have relatively little impact on the United States, and reporters were granted more access to some areas than to others. As a result, reporters were far more likely to be stationed in friendly locations than in neutral or hostile ones.

Fewer bureaus meant less competition, and so did the decline of United Press International—which for years had served as the primary competitor of the Associated Press. It changed hands five times from 1982 to 1992, becoming a subsidiary communication company owned by the Saudi royal family. Annual revenue during the period dropped from $100 million to less than $30 million, and the number of staffers was slashed to fewer than 300, less than one-sixth the number at the beginning of the period.[45]

Apparently few cared. Americans and their media apparently had little interest in international issues that did not involve their own obvious interests, a fact sociologist Herbert Gans noted years earlier. Newspaper coverage of foreign events steadily dropped, making it less likely that Americans would know how, or if, international events affected them.

During one six-year period in the late 1980s and early 1990s, the fall of the Berlin Wall apparently was the only international event not directly involving American troops that still managed to draw significant attention from most Americans. Even a coup attempt to replace Soviet leader Mikhail Gorbachev failed to attract the interest of most Americans, as did—other than a single iconic image—what became known as the Tiananmen Square incident.[46]

In the spring of 1989 Chinese students gathered in Beijing's Tiananmen Square, demanding democratic reforms. After more than a month, soldiers were ordered to drive out the protestors. They fired upon the students, killing an untold number; estimates range from a few hundred to several thousand. U.S. news crews filmed much of the activity, and CBS viewers saw a Chinese official unplug Dan Rather's satellite transmitter. The most enduring image was that of a young man standing alone in front of a line of tanks, stepping quickly sideways as the tanks tried to steer around him. Versions of the picture ran on television and in newspapers around the world, as a single student in the world's most populous country came to stand for an unknown number of protestors. Eventually the protestors were driven from the square, and China again became a politically repressive producer of cheap goods for American consumers, largely ignored by the American news media.

A more important story appeared later the same year, when the Berlin Wall came down. The wall had separated East Germany from West Germany since 1963, becoming a physical symbol of what Winston Churchill had in 1946 called the "Iron Curtain" between Soviet-bloc communist countries and the West. During the next twenty-six years, thousands of people were arrested in the vicinity of the 100-mile wall (about twenty-seven miles in Berlin), and hundreds were killed trying to cross it. In late 1986 East German officials, who had wrestled with the problem of a mass exodus of refugees escaping the country, decided to ease travel restrictions from East to West.[47]

ABC, CBS, and NBC all led their broadcasts with the German story for several consecutive nights. Then, on the night of November 9, television cameras captured a party atmosphere, broadcasting worldwide images of people standing atop the wall, climbing over, and battering it with sledgehammers. Ordered not to shoot, overwhelmed East German border guards stood by and watched. The following day, government workers created new openings in the wall, and within weeks the wall was in ruins.

Many Americans considered cold war policies that helped cripple Soviet Communism to be former President Reagan's most important contribution. The destruction of the wall, which came two years before the break-up of the Soviet Union, prompted networks to air tape of a 1987 Berlin speech in which Reagan demanded of Soviet leader Mikhail Gorbachev, "Mr. Gorbachev, tear down this wall." Further illustrating the importance of the wall, the networks repeatedly ran the same footage in 2004 after Reagan's death.

Anchors of all three major U.S. networks broadcast from the scene of the 1989 incident, demonstrating what had become known as "parachute-drop coverage": When a big event occurred, rather than letting viewers learn about it from the reporters who had already been working in the area, the networks brought in more recognizable and trusted faces to relay the information. Walter Cronkite's 1968 visit to Vietnam had been big news in part because he left the anchor desk, but the somewhat oxymoronic-sounding phenomenon of traveling anchors would become increasingly common. In the case of the Berlin Wall, NBC anticipated events the best, with anchor Tom Brokaw broadcasting from the city starting November 8. Peter Jennings of ABC and Dan Rather of CBS began anchoring their reports from Berlin two nights later, a night after the most dramatic footage had aired. Four nights later, all three anchors were back in their New York studios, and none of the nightly broadcasts began with news from Europe. By the next night, Germany had disappeared altogether from ABC and CBS, though it would continue to pop up on all three networks from time to time for the next few weeks.[48]

Though international news was faring poorly in the media, the same was not true of science and technology. Computers and various forms of entertainment technology were becoming more important to readers and viewers. Environmental groups demanded more attention when they perceived that Reagan and his secretary of the interior were dismantling environmental protections put in place a decade before, and the world seemed to be growing increasingly complicated in many respects. Many newspapers instituted science beats and hired science (sometimes "science and technology") reporters for the first time, and Americans learned about new human possibilities. *Baltimore Sun* reporter Jon Franklin won a 1985 Pulitzer Prize for a series about an entirely new science, molecular psychology, and *New York Times* science writer James Gleick began writing about another new science, called *chaos theory*. Two *Chicago Tribune* reporters won a 1987 Pulitzer for their series about gene therapy and its medical potential, and *Albuquerque Journal* reporter Tamar Stieber linked a rare blood disorder to an over-the-counter dietary supplement, leading to a national recall of the product and a 1990 Pulitzer Prize.

The new coverage sometimes gave Americans new fears, and some of the new reporters made mistakes stemming from the fact that they had relatively little background in the sciences. They sometimes over-dramatized the potential benefits of new scientific discoveries, especially if they could lead to cures, however remote or long-term the possibilities, for frightening diseases such as AIDS or cancer. Another result, however, was that as Americans encountered more amazing scientific discoveries they became increasingly blasé about them. The 1969 Apollo 11 moon landing may have drawn a larger percentage of viewers than any other news or entertainment program in history, but Americans soon considered space travel to be almost routine. A near-disaster in space for Apollo 13 and the 1981 launch of the first Space Shuttle briefly brought more attention, though subsequent launches largely were ignored. An audience faced with ever-increasing entertainment options, an audience that in the 1980s made the VCR the fastest-growing home appliance of all time, was tough to impress. So were journalists.[49]

In 1986, however, came one of the rare moments—John F. Kennedy's 1963 death probably was the best previous example—when television would help people later remember exactly where they were when they "heard the news." Seventy-three seconds after takeoff on the morning of January 28, while still within view of cameras, the space shuttle Challenger shuttle exploded, killing all seven crew members (including elementary teacher Christa McAuliffe, slated to be the first "teacher in space"). Americans quickly gathered around televisions, sharing in joint national grief. A television critic captured what had become notable about the American news audience: "We may not be able to believe that something truly terrible has happened anymore unless we see it six or seven times on television. Yesterday, something truly terrible happened...and the three networks, each sustaining marathon coverage during most of the day, played, replayed and re-replayed videotaped footage, sometimes in slow-motion, sometimes frame by agonizing frame, of this truly terrible occurrence."[50]

The next morning, USA Today's front page offered a nearly full-page, full-color info-graphic of the explosion, complete with timeline, map, and cutaway drawings of the shuttle. An extreme close-up photo caught McAuliffe's parents' reaction to the explosion, while the bold, all-caps headline was a four-word quote of First Lady Nancy Reagan: "OH MY GOD, NO!" Another headline promised "eight full pages" of disaster coverage, while a teaser in a top corner of the page referred to three shuttle stories inside. The first was headlined, "How TV Covered," while another reflected the business emphasis that helped define much of the period: "Shuttle Stocks Dip."[51]

NOTES

    1. Kevin Anderson, "'The Donald' through Deals and Divorces," BBC Online Network, October 8, 1999, accessed at http://news.bbc.co.uk/1/hi/world/americas/468462.stm (accessed March 5, 2006).

    2. Donald L. Barlett and James B. Steele, *America: What Went Wrong?* (Kansas City: Andrews and McMeel, 1992). The book is an expanded version of a 1991

Inquirer series. Trump overcame his financial problems of the early 1990s and by the end of that decade considered a run for the presidency. Continuing to demonstrate the odd nature of fame in America, in 2003 he became the host of a popular "reality show" through which he made a national catchphrase of the words, "You're fired."

3. Richard L. Berke, "Deregulation Has Gone Too Far, Many Tell the New Administration," *New York Times*, December 11, 1988.

4. Editorial, "The 431 Insolvent S&Ls," *Washington Post*, November 8, 1985. Also see Ernest Conine, "At a Time for Outrage on S&Ls and Takeovers, the Silence is Deafening," *Los Angeles Times*, November 2, 1988; Project Censored Web site, http://www.projectcensored.org (March 6, 2006); Robert A. Bennett, "Another Crisis Engulfs the Thrifts," *New York Times*, July 22, 1984.

5. Jonathon Peterson, "The Stock Crash May End Up Benefiting the Economy," *Los Angeles Times*, December 6, 1987.

6. Stephen E. Everett, "Financial Services Advertising Before and After the Crash of 1987," *Journalism Quarterly* 65 (Winter 1988): 920; Stephen D. Reese, John A. Daly, and Andrew P. Hardy, "Economic News on Network Television," *Journalism Quarterly* 63 (Spring 1987): 137–144; J.T.W. Hubbard, "Newspaper Business News Staffs Increase Markedly in Last Decade," *Journalism Quarterly* 63 (Spring 1987): 171–177.

7. New Hampshire had implemented a state lottery in 1964 and a few other states followed suit during the 1970s, especially after federal law was amended to permit radio and television advertising of lotteries in 1975.

8. Editorial, "A Dishonorable Judgment," *St. Louis Post-Dispatch*, March 3, 1991; editorial, "Business as Usual—Four Out of Keating Five Get Off Free," *Seattle Times*, March 2, 1991. An interesting side note: The judge in the state case against Keating was Lance Ito, who later would become famous in the O.J. Simpson case.

9. Peter T. Kilborn, "Big Trader to Pay $100 Million for Abuses," *New York Times*, November 15, 1986.

10. Tom Shales, "The Year of Roseanne, Saddam, Bart and PBS's 'Civil War,' " *Washington Post*, December 30, 1990.

11. Richard Stengel, "Bushwacked!" *Time*, February 8, 1988, 15, 17–20. Also see Thomas J. Johnson, "Exploring Media Credibility: How Media and Nonmedia Workers Judged Media Performance in Iran/Contra," *Journalism Quarterly* 70 (Spring 1993): 87–97; Scott Armstrong, "Iran-Contra: Was the Press Any Match for All the President's Men?" *Columbia Journalism Review*, May/June 1990, 27–35.

12. Everette E. Dennis and Huntington Williams III, "Preface," *Gannett Center Journal* (Spring 1987): 4.

13. Peter W. Kaplan, "Plan for a Fox Network Intrigues TV Industry," *New York Times*, October 11, 1985; Eric Barnouw and others, *Conglomerates and the Media* (New York: New Press, 1997).

14. Ben H. Bagdikian, *The Media Monopoly* (Boston: Beacon, 1983); David Croteau and William Hoynes, *The Business of Media: Corporate Media and the Public Interest* (Thousand Oaks, Calif.: Pine Oaks Press, 2001).

15. John F. Berry, "Skepticism Greets Hype Surrounding Cable News Debut," *Washington Post*, June 1, 1980.

16. Glen T. Cameron, Kuen-Hee Hu-Pak, and Bong-Hyun Kim, "Advertorials in Magazines: Current Use and Compliance with Industry Standards," *Journalism & Mass Communication Quarterly* 73 (Autumn 1996): 722–733.

17. Janine Jaquet, "Broadcast Ownership: A Gift to Big Media," in *Successes and Failures of the 1996 Telecommunications Act*, (Cambridge, Mass.: Massachusetts

Institute of Technology Center for Reflective Community Practice and the Leadership Conference Education Fund, 2002): accessed at http://www.civilrights.org/publications/reports/1996_telecommunications/telecom.html (accessed March 5, 2006).

18. L. Paul Husselbee, "How Newspapers Covered the Telecommunications Act of 1996," conference paper for Association for Education in Journalism and Mass Communication 1997 Convention, http://list.msu.edu/cgi-bin/wa?A2=ind9710a&L=aejmc&F=&S=&P=6953 (accessed March 6, 2006).

19. Jerry Walker, "Newspaper Alliance Sought for Television," *Editor & Publisher*, March 22, 1947, 48.

20. Clark R. Mollenhoff, "The Federal FOI Law: Meaningful IF..." *Quill*, August 1966, 22.

21. Quoted in Victor Jose, "Do Newspapermen Really Want Competition?" *Quill*, August 1965, 21. Also see David R. Davies, *An Industry in Transition: Major Trends in American Daily Newspapers, 1945–1965*, doctoral dissertation, University of Alabama, 1997.

22. Robert O. Blanchard, "The Freedom of Information Act—Disappointment and Hope," *Columbia Journalism Review*, Fall 1967, 16–20; John C. Busterna and Robert G. Picard, *Joint Operating Agreements: The Newspaper Preservation Act and Its Application* (Norwood, N.J.: Ablix Pulishing, 1993); Jose, "Do Newspapermen Really Want Competition?"; Scott, "Today's Journalism," 32.

23. Stephen R. Barnett, "The JOA Scam," *Columbia Journalism Review*, November/December 1991, 47–48.

24. David C. Coulson and Stephen Lacy, "Journalists' Perceptions of How Newspaper and Broadcast News Competition Affects Newspaper Content," *Journalism Quarterly* 73 (Summer 1996): 354–363; William B. Blankenburg, "Predicting Newspaper Circulation After Consolidation," *Journalism Quarterly* 64 (Summer/Autumn 1987): 585–587.

25. David C. Coulson, "Impact of JOAs on Newspaper Competition and Editorial Performance," *Mass Comm Review* 21 (1994): 236–249; David Demers, *The Menace of the Corporate Newspaper: Fact or Fiction?* (Ames, Iowa: Iowa State University, 1996); Martha N. Matthews, "How Public Ownership Affects Publisher Autonomy," *Journalism Quarterly* 73 (Summer 1996): 343–353.

26. Philip Gaunt, *Choosing the News: The Profit Factor in News Selection* (New York: Greenwood, 1990).

27. Ben H. Bagdikian, "News as a Byproduct," *Columbia Journalism Review*, Spring 1967, 5–12.

28. Panel discussion, "Merger and Acquisition Frenzy in the News Business: Where will it End?" *Proceedings of the 1986 Convention of the American Society of Newspaper Editors, 1986*. Also see Richard McCord, *The Chain Gang: One Newspaper versus the Gannett Empire* (Columbia, Mo.: University of Missouri, 2001); Eugene Roberts, Thomas Kunkel, and Charles Layton, eds., *Leaving Readers Behind: The Age of Corporate Newspapering* (Fayetteville, Ark.: University of Arkansas, 2001); John C. Busterna, "Trends in Daily Newspaper Ownership," *Journalism Quarterly* 65 (Winter 1988): 831–838.

29. John Morton comments, panel discussion, "Merger and Acquisition Frenzy."

30. Dennis and Williams, "Preface," 4.

31. John C. Busterna, "Price Discrimination as Evidence of Newspaper Chain Market Power," *Journalism Quarterly* 68 (Spring/Summer 1991): 5–14; John C. Busterna, "National Advertising Pricing: Chain vs. Independent Newspapers," *Journalism Quarterly* 65 (Summer 1988): 307–312, 334.

32. Quoted in Michael L. McKean and Vernon A. Stone, "Deregulation and Competition: Explaining the Absence of Local Broadcast News Operations," *Journalism Quarterly* 69 (Autumn 1992): 713–723. Also see Herbert H. Howard, "Group and Cross-Media Ownership of TV Stations: A 1989 Update," *Journalism Quarterly* 66(Winter 1989): 785–792.

33. Herbert H. Howard, "An Update on Cable TV Ownership: 1985," *Journalism Quarterly* 63 (Winter 1986): 781.

34. Gary Cummings, "The Watershed in Local TV News," *Gannett Center Journal* (Spring 1987): 44.

35. Keith Stamm and Doug Underwood, "The Relationship of Job Satisfaction to Newsroom Policy Changes," *Journalism Quarterly* 70 (Autumn 1993): 528–541. Also see Ted Pease, "Blaming the Boss: Newsroom Professionals See Managers as Public Enemy No. 1," *Newspaper Research Journal* 12 (Spring 1991): 2–21; Doug Underwood and Keith Stamm, "Balancing Business with Journalism: Newsroom Policies at 12 West Coast Newspapers," *Journalism Quarterly* 69 (Summer 1992): 301–317; David C. Coulson, "Impact of Ownership on Newspaper Quality," *Journalism Quarterly* 71 (Summer 1994): 403–410.

36. Doug Underwood, *When MBAs Rule the Newsroom: How the Marketers and Managers Are Reshaping Today's Media* (New York: Columbia University Press, 1993).

37. Francis Pollock, "Knight-Ridder Wants to Know the *Real* You," *Columbia Journalism Review*, January/February 1978, 25–28.

38. Barbara J. Hipsman and Stanley T. Wearden, "Skills Testing at American Newspapers," *Newspaper Research Journal* 11 (Winter 1990): 75–89; Louis Gwin, "Prospective Reporters Face Writing/Editing Tests at Many Dailies," *Newspaper Research Journal* 9 (Winter 1988): 101–111; Lee B. Becker, Vernon A. Stone, and Joseph D. Graf, "Journalism Labor Force Supply and Demand: Is Oversupply an Explanation for Low Wages?" *Journalism & Mass Communication Quarterly* 73 (Autumn 1996): 519–533; "Then and Now," *Columbia Journalism Review*, November/December 1986, 47.

39. Randall Rothenberg, "The Journalist as Maytag Repairman," *Gannett Center Journal* (Spring 1990): 103; Glen T. Cameron and David Blount, "VNRs and Air Checks: A Content Analysis of the Video News Release in Television Newscasts," *Journalism & Mass Communication Quarterly* 73 (Winter 1996): 890–904.

40. Stephen Lacy and Alan Blanchard, "The Impact of Public Ownership, Profits, and Competition on Number of Newsroom Employees and Starting Salaries in Mid-Sized Newspapers," *Journalism & Mass Communication Quarterly* 80 (Winter 2003): 949–968; Howard, "Group and Cross-Media Ownership"; Jim McPherson, "Mergers, Chains, Monopoly, and Competition," in Wm. David Sloan and Lisa Mullikin Parcell, eds., *American Journalism: History Principles, Practices* (Jefferson, N.C.: McFarland & Company, 2002): 116–124.

41. Geneva Overholser, "Good Journalism and Business: An Industry Perspective," *Newspaper Research Journal* 25 (Winter 2004): 8–17; Stephen Lacy, "The Effects of Intracity Competition on Daily Newspaper Content," *Journalism Quarterly* 64 (Summer/Autumn 1987): 281–290; American Society of Newspaper Editors, "Newsroom Employment Census," http://www.asne.org/index.cfm?id=4456#TableO (accessed March 5, 2006).

42. Greg Luft, "Camcorders: When Amateurs Go After the News," *Columbia Journalism Review*, September/October 1991, 35–37.

43. Joseph R. Dominick, "Impact of Budget Cuts on CBS News," *Journalism Quarterly* 65 (Summer 1988): 469–473.

44. Scotti Williston, "Global News and the Vanishing American Foreign Correspondent," Transnational Broadcasting Studies online version, Spring/ Summer 2001, accessed at http://www.tbsjournal.com/Archives/Spring01/ Williston.html (accessed March 5, 2006). Also see Richard A. Schwarzlose, "Cooperative News Gathering," in Sloan and Parcell, American Journalism; Doris A. Graber, Mass Media and American Politics, 4th ed. (Washington, D.C.: Congressional Quarterly Press, 1993): 364.

45. Claude Moisy, "The Foreign News Flow in the Information Age," Discussion Paper D-23, the Joan Shorenstein Center of Press, Politics and Public Policy, Harvard University, November 1996.

46. Herbert Gans, Deciding What's News: A Study of CBS Evening News, NBC Nightly News, Newsweek and Time, Vintage Books ed. (New York: Vintage, 1980); Michael Emery, "An Endangered Species: The International Newshole," Gannett Center Journal (Fall 1989): 151–164.

47. Churchill made the phrase famous after using it in a speech in Missouri, but he was not the first to use the term. German propagandist Joseph Goebbels used it in 1945 and apparently Mrs. Philip Snowden did so in 1920. See the Columbia World of Quotations online, http://www.bartleby.com/66/50/ 25150.html (accessed March 5, 2006); and the Winston Churchill Home Page maintained by the Churchill Centre and Societies, http:// www.winstonchurchill.org (accessed March 5, 2006). The number killed in escape attempts may be impossible to determine. While some estimate the number of deaths at less than one hundred, Berlin officials listed 270 killed, while other "official" German figures list 471. Other groups, counting those killed in escape attempts before the wall was built and border guards who were killed, estimate the total deaths at more than one thousand.

48. Vanderbilt Television News Archive, accessed at http:// tvnews.vanderbilt.edu/ (accessed May 5, 2006).

49. Lee Wilkins and Philip Patterson, eds, Risky Business: Communicating Issues of Science, Risk, and Public Policy (New York: Greenwood, 1991).

50. Tom Shales, "Horror of the Fire in the Sky," Washington Post, January 29, 1986. Also see Christopher Hanson as William Boot, "NASA and the Spellbound Press," Columbia Journalism Review, November/December 1986, 23–29; Haynes Johnson, "Silent Scenes of Tragedy Transfix the Nation," Washington Post, January 29, 1986; Sam Hall Kaplan, "Space Center Triumph Turns to Tragedy," Los Angeles Times, January 28, 1986.

51. USA Today front page, January 29, 1986.

CHAPTER 7

More Content than Context

The 200th anniversary of the Bill of Rights in 1991 would have been a logical starting point for re-educating Americans about the value of the First Amendment, but the press took little notice. Newspapers paid scant attention to the Bill of Rights in general, and even less attention to their own constitutional rights and responsibilities. The *Atlanta Constitution* did run a series of eight editorials about the Bill of Rights, but the one editorial that discussed the First Amendment managed to do so without mentioning the press. The oversight for the news media extended beyond a failure to promote their own interests, however. They also suffered from the fact that many others outside of the press were doing a much better job of promoting their own interests—often with significant assistance from the press.[1]

Public relations professionals had been influencing news coverage to varying degrees for most of the century, but 1991 may have been the first time a PR firm could take significant credit for starting a war. The Persian Gulf War began after Saddam Hussein's Iraq invaded its tiny oil-rich neighbor, Kuwait, in August 1990. A week later President George Bush responded to a Saudi request by sending U.S. troops to Saudi Arabia, to prevent any possible Iraqi invasion of that nation. Hussein then declared war against the United States. In an effort to make Hussein pull his troops out of Kuwait, Western nations began a naval blockade of Iraqi oil. In December, the United Nations set a one-month deadline for withdrawal of Iraqi troops from Kuwait, which Hussein rejected. Bush wanted to go to war, and after initially saying he did not need permission to do so, he decided to ask for congressional approval in January. Nine days after the U.S. Defense Department began censoring news reports from the Gulf, Congress granted Bush the authority to wage a war that began five days later. During the months after the invasion of Kuwait, a huge public relations campaign helped Bush win—by a mere five votes—Senate approval for the war.

Nine days after the invasion, a group calling itself Citizens for a Free Kuwait (though American-style freedom of speech, among other things, did not exist in Kuwait even before the Iraqi invasion) hired Hill & Knowlton, the world's largest public relations firm. Hill & Knowlton apparently was one of the first major companies to combine public relations and political lobbying efforts for its clients. Among its executives was Bush's former vice presidential chief of staff. Coming at a time when the American news media were paying decreasing attention to international news, the Hill & Knowlton effort became the largest foreign-funded PR campaign ever aimed at U.S. public opinion. The *Washington Post* ran one story about it before the war, but few Americans knew about the company's involvement at all, let alone the extent of the campaign or what effect it had on the news they watched and read.[2]

The campaign involved more than a dozen other PR companies and cost more than $12 million. Hill & Knowlton produced dozens of video news releases that aired on news programs around the country, resulting in tens of millions of dollars worth of air time. The company bought advertisements in the *Washington Post, New York Times*, and *USA Today*. Lunches for journalists, speaking engagements, and press kits containing a 154-page book titled *The Rape of Kuwait* also aided the joint PR-lobbying effort. "From pictures of Kuwaiti civilians maimed by Iraqi soldiers to descriptions of captive Americans groveling for food in a far off desert, the images of Iraq's misdeeds in the Persian Gulf are important weapons in an all-out public relations battle Kuwait is fighting to convince Americans its cause is worth dying for," the *Washington Post* reported.[3]

A poll commissioned by Hill & Knowlton found that atrocity stories, a longtime staple of military propaganda, would have the "most emotional meaning" for Americans. Soon the company managed to produce such a tale, a touching "dead baby story" told by a sobbing 15-year-old Kuwaiti girl. The girl, identified only as Nayirah supposedly to protect her family from reprisals, testified in October 1990 before the "Congressional Human Rights Caucus"—a group of politicians and witnesses pulled together by Hill & Knowlton for what resembled a congressional hearing. Unlike a congressional hearing, however, the unofficial nature of the caucus meant "witnesses" faced no penalty for dishonesty, noted one writer: "Lying under oath in front of a congressional committee is a crime; lying from under the cover of anonymity to a caucus is merely public relations."[4] Giving credence to a rumor that had appeared in newspapers the previous month, the girl told a heart-wrenching story about witnessing gun-wielding Iraqi soldiers taking babies out of hospital incubators and leaving them on the floor to die, then stealing the incubators.

Reporters received copies of Nayirah's written comments, though few news sources reported them immediately (perhaps because many already had run rumor-based stories about dead incubator babies during the previous month). In addition to helping "cast and direct" the hearing, however, Hill & Knowlton sent a camera crew and produced its own film, which was promptly sent out as a video news release to Medialink. *Columbia Journalism Review* later noted, "Portions of the VNR featuring Nayirah's testimony were used on the October 10 *NBC Nightly News* and eventually reached a total audience of 35 million—sufficient to win it fourth place on the top ten list of VNR successes in 1990."[5]

During the next few months, President Bush and others freely used Nayirah's story to build support for the war and to criticize those who opposed it. Bush used graphic specifics to be helpful, comparing Hussein to Adolf Hitler as he referred to "newborn babies thrown out of incubators" or "babies pulled from incubators and scattered like firewood across the floor."[6] The news media quoted some of the alleged details, while largely ignored others, as in the case of a speech in which Bush told soldiers who would be asked to fight the war that "Iraq's soldiers pulled the plug on incubators supporting 22 premature babies. All 22 died."[7] He repeated the number in other speeches, though in at least one case he said, "And then they shot the hospital employees," while twelve days later he merely said, "The hospital employees were shocked."[8] Perhaps even more interesting, the president actually referred to "babies heaved out of incubators" in a news conference one day before Nayirah's testimony, noting, "I don't know how many of these tales can be authenticated."[9] Thanks in large part to the Kuwaiti girl's testimony the following day, the atrocity story was repeated in the news media, in United Nations Security Council hearings held to build international support for the war effort, and by Congressmen during several hearings that considered the advisability of going to war. By the end of December, the number of incubator babies killed had somehow surpassed 300, a figure widely reported after the international human rights organization Amnesty International supported the story. After many news organizations published that information, Amnesty International was forced to admit it was wrong.[10]

A few human rights groups and others did question the numbers and details, with the *New York Times* pointing out a month before the war began that "atrocity reports involving occupied territories have frequently been incorrect. In 1914, for example, the Germans were falsely accused by the Allies of murdering Belgian babies at the outset of World War I."[11] Two days later, the director of a human rights organizations reported in a foreign policy forum that interviews with hospital workers in Kuwait had turned up no verifiable accounts of murdered babies or stolen incubators. Yet just two days later, the *Times* ran an Associated Press story in which Amnesty International supposedly verified "300 premature babies who died because incubators were stolen."[12] The press did not seriously examine the story until after the war was over. A month after fighting ceased, ABC aired a report discrediting the story, and later the *Washington Post* reported that a New York-based human rights group had found that "a charge that Iraqi troops killed hundreds of premature babies by stealing their incubators—a widely circulated story repeated by President Bush—has proved 'totally false.' "[13]

A closer look at the original hearing revealed other details previously undisclosed by the news media. The two congressional co-chairs of the Congressional Human Rights Caucus, Democrat Tom Lantos and Republican John Porter, also co-chaired the Congressional Human Rights Foundation, which was housed in Hill & Knowlton's Washington headquarters. The company provided a $3,000 annual rent reduction contribution to the foundation, and Hill & Knowlton's client, Citizens for a Free Kuwait, donated $50,000 to the foundation sometime after Iraq's invasion of Kuwait.[14]

Even Porter apparently did not know Nayirah was the daughter of the Kuwaiti ambassador to the United States (who was sitting in the hearing room at the time and therefore unlikely to face "reprisals"). A *Harper's* magazine reporter and Canadian television finally revealed that fact in January 1992, almost a year after the forty-two-day war ended. Nayirah may not even have been in Kuwait at the time the atrocities allegedly occurred, and apparently was coached by a Hill & Knowlton vice president before she testified. A few days later a clip of her testimony ran on CNN's *Larry King Live*, just minutes before King, apparently also aware of the relationship, interviewed her father about the situation. Almost none of her testimony later could be confirmed. Still, Lantos, who had helped hide the girl's identity even from his co-chair, said it did not matter. In a letter to the *New York Times*, he claimed that the girl's testimony was "consistent" with other witnesses' claims. Besides, he said, the fact that she was the daughter of the Kuwaiti ambassador actually made her a "more credible" witness.[15]

"It was not an implausible claim," Lantos later said about the incubator story, citing Hussein's known history of human rights abuses (most of which had taken place in the 1980s and been largely ignored by the United States, then an ally of Iraq).[16] In fact, as is true of nearly every military action, soldiers did commit some atrocities, though apparently nowhere near the number claimed. And at a time when most Americans questioned the need for military action, especially risking the lives of U.S. soldiers for a mistrusted and little-known Arab emirate, the atrocity stories helped generate support for the war. Hill & Knowlton "had done its job well," noted a *Columbia Journalism Review* critic. "The same could not be said of the U.S. press."[17]

Another area in which the news media fell short, especially until after the war, was in explaining how the U.S. government and American corporations had provided much of Hussein's military strength. "In what may well be the supreme irony of his Presidency, it is becoming increasingly clear that George Bush, operating largely behind the scenes throughout the 1980s, initiated and supported much of the financing, intelligence and military help that built Saddam's Iraq into the aggressive power that the United States ultimately had to destroy," Ted Koppel stated after the war.[18] *Nightline* devoted several episodes to the issue and most newspapers gave it some attention, but the complicated tale of international banking and diplomatic maneuvering failed to hold the attention of either journalists or news consumers.

Of course, as with all wars, both sides used propaganda in various ways before and during the war. American reports of Iraqi troops poised to invade Saudi Arabia proved false. On the other side, even before the fighting began, U.S. soldiers were subjected to radio reports from "Baghdad Betty" and other Iraqi commentators trying to convince them that their cause was unjust, that their wives and girlfriends had abandoned them, and that their own comrades were drunks, drug addicts, and rapists. The broadcasts apparently had little effect. "The only things that cheer the guys up more than Baghdad Betty are letters from home," one officer was quoted as saying. "Officially, of course, we strongly condemn Iraq's perfidious lies, et cetera. Honest, folks, we ain't bayoneting Bedouin babies."[19] The quotes appeared in a *Boston Globe* story twelve days after Nayirah's testimony about Iraqi soldiers dumping babies from incubators.

As with previous wars, censorship and access issues proved to be problems for journalists during the Gulf War, though the news media and the government had worked to improve the relationship. After fielding numerous complaints from the press about the press blackout during the 1983 U.S. invasion of Grenada, officials devised a system that supposedly would allow better access during later incidents. But the National Media Defense Pool had failed miserably in the Bush administration's first military operation, when American troops invaded Panama in 1989 to capture former longtime U.S. ally and Panamanian President Manuel Noriega and arrest him for drug trafficking. Reporters again were blocked from the busiest hours of the fighting during the exercise and ended up relaying reports about suspected packages of cocaine—later identified as tortilla flour—and accepting government figures of about 250 Panamanian deaths (about 80 percent of them civilians). Other sources later estimated a much higher casualty total, numbering deaths in the thousands, but by then Noriega was in a Florida jail and the invasion was old news.

With the Gulf War, the military issued its restrictions in advance. The guidelines established two types of news media pools: eighteen-member pools for ground combat operations and seven-member pools for combat coverage, both mostly "limited to media that primarily serve the American public and that have had a long-term presence covering Department of Defense military operations." Reporters were "strongly discouraged" from trying to join with combat units on their own. Assistant Secretary of Defense Pete Williams also warned that the military would review pool reports "before release to determine if they contain sensitive information about military plans, capabilities, operation, or vulnerabilities."[20]

The American Society of Newspaper Editors quickly protested the rules, arguing that commanders might abuse their power: "In a world where 'spin control' of the news has become commonplace, this form of prior restraint is a tool to gain control over what the American public sees or hears from the battlefield."[21] Raising a point unlikely to inspire optimism among the military, the complaint noted that "few security breaches of any consequence" had arisen in Vietnam, where no similar restrictions existed.[22] The letter also asked that the military allow coverage free of the restraints at some point. The pools had obvious problems. In one case the *New York Times* did not get a position, but a glamour magazine did. The pools were expanded, but the ASNE and some news organizations continued to protest censorship and access issues. The Center for Constitutional Rights filed suit against the military on behalf of several small news organizations and independent journalists (most of whom had no chance of gaining pool positions), though the larger organizations neither joined the suit nor reported it. In addition to complaining to officials, however, television networks made it a point to regularly inform readers and viewers about the restrictions. CNN clearly labeled more than one-third of its wartime Gulf stories "censored." The other networks used the labels far less frequently, but the war marked the first time that Americans had been so clearly forewarned they were getting less than the full story.[23]

At approximately 3 a.m. Baghdad time (7 p.m. in New York) on January 17, 1991, American bombs and missiles began falling on the Iraqi capital city. Prime time television watchers gathered around television sets as CNN reporters Peter Arnett, Bernard Shaw, and John Holliman, whom Hussein let stay in Baghdad, described the bright flashes of tracers and sounds of explosions outside their hotel window in coverage later called "reminiscent of Edward R. Murrow's reports from London in WW II."[24] Of course, Murrow had been broadcasting from the capital city of America's ally, not that of its enemy. Arnett drew considerable criticism, even from some journalists, for ensuing reports from Iraq.

U.S. Senator Alan Simpson and others called him an Iraqi sympathizer, saying he also had sympathized with the enemy in Vietnam (where his coverage won a Pulitzer). Each of Arnett's stories had to be cleared by an Iraqi censor, though the reporter said he never was told what to say or forced to broadcast at gunpoint. "Cruise missiles were aimed at my head," he told the National Press Club, referring to the steady attacks coming from American forces.[25]

CNN covered the war twenty-four hours a day, and most Americans believed the network did the best job of reporting the conflict. In some cases even other journalists had little choice other than to report what they (and other Americans) had seen on CNN. The network's ratings jumped 500 percent, prompting an increase in price from $3,500 to $20,000 for a single thirty-second ad.[26]

Through all news media, Americans saw an unprecedented amount of coverage; the war produced more network stories than any other event in history over the same period of time. ABC, CBS, and NBC broadcast 337 related stories, covering more than eleven hours, during the first week alone. ABC's nightly broadcast drew the largest audience of the three, despite the fact that Peter Jennings stayed in New York while Dan Rather and Tom Brokaw reported from the Gulf region. The amount of coverage also made celebrities of television reporters other than Arnett, including NBC's Arthur Kent, who picked up the nickname "Scud Stud" after broadcasting from an area threatened by Iraqi Scud missiles. Newspapers could not match the immediacy or breathlessness of the TV coverage, but they saw their circulations jump nevertheless. The *New York Times* published fifty war-related stories and columns in a single day. Often those newspaper stories served to correct reports from the previous night on television.[27]

The quality of the coverage could not match its quantity, in part because government and military officials managed it so well. After the war started, Iraq launched missiles into Israel, but the Israeli government proved even more censorious than U.S. officials. The military waged most battles from afar with bombs and missiles and turned to ground troops only at the end of the war, and reporters had little means of access to the battlefield even if they wanted to go. As a result, much of the war had to be covered by journalists stationed in Saudi hotels. Pool restrictions, the number of reporters, suspicious commanders, and equipment problems all contributed to friction, misinformation, and delays. Journalists also were frustrated by what had become a recurring theme: The public was more likely to support censorship than to favor less control of the press.[28]

The military provided the majority of the most dramatic pictures of the war, and in many cases journalists became as captivated by televised images as did people watching the news. Bombs and missiles were fitted with TV cameras, so targets could be filmed as the weapons approached. In one example, the first U.S. deaths in the ground campaign, Allied Forces Commander "Stormin' Norman" Schwarzkopf replaced the staff officer who typically gave the press its daily briefing. Before mentioning the dead soldiers, Schwarzkopf went through several charts describing mission operations and equipment and showed videotape of so-called smart bombs and fighter planes destroying their targets. He described the Iraqi losses as "rather sensational" and offered estimates of enemy dead and equipment losses. Finally, more than twenty minutes into the briefing, the general reported: "The Marines lost two light armored vehicles. Unfortunately, I'm very sad that I have to report to you that they lost twelve KIA [killed in action] in that engagement."[29] Two *Newsweek* correspondents noted that the networks gave the "bombs-away" video as much attention as they gave the American dead.[30]

In fact, the dead drew little attention throughout the war, in words or images. Citing concerns for the privacy of soldiers' families, while conscious of the effect of flag-covered coffins during the Vietnam War, government officials instituted a new policy that prohibited photography of those coffins as they arrived back in the United States. Most also died off camera, but even when journalists got pictures of soldiers or civilians who had been killed, they frequently withheld the footage. Instead, stories and pictures often focused on the impressive weapons and technology boasted by the allies. Along with the footage from planes and precision-guided bombs, news cameras showed U.S. Patriot missiles apparently blowing up Scuds in mid-air. Because of the pictures, some called the conflict a "Nintendo war" or a "video-game war." Not until the war was over did the press find out that in fact many—perhaps almost all—of the Patriots missed their targets. "Patriot was about as effective as Fourth of July fireworks," one scientist later told CNN. "It looked great on TV, made people feel good; but it turned out that Patriot missed almost all the SCUDS that it was fired at."[31] Though smart bombs provided dramatic video of structures being destroyed with pinpoint accuracy, even many of the smart bombs also missed. Besides, the military later admitted, only 7 percent of the weapons used were smart bombs. Most of the damage was inflicted by far-less-accurate traditional weapons, and a *Washington Post* reporter figured that 70 percent of the 88,500 tons of bombs dropped missed their targets.[32]

The technology that provided the most notable pictures of the war also provided much of the language used by journalists, who often resorted to what Gulf War reporter Bob Deans called "numbingly innocent" military terminology: "Enemy aircraft aren't blown up, they're 'knocked down.' Buildings with people in them don't explode and crumble; rather, 'ground positions' are 'taken out.' "[33] Other language demonstrated that U.S. journalists were Americans before they were journalists. Especially for television reporters, U.S. troops and machinery became "our boys" and "our weapons." As the enemy, Iraqi troops could be compared to vermin without challenge: CBS cited a pilot who said, "It's almost like you flipped on the light in the kitchen late at night and the cockroaches start scurrying and we're killing them."[34] Military sources provided most of the information about the technology and strategies of war, but other "experts" also were used more than ever before. Their expertise went far beyond explaining factual circumstances.

As when covering politics, journalists offered their interpretations of war news for readers and viewers, but one noteworthy trend that continued after the war was the tendency toward letting non-journalists help with the interpretation. News directors called upon more and more "experts," referred to by journalism scholar Lawrence Soley as "news shapers," to lend credibility to the analysis of issues.[35] Typically retired military officers, university professors, or representatives of "think tanks" such as the Brookings Institution and the Center for Strategic and International Studies, those experts frequently spent more time on camera than did policy makers.

Because of the months leading up to the fighting, producers and editors had time to develop lists of experts they could call upon when circumstances warranted, even if the circumstance primarily was a need to fill airtime while waiting for significant news to occur. For television, of course, the experts had to look and sound good on camera. They had to be able to summarize ideas or arguments quickly, ideally with memorable voices and phrasing. When seeking out the experts, both newspaper and television reporters sometimes found titles more appealing than credentials. Regardless of the sources' achievements, news producers preferred Harvard and Johns Hopkins University professors to professors from institutions considered less prestigious, and people with more prestigious-sounding titles were more likely to be quoted.[36]

Those the media hired were far from the only ones shaping news. Even if public relations could not be blamed for starting the war, PR was important throughout and after the conflict. The Pentagon alone boasted more than 3,000 public relations staffers, while other government agencies and industries also relied heavily on PR to spread or filter their message. At a time when journalists could not easily gain access to information, they often had little recourse but to rely on public information officers or press releases.[37]

Though the war ended, often the reliance on mediated information continued. Journalists rarely acknowledged how much of the news, on both national and local beats, was generated by PR professionals. Even in cases in which the journalist initiated the story, he or she often had to deal with a public relations person before (or instead of) talking to a government or industry official—an official who then might be available to the press after being briefed by the PR person about what to say and how to say it. Exxon provided a popular textbook case study of how not to practice public relations when the oil supertanker "Exxon Valdez" ran aground in 1990 and spilled 11 million gallons of oil. The spill killed thousands of birds and animals, contaminated hundreds of miles of rugged Alaskan coastline, and netted the *Seattle Times* a Pulitzer Prize. Other PR professionals learned from Exxon's mistakes.[38]

Public officials also found other ways to use the news media, or in some cases to bypass most reporters completely. A multitude of new media options helped because so many cable stations and networks competed to first bring information to viewers. Newsmagazines turned "get" into a noun: Someone who was in the news became a "get" who might boost that week's all-important ratings. Increasingly the sources were actors or musicians (not an altogether new phenomenon, as even Edward R. Murrow had interviewed popular entertainers). Some shows paid sources, further blurring the already fading line between news and entertainment. Others ended up helping the source promote a book or film, typically one produced by the publishing arm or the entertainment division of whichever corporation happened to own the network on which the source appeared.

CNN, which had established its reputation during the Gulf War, staged another coup in 1992 when Texas billionaire businessman H. Ross Perot chose to announce his candidacy for president on *Larry King Live*, a show that featured an audience call-in segment. Perot appeared on the show several times, and on one visit he said he would run as an independent if his supporters organized a campaign to put him on the ballot in every state. After they did so, he took calls on C-SPAN and appeared on other shows and in the presidential debates, eventually drawing enough votes in the election to perhaps cost George Bush re-election. After Perot "legitimized" the practice other candidates for various offices appeared on similar call-in shows. Democratic nominee Bill Clinton answered viewer questions on King's show, on the ABC, CBS, and NBC morning shows, and on a CBS "Town Hall." Bush fielded audience questions on King's show, on ABC's *Good Morning America*, and from the White House Rose Garden for *CBS This Morning*.[39]

Audience members typically offered softer questions than did professional interviewers, allowing the candidates to look approachable and brave while limiting their access to traditional political reporters. "No wonder that in this talk-show campaign," noted *New York Times* writer Richard Berke, "[the candidates] often bypass national reporters, leaving their jobs to ordinary citizens."[40] At the same time, audience members often asked the questions most relevant to what candidates might be expected to do after taking office. They asked questions relevant to their own lives, while reporters tended to ask questions about polls, strategy, and the "story of the day" (often defined by the campaigns through pseudo-events or other activities). While reporters tried to get answers about Bill Clinton's infidelity, ABC's Peter Jennings said, "The voters in New Hampshire wanted to know about the economy. And we were getting in their way."[41]

The candidates did not limit their appearances to news or pseudo-news programs. Just as newsmagazines turned increasingly to entertainers as news, political figures increasingly began to appear on entertainment programs. On those shows the candidates could reach new potential voters, while coming across as casual and friendly. They also could typically count on softer questions from entertainment hosts than they would get from political reporters, especially after Phil Donahue was booed by his own audience for asking Clinton tough questions about his sex life. Clinton played his saxophone on *The Arsenio Hall Show*, and he and running mate Al Gore both appeared on MTV.

Journalists worried about the shift from news to infotainment, finding fault with their own corporate bosses, among others. They lamented the fact that the networks, especially through their morning programs, so freely relinquished news coverage time to non-journalists. "What shall we call this stuff—the Unquestioning Media? The Easy Media?" asked longtime NBC reporter John Chancellor, noting that while candidates liked the casual approach and the easier questions, networks enjoyed higher ratings: "You have a nice combination of commercial success and candidates wanting to do this," he said, "and guys like me are left standing outside, somewhere near the gutter."[42] Columnist Russell Baker was even more blunt, stating, "It becomes harder and harder for press and television to play any role in Presidential politics that is not utterly contemptible."[43] Voters probably were less likely to make their decisions based on information gleaned from entertainment programs than on details gained from traditional news sources, but a side benefit for the candidates proved to be how often the news programs ended up covering the appearances on the entertainment shows—again, typically covering strategy rather than meatier issues.

Occasionally, non-professional interviewers did provide surprises, perhaps most notably less than a month before the election when one of the presidential debates adopted much of the talk show format while featuring a live audience. An audience member asked the candidates whether economic problems affected them, and how they could understand those problems without having suffered personal economic struggles. After Bush, who remained seated on his stool and checked his watch as if he had someplace better to be, struggled with the question, Clinton walked close to the questioner and personalized his answer. His empathy came through to the audience on the scene and on television, based on what Larry King later noted "would have been a cheap question on the lips of just about anyone in the media. When the public asked, however, it worked."[44] Most viewers agreed that Clinton won the debate, on his way to winning the presidency.

Candidates tried other ways to bypass journalists in 1992, sending out their own video news releases in the hope that local stations would use them. More effective was the use of direct satellite transmissions, through which a Congressman/candidate could sit down in a congressional studio in Washington to answer questions from local newscasters. Happy to have access to their senator or representative, those newscasters typically asked softer questions than did national political reporters. By doing so they contributed to a culture in which people continued to like their own representatives, even as their trust in Congress and other governmental institutions decreased. If local reporters or anchors did ask tough questions, of course, a competing station would likely get most of the future interview opportunities.

The news media and pseudo-news media also began letting their audiences participate in the news in ways other than by interviewing candidates. One perhaps troubling method was the introduction of the audience "vote" about events in the news. In a typical example, *Dateline* viewers watching a program about a murder case would be invited to call in, paying fifty cents per call, to vote on the guilt of the accused. Of course, editing left the issue of guilt or innocence in doubt until the final few minutes of the program. Later, with the arrival of the Internet, viewers could log on to the program's Web site to vote. Networks and some local stations used the same technique to gain nearly instant feedback about news ranging from viewers' trust in astrology to political speeches to the advisability of the country waging a war, though any social scientist could point out that the chances of such "polling" being accurate often could be compared to the accuracy of determining a suspect's guilt by flipping a coin.

A more important form of what became known as "interactivity" between the news media and news users arrived in the form of civic journalism, sometimes called public journalism or community journalism. Newspaper publishers and editors sought ways to combat stagnant sales and to become more relevant to readers' lives. Recognizing that standardized journalism education, media conglomeration, and other factors had contributed to a sameness of news from city to city—with, as journalist Davis Merritt noted, "its shape and tone determined by what happened at the top of the pyramid, not by the needs of any specific place or time—some worked to figure out what readers wanted, expected or sometimes needed from their news.[45] Like local broadcast stations, sometimes newspaper professionals turned to consultants. More notably in the case of civic journalism they turned to their own readers and then began producing what for many was an entirely new form of journalism. Some local broadcasters soon followed their lead.

Like investigative journalists, civic journalists worked to improve the communities in which they worked. Rather than merely pointing out problems and raising questions, however, they also tried to provide answers. And rather than serving as dispassionate observers, the civic journalists became actively involved in their communities. After all, one reporter noted after riots in Los Angeles and Detroit, "It is cruelly ironic that newspapers such as the *Detroit Free Press* won prestigious awards for coverage of the events that devastated their own markets."[46] Civic journalism also invited readers and viewers to become more involved with their communities, and with the journalistic process. "At its heart is a belief that journalism has an obligation to public life—an obligation that goes beyond just telling the news or unloading lots of facts," argued the Pew Center for Civic Journalism, one of the organizations most responsible for acceptance and expansion of the latest form of "new journalism."[47] Some argued that increased civic engagement by journalists and their readers might even be necessary to save journalism—and perhaps to save democracy, or at least to avoid what Robert M. Entman termed a "democracy without citizens" in which Americans continued to withdraw from the political process.[48] "Civic journalism grew out of a sense that, as we in the press have dutifully reported for so long, our democracy actually *is* going to hell in a handbasket," noted writer Mike Hoyt.[49]

The sense of participatory societal obligation was not entirely new for journalists, of course. Some, such as writer Enid Sefcovic, argued that a civic journalism-related concept of a "marketplace of ideas" was rooted in early American press traditions and provided the justification for the fact that "the news industry is the only business protected by the Founding Fathers in the Constitution with First Amendment guarantees."[50] The "yellow journalists" of the early twentieth century also became involved in community campaigns. Many American newspapers throughout their history have sponsored and promoted Christmas drives and similar activities, and local publishers and broadcast station owners traditionally have in various ways reflected the pro-development perspectives of their chamber of commerce colleagues. Still, a primary difference in those activities may be that their focus was more social or economic than political, though such distinctions inevitably are fuzzy.

Modern civic journalism may have started in 1990 with the *Wichita Eagle*, a Knight-Ridder chain newspaper located in Kansas' largest city. Frustration about the apparent lack of depth of some political candidates, along with a desire to help readers know more about the candidates, issues, and process of the election, prompted the *Eagle* to initiate its "voter project." The newspaper's ambitious goals included improving the tone and content of the campaigns, generating increased interest and knowledge among voters, and increasing the relevance—and the readership—of the publication. In 1990, 1991, and 1992, the *Eagle* asked readers to help determine elections issues that candidates and the newspaper should address, and then it covered those issues in more depth than it typically would have. Under the heading "Your Vote Counts," it ran regular election-related items such as a weekly "Where They Stand" feature, told readers on its front page how to register and vote, and let them know they could register at the newspaper itself. With each of the three elections, the *Eagle* published and distributed a simplified voters' guide to about 135,000 non-subscribing households and to adult literacy classes, and then it joined forces with a local television station.[51]

Generally pleased with the initial reaction, the *Eagle* later interviewed hundreds of area residents and expanded the idea, under the term "The People Project," to other non-election issues such as education, family issues, and crime (including the death penalty). It used special sections to discuss the issues in depth, relying more heavily on stories about, and quotes from, ordinary residents than on information from the "usual suspects": political leaders and bureaucrats. The names and contact information of policy makers and others such as non-profit organizations ran along with relevant stories, so that readers knew where to turn for help or answers to questions raised by the stories. Besides the initial interviews, the *Eagle* also hosted community discussions and used questionnaires that readers could clip and mail in. Local television and radio stations broadcast the community discussions. Reporters began to seek out places such as coffee shops where less formal civic discussions took place. Results were mixed, as voter participation continued to drop in the newspaper's circulation area, but not as much as participation fell in other parts of the state. The new reader-centered journalism also failed to forestall further decreases in circulation.[52]

Like the *Wichita Eagle*, the *Charlotte Observer* also focused first on electoral politics and also teamed with a local television station, as it brought civic journalism to North Carolina a year after the experiment arrived in Kansas. Looking for voter-driven coverage, the *Observer* polled readers about news themes, gave attention to the themes identified, involved residents in various aspects of the news coverage, and pressed candidates on the issues identified by readers. "Citizens Agenda" themes such as the economy, crime and drugs, education, the environment, and "family values" became the centerpiece of a six-week series. The reporters with the most expertise on those issues, rather than political reporters, covered and wrote the stories. The *Observer* later brought six other newspapers, five other television stations, and three radio stations (which, among them, covered most of the eastern half of the state) into the project.[53]

One state to the north, the Norfolk *Virginian-Pilot* also began experimenting with civic journalism in the early 1990s. Its most notable contribution probably was the reorganization of beats into "coverage teams," each composed of several reporters and an editor. Instead of the traditional institutional or geographic beats such as city hall or a specific part of the county, each team devoted its efforts to a more issue-driven focus. New beats included public safety, public life, "real life" (e.g., traffic, home, and consumer news), and "women, family, and children." Traditional beats of education and criminal justice (informally called "cops and courts" at many newspapers) still existed, though the focus shifted toward reader concerns and away from traditional institution-based reporting.[54]

Many newspapers and broadcast stations throughout the country began shifting at least part of their journalistic focus to new reader-centered forms, especially during election years. Notable projects came from the *Boston Globe, Tallahassee Democrat, Seattle Times, St. Louis Post-Dispatch*, and *Portland* (Maine) *Press Herald*, among numerous others. The *San Francisco Chronicle*, KRON-TV, and KQED-FM radio combined for a 1994 political project, providing information in Cantonese, Vietnamese, and Spanish. "We the People/Wisconsin," initiated in 1992, eventually included the *Wisconsin State Journal*, Wisconsin Public Television, Wisconsin Public Radio, commercial station WISC-TV, and its own Web site. The Pew Charitable Trusts started the Pew Center for Civic Journalism in 1993. It produced newsletters and videotapes, offered workshops and prizes, and provided funding for joint print-broadcast civic journalism projects around the country. Many news viewers began seeing more women and minorities as sources in their local news, and many university journalism programs made civic journalism part of the curriculum.[55]

Though many news organizations changed their focus and methods, civic journalism drew at least as many critics as converts among the working press. Some news people wondered why they had studied journalism when publishers or editors seemed to consider ordinary citizens to be as qualified as journalists in determining news coverage. Some editors said they did not need polls to tell them what readers wanted, though at least one study indicated that editors were not particularly good at predicting readers' preferences. Others worried about news media catering more to readers' desires than to their needs, especially if those media faced competition, or even whether journalists could count on readers to be honest. "If the choice is between what people tell interviewers they want and what the ratings reveal, any career-minded producer is bound to choose the ratings," argued the *New York Times'* Walter Goodman, who suggested that the citizens' forums "sound like get-togethers of the Rotarians and Alcoholics Anonymous."[56] Other journalists criticized the inherent lack of neutrality or objectivity that came from participating in news rather than simply reporting it. Some critics disliked the fervor of the movement, while others wished the same enthusiasm and financial resources could be devoted to investigative journalism or other traditional news. One book, calling forth suggestions of a Communist threat by calling it "people's journalism," suggested that the movement could curtail press power and freedom.[57]

The high-profile Pew Center for Civic Journalism closed a decade after it began, and some journalists happily declared the movement dead. Still, the Pew Center claimed that at least a fifth of all U.S. dailies practiced some form of civic journalism between 1994 and 2001, and other organizations remained devoted to the maintenance and spread of the practice. Probably most newspapers, including those critical of the movement as a whole, adopted some civic journalism aspects such as more reader-friendly listings of useful consumer information, more ways for readers to voice their opinions, more stories about lifestyle issues, and a broader variety of types of sources used for news stories. Many newspapers also followed the lead of the Norfolk *Virginian-Pilot* in dumping traditional beats in favor of coverage teams, though many independent-minded journalists disliked the loss of individual autonomy associated with the shift. Others thought that the team system increased the number of errors in the newspaper and the complexity of their jobs while slowing and softening the news. "We simply miss breaking stories because there's no one in charge to point out the errors and there is pressure at meetings to simply be agreeable," one journalist complained.[58] All in all, the greatest value of civic journalism may have been the discussions it prompted about how to improve the news media.

A year after the *Wichita Eagle* introduced civic journalism, something arrived that would change American news media even more dramatically than public-centered news. Tim Berners-Lee and others at the European Laboratory for Particle Physics introduced a computer "hypertext" system based on "links" to information, effectively creating the World Wide Web. The Web, later commonly referred to as the Internet, would allow the civic journalism buzzword of "interactivity" to take myriad new forms. It continues to change the form and functions of journalism while making journalism better in some respects, perhaps worse in others.

The Internet actually arrived in the 1960s through research by the Defense Advanced Research Projects Agency as a means of allowing scientific and military computers to share information. First online the "ARPANET" were four computers in the Southwest, at the University of Utah, the University of California at Santa Barbara, UCLA, and the Stanford Research Institute. Soon MIT, Stanford University, Harvard, Systems Development Corp., and others logged on, and growth continued exponentially. Originally government-funded, at first the Internet was limited to research, education, and government uses. Because of those limitations and the complexity of using the system, early users were technically savvy computer experts, librarians, engineers, and scientists.[59]

Ease of access improved during the 1980s, and academics around the world began sharing information via e-mail. In 1991 the University of Minnesota introduced a relatively simple menu system for seeking information (titled "gopher" after the school's "Golden Gopher" mascot), which opened up the Internet to even fairly casual users. Berners-Lee agreed in 1994 to help create and direct the World Wide Web Consortium, established to figure out guidelines and computer codes to make the Web widely functional. New independent commercial networks opened the Web for uses other than research or education, and Mosaic became the first modern "graphical browser," followed by Netscape Navigator and Microsoft Internet Explorer.[60]

Newspapers quickly made use of the Internet. Reporters found they could save time and add depth to stories with research done from their desks. Soon many reporters turned to the Internet on a daily basis. Because of the nature of the research, even reporters for small newspapers could do it (though some larger newspapers hired people to help their reporters with Internet research). As the number of Web pages grew, so did the possible research sites, greatly enhancing computer-assisted reporting. Congress passed the Electronic Freedom of Information Act, requiring government agencies to use the Internet to make many documents available. Those agencies, non-profit organizations, research libraries, and numerous private companies and individuals produced Web pages that reporters, along with anyone else who had a computer with Internet access, could use. Or misuse. Despite the fact that no one knew where much of the information came from, many Web users inexplicably viewed that information as more credible than what they read in their morning newspaper. The same trust in technology that had appeared years earlier with the arrival of television reappeared with the Internet. Though journalists were likely to be skeptical of information from cyberspace, ordinary Americans sometimes trusted too much of what they found. Even reporters encountered errors (often the result of data entry problems) on sites they thought were credible, and were frustrated by difficulties in verifying Web information.[61]

Of course, one of the things Americans could soon find was the Web site of their own local newspaper or television station—or of a newspaper in another part of the world. Newspapers found they could offer news on the Web, and get it to readers nearly as quickly as television could get it on the air. That sometimes led to problems as breaking news might not be read or edited as carefully as would the next day's paper, especially because it was common for one or two staff members to oversee all news on the Web. In mid-1995, fewer than 100 newspapers had Web sites, but the number jumped to almost 400 by a year later. Soon most newspapers had Web sites, though most of them adapted to the new technology more slowly than did broadcast stations. Many newspapers simply dumped the stories from the paper onto the Web site, creating a medium only slightly more interesting than the earlier videotext systems that generally had failed miserably. Broadcast stations often became more creative more quickly, probably because the Internet emphasis on print stories forced stations to view it as a new medium from the beginning. They also used the Web more for company self-promotion than did newspapers, probably because most of the newspapers had little or no print competition.[62]

Though newspapers did use their Web sites to promote the print versions of their product, the primary goals involved reaching more readers and generating more revenue. A few newspapers charged customers for access to their Web versions, though most did so only for archived articles. Some asked readers to register, often by including some personal information that the publication might use to determine readership. Most of the online versions also carried advertising, along with electronic forms that readers could use to subscribe to the print version. Because the newspapers already generated large amounts of written copy and many photos, coming up with content for a Web site was relatively easy. In fact, many newspapers soon began including items on the Web such as longer stories, extra sidebars, or more photos, which they could not fit into the print version. Web page designers found they could do much more than simply dump content on pages, however.[63]

For some newspapers, the Web versions looked much like the printed version, with large blocks of text on screen, but others used space more efficiently, listing headlines and perhaps brief summaries with links that the reader could use to see the full version of a story. Some opened with listings of directories to sections like those of the print version, while others included the section directory on every page. Most also soon began including "hyperlinks" that could take the reader elsewhere, even to sites far from the newspaper's own site. For example, someone reading about the Persian Gulf War five years after it ended might see—on the same page, or even within the story—links to stories written during the war and to Web sites from the Pentagon, the White House, an antiwar organization, and an organization devoted to war history. Through what became known as "transaction technology," someone could read a book review and then click on a link to a bookseller that sold the book. Later "streaming" technology allowed the use of video on a site, so that even a newspaper site might include CNN videotape. Not surprisingly, newspapers with more resources tended to have much more complex sites that offered readers more options.[64]

The use of links also raised concerns for media professionals. The hyperlink technology gave readers much more control over what they chose to read or see, putting more of the editing function in their hands. Some editors worried that readers, especially those with short attention spans or a desire to be entertained by their news media, might wander away. For example, a reader who began with a story about a favorite baseball team might connect to the team's linked Web site, go from link to link, and never came back to the original news site. A viewer who became bored with a thirty-second video easily could just go to something else rather than waiting to see what story the TV station would offer next. Even if readers chose to read the opinion section before the local news, newspapers and traditional television news were primarily linear in form. With the Internet, link-to-link reading became nonlinear. Perhaps in part because of that nonlinear form, readers seemed less likely to remember what they read on a Web newspaper than in a paper version. Though editors worried that some readers might choose the free electronic version of the paper instead of paying for a regular subscription, Internet news apparently had a bigger negative impact on television. Those who read Internet news also tended to read newspapers.[65]

Photos typically looked better on the Web version of a newspaper than on newsprint, in large part because of digital photo technology that arrived just before the Internet. The Associated Press and United Press International both began sending all photos via digital transmission in the early 1990s and most newspapers soon had electronic darkrooms. AP helped with the process by providing necessary hardware to subscribers. With digital technology photos could be shot and placed on a page much more quickly than before. If a story lacked a good photo, a photographer could be dispatched to shoot one and the editor could have it on his or her computer screen within the hour. The photo could go immediately onto the newspaper Web site or on the next day's front page. Under the old system, processing time alone might mean the lack of a strong photo could prompt an editor to delay the story for an extra day.[66]

With a digital camera, the photographer could determine while still on the scene if he or she had captured the desired photo, avoiding some darkroom surprises. And because digital cameras required less on-site equipment and produced images that could be easily translated via phone lines or by satellite, they proved especially useful for photographers covering war or other rigorous activities. "It's fast, economical, and lets you transmit instantly instead of sending your film on a two-week safari to the Saudi desert," photographer Brian Storm said.[67] Eventually most newspapers turned entirely to digital photography, leaving old-fashioned chemical darkrooms largely to hobbyists, though newspaper photographers found that much of the time they saved with processing of film now went to saving photos on disks or in electronic databases.[68]

Digital technology also opened up new ethical issues, especially after the arrival of Adobe Photoshop in the early 1990s let photographers easily modify photos in new ways. The National Press Photographers Association adopted a Digital Manipulation Code of Ethics in 1991, noting that "it is wrong to alter the content of a photograph in any way that deceives the public," but such alterations provided fairly regular discussion for trade journals and ethics books.[69] Even without Photoshop, *National Geographic* provided one of the first well-known examples, moving two pyramids closer together for a 1982 cover shot. Later *Time* altered O.J. Simpson's mug shot. *Newsweek* digitally straightened and whitened the teeth of a mother of septuplets. Newspapers added people (or clothing for "under-dressed" people) to photos or cut them out. Even more troubling for many was the fact that, unlike with film cameras, no negatives existed. After digital images were changed, no identifiable hard-copy version might exist. "It literally will be possible to purge information, to alter a historic event that occurred five years ago because no original exists," said an editor of the *Asbury Park* (N.J.) *Press*, whose own newspaper had changed its policy after digitally removing someone from a photo. "There's enormous potential for great wrong and great misuse."[70] Most of the intentional misuse came not from the news media but from amateurs with home computers who spread hoax photos via the internet. Digital technology also spread to movies and to television, allowing fantastic but frugal fictional special effects and new forms of product placement—including on the news. On New Year's Eve 2000, Dan Rather broadcast the *CBS Evening News* from Times Square, where the CBS logo hung above his shoulder. What viewers did not know, until the *New York Times* revealed the secret, was that the network had digitally added its own logo to block out NBC advertising.[71]

Some news organizations took advantage of the Internet and other technology through cooperation or even through what became known as "convergence," in which print and broadcast media belonging to the same company combined forces. Under the new model, some journalists became "content providers," perhaps writing news for the newspaper and the Web site, the nightly newscast and the Web site, or for all three. In some companies, each entity had its own news staff, but the staffs shared information and perhaps a newsroom. With the Web address on the screen during the newscast and perhaps on the front page of the newspaper, the three media could reinforce one another, or a reader who stumbled upon the Web site could be referred to the other media. Typically the newspaper and television station each had its own

Web site, though one might link to the other to make it easy for readers to go back and forth.[72]

Journalism schools, many of which had long since become "schools of communication," also changed their focus. News writing classes became "media writing" courses that might involve any combination of print news, broadcast news, writing for the Web, advertising, and public relations writing. Not all journalists or would-be journalists liked the change. For example, at Brigham Young University, which revamped its journalism program to train content providers in a combined newspaper/ television setting, some faculty members and students complained. "All my life I dreamed of being a news anchor in a television news station," one student said. "I worked hard, got into a good program, and now I am on a team that does a half dozen things I'm not interested in."[73]

Most media companies dropped their experiments in print/broadcast convergence, though universities continued to try to teach students some basics of all the news media. For many students that meant cutting elective courses such as history, political science, sociology, and literature, classes that might be expected to give future journalists—who would be expected to do more news analysis than their journalistic forefathers had done—the ability to provide much-needed context and to do so in a way that people actually enjoyed reading or hearing. The alternative for other students was to pull away from another form of specialization, in which they might study one subject heavily in hopes of becoming a business reporter or science writer.

Not surprisingly, corporations and interest groups found the Internet to be a valuable advertising and public relations tool. A company in the news could use its Web site to tell its side of a controversial story, along with providing potential customers or investors information unavailable elsewhere. Some included copies of all their press releases, even those releases that never made it into the newspapers. Always interested in ways to bypass the press and to reach constituents and potential voters directly, political candidates found their way to the Web in 1994. Former Tennessee governor Lamar Alexander announced his Republican presidential candidacy via the Web in 1995 and most candidates had Web sites by the 1996 election, though those sites had little effect on voters or the process. By four years later, both major candidates offered Web sites in Spanish as well as in English, and many voters relied on the Internet for much of their political information. Of course, so did many journalists.[74]

The Internet also permitted the creation of new news and pseudo-news sites. Search engines such as Yahoo!, through which users could find Web sites on almost any topic, also offered links to regularly updated news stories gleaned from newspapers and broadcast companies throughout the world. The reader could even tell how many minutes earlier the story had been posted on the Web. The Web gave the serious news consumer more options than ever before, prompting some to predict that the Internet might do more than any other medium for the democratic process. A reader, for example, easily could access competing stories about a presidential decision and then could go to the White House Web site to see the actual text of the speech—something almost every newspaper had eliminated years before.

The Internet also meant that almost anyone could become an information provider (and the easy cut-and-paste technology of modern word processing meant material could be plagiarized more easily than ever before). Thinkers ranging from colonial believers in a free exchange of ideas to the originators of public access television in the 1960s to the 1990s developers of civic journalism had shared a desire to involve more voices in the civic discourse. The Web made the "marketplace of ideas" possible in ways never previously imagined, though one concern for media professionals and political scientists was that people might tend to stick to sites produced by those with whom they agreed, reinforcing prejudices more than broadening perspectives.

In the process, the Internet gave a voice to some "journalists" who never would have been hired by established news organizations. Some created electronic magazines, or "e-zines," while others produced sites that looked similar to mainstream news sites. The most notable of those was Matt Drudge, whose *Drudge Report* combined links to credible news with poorly researched but inflammatory articles and opinion pieces aimed at a politically conservative audience. Drudge—referred to by another Web journalist as "the troll under the bridge of Internet journalism"—might have faded into obscurity except that in 1998 he broke a story that more reputable news organizations had withheld for lack of confirmation: the story of President Bill Clinton's affair with White House intern Monica Lewinsky.[75] After Drudge's report appeared, mainstream journalists, arguing that the story was now "out there," felt free to pursue the issue (discussed further in the next chapter).

Another new form of journalism wrought by the Internet was the Web log, or "blog." Spawned by a culture that had produced numerous people willing to expose their foibles and innermost thoughts on offensive television talk shows, most early blogs appeared as personal diaries of their creators. A typical blogger sat down each day, offering bits of information about his or her personal life and whatever random thoughts happened to be in the blogger's head at the time. Soon, however, many of the bloggers devoted their commentary to events in the news, and many of the most thoughtful and best writers among them developed substantial followings. They commonly linked their sites to those of other bloggers, creating an ever-expanding community. Newspapers hired a few, and some newspapers began hosting links to bloggers on their own Web sites. "Rather than be afraid of it or work against it, we should be going with the flow," said one newspaper Web editor. "If this is where communication in our society is going, we should try to figure out how to facilitate it."[76] The 2004 Democratic National Convention also granted access to some bloggers. Some worried that Internet options might leave traditional journalism out in the cold, but others argued that, in the words of communication scholar Andrew Gordon, the quantity of information available made trained media professionals more necessary—that journalists "experienced with dealing with massive amounts of chaotic information and organizing it into a manageable form," had skills "desperately needed" in an Internet world.[77]

NOTES

1. James B. McPherson, "Crosses Before a Government Vampire: How Four Newspapers Addressed the First Amendment in Editorials, 1962–1991," *American Journalism* 13 (Summer 1996): 304–317; Editorial, "Free Religion and Speech in Retreat," *Atlanta Constitution*, December 9, 1991.

2. Gary Lee, "Kuwait's Campaign on the PR Front," *Washington Post*, November 29, 1990.

3. Ibid. Also see John R. MacArthur, *Second Front: Censorship and Propaganda in the Gulf War* (Berkeley: University of California Press, 1992); John Stauber and Sheldon Rampton, *Toxic Sludge is Good for You: Lies, Damn Lies and the Public Relations* Industry (Monroe, Maine: Common Courage Press, 1995).

4. MacArthur, *Second Front*. Also see James W. Tankard Jr. and Bill Israel, "PR Goes to War: The Effects of Public Relations Campaigns on Media Framing of the Kuwaiti and Bosnian Crises," conference paper for Association for Education in Journalism and Mass Communication 1997 Convention: http://list.msu.edu/cgi-bin/wa?A2=ind9709c&L=aejmc&F=&S=&P=3857 (accessed May 5, 2006).

5. Arthur E. Rowse, "How to Build Support for a War," *Columbia Journalism Review*, September/October 1992, 28. Also see Tankard and Israel, "PR Goes to War."

6. George Bush, excerpts from speech given on November 22, 1990 at Saudi Arabia Marine outpost, *New York Times*, November 23, 1990; George Bush, speech at Hickam Air Force Base, Hawaii, October 28, 1990, obtained via Federal Information Systems Corporation Federal News Service: http://web.lexis-nexis.com (accessed August 5, 2002).

7. Bush speech at Hickam Air Force Base.

8. Bush speech at Hickam Air Force Base; George Bush, fund-raising in Iowa, October 16, 1990, obtained via Federal Information Systems Corporation Federal News Service: http://web.lexis-nexis.com (accessed August 5, 2002).

9. George Bush, presidential press conference, White House, October 9, 1990. Also see Paul Bedard, "Bush Talks of Atrocity Trial for Saddam," *Washington Times*, October 16, 1990.

10. Associated Press Story, "Standoff in the Gulf: Amnesty Report Says Iraqis Tortured and Killed Hundreds," *New York Times*, December 20, 1990.

11. Judith Miller, "Standoff in the Gulf; Atrocities by Iraqis in Kuwait: Numbers Are Hard to Verify" *New York Times*, December 16, 1990.

12. "Standoff in the Gulf." Also see Andrew Whitley, speech as part of Foreign Policy Research Forum, Washington, D.C., December 18, 1990,

obtained via Federal Information Systems Corporation Federal News Service: http://web.lexis-nexis.com (accessed August 5, 2002); *World News Tonight with Peter Jennings* transcript, March 15, 1991.

13. William Branigin and Nora Boustany, "Groups Probe Torture in Kuwait," *Washington Post*, April 2, 1991. A *Washington Post* column also questioned the dead baby story a month before Nayirah's testimony, noting that both sides were accusing one another of similar atrocities: Glenn Frankel, "Iraq, Kuwait Waging an Old-Fashioned War of Propaganda," *Washington Post*, September 10, 1990.

14. John R. MacArthur, "Remember Nayirah, Witness for Kuwait," *New York Times*, January 6, 1992; Editorial, "Deception on Capital Hill," *New York Times*, January 15, 1992.

15. Tom Lantos, letter to editor, "Kuwaiti Gave Consistent Account of Atrocities," *New York Times*, January 15, 1992. Also see *Larry King Live*, CNN transcript, October 16, 1990.

16. Quoted in Dana Priest, "Legislator to Probe Allegations of Iraqi Atrocities" *Washington Post*, January 7, 1992.

17. Rowse, "How to Build Support." Also see Paul Bedard, "As Number of Troops in Gulf Rises, Support for Bush Falls," *Washington Times*, November 15, 1990.

18. *Nightline*, ABC transcript, June 9, 1992. Also see Russ W. Baker, "Iraqgate: The Big One that (Almost) Got Away," *Columbia Journalism Review*, March/April 1993:   http://www.cjr.org/archives.asp?url=/93/2/iraqgate.asp   (accessed March 5, 2006).

19. Colin Nickerson, "A GI Morale Booster: Iraqi Propaganda," *Boston Globe*, October 22, 1990.

20. Pete Williams, "Ground Rules and Guidelines for Desert Shield," in Hedrick Smith, ed., *The Media and the Gulf War: The Press and Democracy in Wartime* (Washington, D.C.: Seven Locks Press, 1992): 4–12.

21. Burl Osborne and Larry Kramer, letter to Pete Williams, January 8, 1991, in Smith, *The Media and the Gulf War*, 13–14.

22. Ibid.

23. "War Stories," Newseum Web site: http://www.newseum.org (accessed March 5, 2006).; Burl Osborne, letter to Pete Williams, January 25, 1991, in Smith, *The Media and the Gulf War*, 14–15; Martin A. Lee and Norman Solomon, *Unreliable Sources: A Guide to Detecting Bias in News Media* (New York: Carol Publishing, 1991); John E. Newhagen, "The Relationship between Censorship and the Emotional and Critical Tone of Television News Coverage of the Persian Gulf," *Journalism Quarterly* 71 (Spring 1994): 32–42.

24. Newseum, "War Stories."

25. Peter Arnett, "Speech at the National Press Club," in Smith, *The Media and the Gulf War*, 315–329. Also see Peter Arnett, *Live from the Battlefield: From Vietnam to Baghdad—35 Years in the World's War Zones* (New York: Simon & Schuster, 1994); Jeff Kamen, "CNN's Breakthrough in Baghdad," in Smith, *The Media and the Gulf War*, 350–357.

26. Kamen, "CNN's Breakthrough."

27. Robert Lichter, "The Instant Replay War," in Smith, *The Media and the Gulf War*, 224–230; Howard Kurtz, "Newspapers, Getting it Late but Right," in Smith, *The Media and the Gulf War*, 274–276.

28. John J. Fialka, *Hotel Warriors: Covering the Gulf War* (Washington, D.C.: Woodrow Wilson Center Press and Johns Hopkins University Press, 1992); Douglas M. McLeod, William P. Eveland Jr., and Nancy Signorielli, "Conflict

and Public Opinion: Rallying Effects of the Persian Gulf War," *Journalism Quarterly* 71 (Spring 1994): 20–31; John E. Newhagen, "The Relationship Between Censorship and the Emotional and Critical Tone of Television News Coverage of the Persian Gulf War," *Journalism Quarterly* 71 (Spring 1994): 32–42.

29. *CBS News Special Report* transcript, January 30, 1991. Schwarzkopf's count was off by one, as eleven soldiers actually died.

30. Ann McDaniel and Howard Fineman, "The President's 'Spin' Patrol," in Smith, *The Media and the Gulf* War, 154–156.

31. John Pike, quoted on CNN news transcript, October 28, 1994.

32. Barton Gellman, "U.S. Bombs Missed 70 Percent of the Time," in Smith, *The Media and the Gulf War*, 197–199. Also see Tom Wicker, "An Unknown Casualty," in Smith, *The Media and the Gulf War*, 194–196; Michael Griffin and Jongsoo Lee, "Picturing the Gulf War: Constructing an Image in *Time, Newsweek,* and *U.S. News & World Report*," *Journalism & Mass Communication Quarterly* 72 (Winter 1995): 813–825.

33. Bob Deans, commentary, "The Sanitized Lexicon of Modern War," *Newspaper Research Journal* 12 (Winter 1991): 10–12.

34. Leslie Stahl, *America Tonight* transcript, January 31, 1991. Also see Robert Fisk, "Out of the Pool," in Smith, *The Media and the Gulf War*, 143–148.

35. Lawrence C. Soley, "Pundits in Print: 'Experts' and Their Use in Newspaper Stories," *Newspaper* Research Journal 15 (Spring 1994): 65–75.

36. Janet E. Steele, "Experts and the Operational Bias of Television News: The Case of the Persian Gulf War," *Journalism & Mass Communication Quarterly* 72 (Winter 1995): 799–812.

37. Lee and Solomon, *Unreliable Sources.*

38. William J. Small, "Exxon Valdez: How to Spend Billions and Still Get a Black Eye," *Public Relations Review* 17 (1991): 9–25.

39. Larry King and Mark Stencel, *On the Line: The New Road to the White House* (New York: Harcourt Brace & Company, 1993).

40. Richard L. Berke, "The 1992 Campaign: The Media; Why Candidates like Public's Questions," *New* York Times, August 15, 1992.

41. Ibid.

42. Quoted in Christopher Lydon, "A Walk through the Garden," *Columbia Journalism Review*, September/October 1992, 9.

43. Russell Baker, "Against the Grain," (a tribute to deceased newsman Eric Sevareid): *New York Times*, July 14, 1992.

44. King and Stencel, *On the Line*, 170. Also see debate transcript, Federal Information Systems Corporation Federal News Service, October 19, 1992: http://web.lexis-nexis.com (accessed August 9, 2003); *CBS This Morning* transcript, October 16, 1992.

45. Davis Merritt, "Public Journalism—Defining a Democratic Art," *Media Studies Journal* (Summer 1995): 125–132. Merritt was editor of the *Wichita Eagle* and one of the founders of the civic journalism movement. See also Edmund B. Lambeth, Philip E. Meyer, and Esther Thorson, eds., *Assessing Public Journalism* (Columbia, Mo.: University of Missouri Press, 1998).

46. Quoted in John Bare, "Case Study—Wichita and Charlotte: The Leap of a Passive Press to Activism," *Media Studies Journal* (Fall 1992): 149–160.

47. Pew Center for Investigative Journalism Web site: http://www.pewcenter.org (accessed March 6, 2006).

48. Robert M. Entman, *Democracy without Citizens: Media and the Decay of American Politics* (New York: Oxford University, 1989).

49. Mike Hoyt, "Are You Now, or Will You Ever Be, A Civic Journalist?" *Columbia Journalism Review*, September/October 1995, 27. Also see George Everett and W. Joseph Campbell, "The Age of New Journalism 1883–1900," in Wm. David Sloan, ed., *The Media in America: A History*, 5th ed. (Northport, Ala.: Vision Press, 2002); Public Journalism Network Web site, http://www.pjnet.org (accessed March 5, 2006).

50. Enid Sefcovic, "Journalism Needs Respite from Media," *Palm Beach Post*, March 17, 1998.

51. Michael Hoyt, "The Wichita Experiment," *Columbia Journalism Review*, July/August 1992, http://archives.cjr.org/year/92/4/wichita.asp (accessed March 5, 2006); Jay Rosen, "Public Journalism as a Democratic Art," in Cheryl Gibbs, ed., *Public Journalism, Theory and Practice* (Dayton, Ohio: Kettering Foundation, 1997); John C. Merrill, Peter J. Gade, and Frederick R. Blevens, *Twilight of Press Freedom: The Rise of People's Journalism* (Mahwah, N.J.: Lawrence Erlbaum, 2001); Davis Merritt, *Public Journalism and Public Life: Why Telling the Truth is Not Enough*, 2nd ed. (Hillsdale, N.J.: Lawrence Erlbaum, 1997).

52. Hoyt, "The Wichita Experiment."

53. Dennis Zehner, *Shining the Big Spotlight: Case Studies of Attitudes Toward Civic Journalism in American Newsrooms*, undergraduate honors thesis, Lehigh University, 1999; Merrill, Gade, and Blevens, *Twilight of Press Freedom.*

54. Zehner, *Shining the Big Spotlight.*

55. Ibid.; We the People Wisconsin Web site, http://www.wtpeople.com/ (accessed March 5, 2006); Pew Center Web site; Hoyt, "Are You Now...";
David D. Kurpius, "Sources and Civic Journalism: Changing Patterns of Reporting?," *Journalism & Mass Communication Quarterly* 79 (Winter 2002): 853–866; Tom Dickson, Wanda Brandon and Elizabeth Topping, "Editors, Educators Agree on Outcomes but Not Goals," *Newspaper Research Journal* 22 (Fall 2001): 44–56.

56. Walter Goodman, "Inverse Relation of Heat and Light," *New York Times*, February 14, 1996.

57. Merrill, Gade, and Blevens, *Twilight of Press Freedom.* Also see Don H. Corrigan, *The Public Journalism Movement in America: Evangelists in the Newsroom* (Westport, Conn.: Praeger, 1999); Joseph P. Bernt, Frank E. Fee, Jacqueline Gifford, and Guido H. Stempel III, "How Well Can Editors Predict Reader Interest in News?" *Newspaper Research Journal* 21 (Spring 2000): 2–10.

58. Anonymous survey respondent quoted in Kathleen A. Hansen, Mark Nuezil, and Jean Ward, "Newsroom Topic Teams: Journalists' Assessments of Effects on News Routines and Newspaper Quality," *Journalism & Mass Communication Quarterly* 75 (Winter 1998): 803–821. Also see Peter J. Gade and Earnest L. Perry, "Changing the Newsroom Culture: A Four-Year Case Study of Organizational Development at the *St. Louis Post-Dispatch*," *Journalism & Mass Communication Quarterly* 80 (Summer 2003): 327–347; Brian L. Massey and Tanni Haas, "Does Making Journalism More Public Make a Difference? A Critical Review of Evaluative Research on Public Journalism," *Journalism & Mass Communication Quarterly* 79 (Autumn 2002): 559–586.

59. Walt Howe, "A Brief History of the Internet," http://www.walthowe.com/navnet/history.html (accessed March 6, 2006); World Wide Web Consortium Web site, http://www.w3.org/ (accessed March 6, 2006).

60. Ibid.

61. Bruce Garrison, "Online Services, Internet in 1995 Newsrooms," *Newspaper Research Journal* 18 (Summer/Fall 1997): 79–93; Bruce Garrison, "Computer-assisted Reporting Near Complete Adoption," *Newspaper Research Journal* 22

(Winter 2001): 65–79; Martin E. Halsuk and Bill F. Chamberlin, "Open Government in the Digital Age: The Legislative History of How Congress Established a Right of Public Access to Electronic Information Held by Federal Agencies," *Journalism & Mass Communication Quarterly* 78 (Spring 2001): 45–64; Scott R. Maier, "Digital Diffusion in Newsrooms: The Uneven Advance of Computer-assisted Reporting," *Newspaper Research Journal* 21 (Spring 2000): 95–110; Stan Ketterer, "Oklahoma Small Dailies, Weeklies Use Internet as Reporting Tool," *Newspaper Research Journal* 24 (Spring 2003): 107–113; S. Shyam Sundar, "Effect of Source Attribution on Perception of Online News Stories," *Journalism & Mass Communication Quarterly* 75 (Spring 1998): 55–68; Thomas J. Johnson and Barbara K. Kaye, "Cruising is Believing?: Comparing Internet and Traditional Sources on Media Credibility Measures," *Journalism & Mass Communication Quarterly* 76 (Summer 1998): 325–340; Andrew J. Flanagin and Miriam J. Metzger, "Perceptions of Internet Information Credibility," *Journalism & Mass Communication Quarterly* 77 (Autumn 2000): 515–540; Bruce Garrison, "Journalists' Perceptions of Online Information-Gathering Problems," *Journalism & Mass Communication Quarterly* 77 (Autumn 2000): 500–514.

62. Jane B. Singer, "Campaign Contributions: Online Newspaper Coverage of Election 2000," *Journalism & Mass Communication Quarterly* 80 (Spring 2003): 39–56; Garrison, "Online Services, Internet"; Hsiang Iris Chyi and Dominic Lasorsa, "Access, Use and Preferences for Online Newspapers," *Newspaper Research Journal* 20, (Fall 1999): 2–13; Carolyn A. Lin and Leo W. Jeffres, "Comparing Distinctions and Similarities Across Websites of Newspapers, Radio Stations, and Television Stations," *Journalism & Mass Communication Quarterly* 78 (Autumn 2001): 555–573; Karen Vargo and others, "How Readers Respond to Digital News Stories in Layers and Links," *Newspaper Research Journal* 21 (Spring 2000): 40–54.

63. Foo Yeuh Peng, Naphtali Irene Tham, and Hao Ziaoming, "Trends in Online Newspapers: A Look at the U.S. Web," *Newspaper Research Journal* 20 (Spring 1999): 52–63.

64. Ibid.

65. Robert Huesca, "Reinventing Journalism Curricula for the Electronic Environment," *Journalism & Mass Communication Educator* 55 (Summer 2000): 4–15; Xigen Li, "Web Page Design and Graphic Use in Three U.S. Newspapers," *Journalism & Mass Communication Quarterly* 75 (Summer 1998): 353–365; Eric S. Fredin, "Rethinking the News Story for the Internet: Hyperstory Prototypes and a Model of the User," *Journalism & Mass Communication Monographs* 163 (September 1997); David Tewksbury and Scott L. Althaus, "Differences in Knowledge Acquisition Among Readers of the Paper and Online Versions of a National Newspaper," *Journalism & Mass Communication Quarterly* 77 (Autumn 2000): 457–479; Guido H. Stempel III, Thomas Hargrove, and Joseph Bernt, "Relation of Growth of Use of the Internet to Changes in Media Use from 1995 to 1999," *Journalism & Mass Communication Quarterly* 80 (Spring 2003): 71–79.

66. Shahira Fahmy and C. Zoe Smith, "Photographers Note Digital's Advantages, Disadvantages," *Newspaper Research Journal* 24 (Spring 2003): 82–96.

67. Quoted in J.D. Lasica, "Portraying the Graphic Face of War," *Online Journalism Review*, March 20, 2003, http://ojr.org/ojr/lasica/1048185413.php.

68. John Russial, "How Digital Imaging Changes Work of Photojournalists," *Newspaper Research Journal* 21 (Spring 2000): 67–83.

69. National Press Photographers Association Web site, http://www.nppa.org/professional_development/business_practices/digitalethics.html (accessed March 5, 2006).

70. Quoted in J.D. Lasica, "Photographs that Lie," *Washington Journalism Review*, June 1989, 24.

71. Paul Vercammen, "Digital Developments: Networks Changing Images Before Your Eyes," CNN.com, January 25, 2000, http://www.cnn.com/2000/SHOWBIZ/TV/01/25/digital.inserts (accessed March 5, 2006).

72. Aly Colon, "The Multimedia Newsroom," *Columbia Journalism Review*, May/00, http://www.cjr.org/archives.asp?url=/00/2/2/colon.asp (accessed March 6, 2006); David Tewksbury, Andrew J. Weaver, and Brett D. Maddex, "Accidentally Informed: Incidental News Exposure on the World Wide Web," *Journalism & Mass Communication Quarterly* 78 (Autumn 2001): 533–554.

73 Quoted in Scott C. Hammond, Daniel Petersen, and Steven Thomsen, "Print, Broadcast and Online Convergence in the Newsroom," *Journalism & Mass Communication Educator* 55 (Summer 2000): 16–26.

74 Stuart L. Esrock and Greg B. Leichty, "Corporate World Wide Web Pages: Serving the News Media and Other Publics," *Journalism & Mass Communication Quarterly* 76 (Autumn 1999): 456–467; Thomas J. Johnson, Mahmoud A.M. Braima, and Jayanthi Sothirajah, "Doing the Traditional Media Sidestep: Comparing the Effects of the Internet and Other Nontraditional Media with Traditional Media in the 1996 Presidential Campaign," *Journalism & Mass Communication Quarterly* 76 (Spring 1999): 99–123; Gary W. Selnow, *Electronic Whistle-Stops: The Impact of the Internet on American Politics* (Westport, Conn.: Praeger, 1998); Maria E. Len-Rios, "The Bush and Gore Presidential Campaign Web Sites: Identifying with Hispanic Voters During the 2000 Iowa Caucuses and New Hampshire Primary," *Journalism & Mass Communication Quarterly* 76 (Winter 2002): 887–904; Thomas J. Johnson and Barbara K. Kaye, "A Boost or Bust for Democracy?: How the Web Influenced Political Attitudes and Behaviors in the 1996 and 2000 Presidential Elections," *Harvard International Journal of Press/Politics* 8 (July 2003): 9–34; Singer, "Campaign Contributions."

75 Jules Witcover, "Where We Went Wrong," *Columbia Journalism Review*, March/998; *Drudge Report* Web site, http://www.drudgereport.com (accessed March 5, 2006).

76 Dan Webster, "Blogger's Choice," Spokane (Wash.) *Spokesman-Review*, April 10, 2004.

77 Andrew C. Gordon, "Journalism and the Internet," *Media Studies Journal* (Summer 1995): 173–176.

CHAPTER 8

Return to Social Conflict

A decade that began in the mid-1990s brought turbulence that Americans had not seen for at least twenty years. New political battles arose and led to a shift in congressional power. A sex scandal threatened a presidency and helped the Republican Party regain the White House. The Supreme Court was pulled into a contested presidential election won by the candidate who lost the popular election. Foreign and domestic terrorists blew up planes and buildings, and for many people around the world a pair of hyphenated numbers—"9-11"—and events that followed came to symbolize what was best and worst about America. The United States again waged war in Iraq. All those events changed the country and they also changed American journalism.

President George Bush had enjoyed an approval rating of over 90 percent during the Persian Gulf War, but he lost to accused philanderer Bill Clinton in 1992. Clinton won only 43 percent of the popular vote, but third-party candidate Ross Perot garnered almost 19 percent, most of it drawn from Bush. Democrats' satisfaction about winning the White House for the first time in twelve years was short-lived, however, as two years later the Republicans captured a majority in the House of Representatives for the first time in four decades. "Something that hasn't happened in about 40 years happened last week on Capitol Hill: House Republicans talked and everyone listened," the *Washington Post* noted after the election.[1] Republicans gained more than fifty House seats, winning 230 of the 435 positions. Speaker of the House Tom Foley became the first sitting speaker to lose re-election in 134 years. Republicans also gained control of the Senate for the first time since the 1980s, giving them control of the entire legislative branch. House Minority Whip Newt Gingrich, the primary architect of the "Republican revolution," became one of the most powerful and controversial speakers of the house in American history.

The scope of the sweep surprised most people in government and in the press, but the Republicans had waged a cohesive nationwide campaign in which their opponents were linked with the perceived weakness of Bill Clinton, who immediately after taking office in 1992 began to butt heads with Washington insiders. He staked much of his early legislative efforts on a national health care proposal, putting his wife, Hillary, in charge of developing the plan. Public opinion polls supported the idea before the election and contributed to Clinton's electoral win. Afterward, however, a massive public relations campaign funded by the insurance industry helped kill the health plan, an obvious failure for the Clintons.

Clinton struggled with media portrayals suggesting indecisiveness and a lack of character even before his presidency, when he fended off allegations of infidelity, marijuana use, and Vietnam draft dodging. His election failed to win over many of his press critics, though "the president has been pounded far more on the issues than on questions of personal character, with scandal stories accounting for only 5 percent of the network total," the *Washington Post* reported, based on a 1994 Center for Media and Public Affairs study. "But he has taken a beating on virtually all issues: 68 percent negative on health care, 60 percent negative on the economy, 64 percent negative on other domestic issues, 66 percent negative on foreign policy, and 56 percent negative on character questions."[2] From Inauguration Day through late June 1994, Clinton drew more than 2,400 negative comments on the network evening newscasts, an average of almost five per night. Despite a common belief in a post-election period during which journalists treat a new president more kindly than they might later—and apparently every president except two since Eisenhower had enjoyed such a "honeymoon" period—Clinton became an instant media target. The only other post-1952 president who did not experience an obvious press honeymoon was another southern Democrat, Jimmy Carter in 1977. Even politically liberal Pulitzer Prize-winning cartoonist Garry Trudeau portrayed Clinton not as a human caricature but as a waffle floating in the air, apparently the winning icon among readers asked to vote for their choice between a waffle and a flipping coin. (Trudeau was even harder on Republicans, portraying President George Bush as a flag-draped invisible man with an "evil twin" named "Skippy," Vice President Dan Quayle as a feather, and Gingrich as a bomb with a lit fuse.) Whether because of his actions or because of media bias, Clinton's approval ratings corresponded with the tone of the coverage, falling throughout the first two years of his presidency leading up to the 1994 election (though he still remained personally popular and scored higher than journalists in credibility surveys).[3]

Besides tying their opponents to Clinton, Republicans also "nationalized" the election by coming together to produce a rhetorically appealing populist theme summarized in an eight-point "Contract with America." "Republican members of Congress and would-be Republican members are not merely running against someone; they have united to say that they are running for something as well," noted a *Washington Times* editorial.[4] Led by Gingrich, more than 300 congressional candidates gathered on the steps of the U.S. Capitol to sign the "contract." Though critics called the action political showboating and Democrats referred to the document as a "contract on America" that if implemented would do more harm than good, voters liked the plan. It outlined ten specific legislative bills to be introduced during the first 100 days of a Republican majority. It called for lower taxes and decreases in overall government spending. It called for increased spending for the military and for prisons and stated that Congress would implement a balanced budget and term limits. Stressing the aspect of credibility, the first two tenants of the "contract" called for "all laws that apply to the rest of the country also apply equally to the Congress" and "a comprehensive audit of Congress for waste, fraud or abuse." Voters distrustful of American institutions were left to assume for themselves that congressional lawbreaking and waste were rampant—perhaps the truth, but with little American investigative journalism focused on government at any level, the news media had little to offer on the subject other than the now-customary reporting of prepared statements by officials.[5]

The new Republican majority led by Gingrich (*Time* magazine's 1995 "Man of the Year") quickly began to assert its strength. The Contract with America itself had little legislative impact, as the House passed nine of the ten proposed bills only to see the Senate reject some of them and Clinton veto another. Still, even though the Republicans could not pass many of the proposals called for in the contract, they did manage to change the way Congress functioned so that seniority became less important for holding positions of power. Public appeals via the press became more common, and Gingrich and some other members of Congress became increasingly visible.

At times, the increased media visibility of the legislative branch proved to be a double-edged sword. Clinton won re-election in 1996, in part because Gingrich and the Republicans drew most of the blame for a budget impasse that led to a shutdown of the federal government. Gingrich, popular with many Americans but not with the mainstream press, suffered the most negative portrayals in the budget fight, but the GOP maintained control of both houses of Congress throughout Clinton's term and again in 2000 and 2002. That Republican control and Clinton's sex life clashed to define one of the most dismal periods for the American presidency and for the American press, and to help Republicans gain control of the executive branch, as well.

Internet tabloid-style "journalist" Matt Drudge broke the story that *Newsweek* had withheld a story about President Bill Clinton's alleged affair with White House intern Monica Lewinsky in January 1998, more than two years after the affair apparently began. Several main-stream media organizations soon reported the allegations. Clinton already was under investigation for alleged financial misdealing in what became known as the Whitewater affair and was being sued for alleged sexual harassment of Arkansas state employee Paula Jones while he was governor of that state. He denied wrongdoing in both criminal cases, and both eventually were dropped (though Clinton settled out of court with Jones for $850,000 with no admission of guilt), but they led independent prosecutor Kenneth Starr, who became a significant media figure in his own right, to other investigations ranging from White House travel vouchers to missing FBI files to the suicide of a Clinton advisor. Those investigations also failed to turn up criminal wrongdoing by Clinton and largely were ignored by the public, but after four years of investigation (and more than $30 million) Starr turned up evidence of the affair with Lewinsky.

At first Clinton denied knowing Jones or having a sexual relationship with Lewinsky, famously glaring into television cameras and stating with a voice quivering with emotion, "I did not have sexual relations with that woman." Hillary Clinton also appeared on television, blaming the accusations and the series of investigations on a "right-wing conspiracy." A supposed friend of the intern had secretly recorded conversations she had with Lewinsky about the affair, however, and a transcript seemed to support the accusation that Clinton tried to persuade Lewinsky to commit perjury by lying about the affair. "Now, there's Zippergate," wrote one columnist. "Instead of finding something in the Clintons' laundry, Starr may have found a smoking gun in Monica Lewinsky's. While many Americans' ears are tuned to hear this young woman's taped confessions of alleged trysts with Clinton, earlier tales of lost files and found billing records only glazed their eyes."[6] The networks turned up a video of Clinton hugging Lewinsky on the White House lawn. The video played repeatedly for months, probably making the woman's black beret the most recognizable headwear in America. "It was during a public occasion and there were hundreds of people around, but the gesture took on an intimate nature in slow motion and Monica's body language and expression also seemed to indicate a hidden agenda," one report later noted.[7] In a televised speech, Clinton finally admitted lying about the affair but claimed not to have violated any laws.

The media and the public also flocked to the leaked full 445-page report of the Clinton-Lewinsky investigation, in which Starr told Congress that the president had committed eleven impeachable acts, including perjury and obstruction of justice. Many newspapers and Web sites carried the full text of the "Starr report," along with warning about the graphic sexual content within. Among those graphic details were statements that Lewinsky performed oral sex on the president on at least nine occasions, that she and Clinton had engaged in "phone sex" numerous times and that a semen stain on one of her dresses contained Clinton's DNA. Even news sources that did not carry the full text of the report quoted liberally from it, though some toned down or bypassed the most graphic sexual material. Starr also released a videotape of Clinton's grand jury testimony, which some cable stations ran repeatedly. Some readers and viewers complained about the inclusion of sexual details in their news, and other critics found more fault with other aspects of the coverage. Besides the sensationalist tone of many of the news stories, much of the coverage also relied heavily on leaks and unidentified sources. One study found that most of the anonymous sourcing was cloaked in vague terms such as "sources said," that less than 20 percent of sourcing "offered even the slightest hint of the source's allegiances" and that the use of anonymous sources by the mainstream press varied little from that of the tabloid press.[8]

Like Ronald Reagan, Clinton made effective use of pseudo-events, excelled with TV-friendly emotional appeals, and seemed to enjoy being in front of cameras. He used travel and public appearances—most notably a trip to China in which he conducted a seventy-minute news conference—to try to distract attention from elsewhere (though critics pointed out the irony of the China news conference for a president who, like Reagan and other recent presidents, tended to avoid press conferences at home, especially after the Lewinsky scandal broke). Clinton also shared something else with the former Republican president: Regardless of how much criticism he drew from his political opponents and in the press, his public approval ratings usually were higher than those critics could understand or explain. Much to the dismay of Republicans, in some respects Clinton became the Democratic version of a "Teflon" president whose many foibles Americans overlooked. "Americans think Mr. Clinton is doing a good job and that he is a sleazeball," a *Washington Times* columnist noted.[9] Even so, Clinton's visible flaws and the number and passion of his enemies exceeded Reagan's, and his popularity with many voters could not prevent him from becoming the second U.S. president in history to be impeached by the House of Representatives. (Andrew Johnson was the first, in 1968; Richard Nixon might have been impeached in 1974 had he not resigned.)

Democrats and Republicans took to the airwaves to voice their opinions, and rancor that had been triggered as early as the 1994 congressional election grew as some journalists and others began investigating the extramarital sexual activities of various members of Congress. Some of those members (including Gingrich, eventually) saw past infidelities exposed. The House considered four articles of impeachment: perjury before the grand jury, obstruction of justice, perjury in a civil suit, and abuse of power. Voting split largely along party lines, and the House impeached Clinton on the first two charges in December 1998. The Senate took up the case, with Supreme Court Chief Justice William Rehnquist presiding over the televised Senate trial. Though the head of the most secretive of the three branches of government, Rehnquist demonstrated that he understood the value of showmanship in public appearances; he added four gold stripes to each sleeve of his black judicial robe, apparently modeled after the garb of a "Lord Chancellor" in a Gilbert and Sullivan opera. Clinton gave his State of the Union Address while the proceedings went on but did not mention the impeachment.[10]

Public opinion polls showed that most Americans thought Clinton should be punished but not removed from office, and his job approval ratings and personal popularity remained generally high (despite the predictions of Sam Donaldson and other news commentators that the scandal would force the president to resign). "There's only one way Bill Clinton could get more popular right now, only one way the president could get more scorchingly HOT!—and that's if the U. S. Senate votes to convict him and remove him from office. Because impeachment is proving a great political tonic for the president's health," a *Washington Post* reporter wrote.[11] With a two-thirds Senate vote required to remove him, there was little doubt that Clinton would retain his office. The Senate voted 55–45 to acquit him on the perjury charge, with ten Republicans joining all forty-five Democrats. Five of those same Republicans also voted with the Democrats on the obstruction charge, resulting in a 50–50 vote for acquittal.

The case deepened already existing divisions between the two major parties and among Americans. Many expressed mixed emotions, generally glad the legal fight was over. Many were angry, either because the case had gone so far or because of the end result. "American democracy failed a major test," complained a *Washington Times* writer, who, like others, found fault with both the Senate and the media.[12] Conservatives complained that CNN became the "Clinton News Network," while political liberals blamed talk radio and tabloid tendencies among other news media for inciting and promoting much of the political debacle. Those who thought the rancor had hit its high point were less than two years away from being proven wrong, however.

By the arrival of the 2000 presidential election between Clinton's vice president Al Gore and Texas Gov. George W. Bush (the son of the man Clinton had defeated for his first term as president), most political watchers thought it would be close. Gore expressed deep disappointment about

Clinton's behavior but found himself criticized by Republicans as part of the Clinton administration and by Democrats for not being as charismatic as Clinton. Bush fended off stories about a drunken driving arrest in his unfocused youth, and both candidates made heavy use of negative political ads to win their primary election challenges. The tightness of the polls meant journalists, relying on their now-typical devotion to horse-race aspects of electoral politics, spent more time than usual discussing the Electoral College, the uniquely American electoral process that awards presidential votes based on the winners of individual states rather than on a popular vote. Though the instances in which a candidate won a plurality of the popular vote but lost the presidency were only slightly more common than presidential impeachment proceedings—such elections had occurred only three times, in the cases of Andrew Jackson in 1824, Samuel Tilden in 1876, and Grover Cleveland in 1888—some worried it might happen in 2000 and that such an occurrence could create even greater splits in an already divided nation. The *New York Post* noted days before the election, "Quietly, some of George W. Bush's advisers are preparing for the ultimate 'what if' scenario: What happens if Bush wins the popular vote for President, but loses the White House because Al Gore's won the majority of electoral votes?"[13] Bush supporters said they would fight for the election in such a case: "A massive talk-radio operation would be encouraged. 'We'd have ads, too,' says a Bush aide, 'and I think you can count on the media to fuel the thing big-time. Even papers that supported Gore might turn against him because the will of the people will have been thwarted.'"[14] Democrats promised to do the same if they came out on the wrong side of such a result. Still, most pundits considered such an outcome highly unlikely, with the discussions providing just another arcane electoral topic for political insiders.

On election night, however, as Hillary Clinton was becoming the first president's wife to be elected to the Senate, the "what if" scenario played out in one of the most controversial presidential elections in U.S. history. The news media contributed to the confusion, using exit polling to declare apparent winners as polls closed in various states. "ABC News projects that Al Gore wins the state of Florida and its 25 electoral votes," Peter Jennings declared at 8 p.m. Eastern Time. "Give him the first big state momentum of the evening."[15] The other networks also projected Gore as the winner of Florida, even hinting that the projected win, along with projected victories in Michigan, Illinois, and elsewhere, could lead to a landslide. "He is threading the needle up to this hour," Tom Brokaw said about Gore. "He is running the table. Whether or not it can continue, we'll have to wait and see."[16] One of the most common complaints about television projections always has been that they may decrease turnout in areas that have not yet voted, and the early Florida projections angered Republicans who pointed out that the state's panhandle polling locations in the Central Time Zone had not yet closed. Regardless, Bush edged ahead in the count a couple of hours later, forcing the networks to retract their earlier projections and classify the state "too close to call."

As results came in from other states, it became clear that Gore would win the popular vote, but whichever candidate won Florida likely would claim enough electoral votes to win the presidential election. A few hours later, led by Fox News, the networks and several newspapers declared Bush the winner of the state and the election. Dan Rather of CBS did so the most blatantly: "Sip it, savor it, cup it, photostat it, underline it in red, press it in a book, put it in an album, hang it on the wall: George W. Bush is the next president of the United States."[17] Unfortunately, despite Rather's folksy phrasing, the result was still very much in doubt.

Fox News, which made the first Bush projection, later drew considerable criticism when reporters discovered that the Fox staffer behind the projection was a Bush first cousin who had spoken to both Bush and his brother, Florida Governor Jeb Bush, shortly before recommending the projection for Bush. "Even as he was leading the Fox decision desk that night, John Ellis was also on the phone with his cousins—'Jebbie,' the governor of Florida, and the presidential candidate himself—giving them updated assessments of the vote count," wrote a *Washington Post* critic. "Ellis's projection was crucial because Fox News Channel put Florida in the W. column at 2:16 a.m. followed by NBC, CBS, CNN, and ABC within four minutes. That decision, which turned out to be wrong and was retracted by the embarrassed networks less than two hours later, created the impression that Bush had 'won' the White House."[18] More than a year before joining the network, Ellis had resigned as a political columnist for the *Boston Globe*, writing: "I am loyal to my cousin, Governor George Bush of Texas. I put that loyalty ahead of my loyalty to anyone else outside my immediate family. That being the case, it is not possible for me to continue writing columns about the 2000 presidential campaign." Ironically, at that time he also noted, "There is no way for you to know if I am telling you the truth about George W. Bush's presidential campaign because in his case, my loyalty goes to him and not to you."[19] Shortly after the networks made their projections for Bush, Gore decided to give a concession speech, but he changed his mind when new numbers came in and again made the election too close to call. Fox, the first network to project the state for Bush, also was the first to retract its projection. At CBS, a humbled Rather told viewers, "If you're disgusted with us, frankly I don't blame you."[20]

The controversy was far from over, as the news media descended on Florida seeking and reporting other election irregularities. A confusing "butterfly ballot" in one heavily Democratic county apparently prompted some voters to accidentally mark conservative candidate Pat Buchanan's name instead of Gore's. Katherine Harris, the Florida secretary of state who made the first "official" declaration that Bush won, was a Republican appointed by Jeb Bush and the co-chair of George Bush's Florida campaign. Before the election, she ordered that the voter rolls be purged of illegal voters. In the process, thousands of voters (some estimated as many as 90,000, with disproportional numbers of blacks, Latinos, and Democrats) apparently were improperly prevented from casting ballots. The state later settled a class action lawsuit and promised to reinstate those wrongfully excluded, but long after the election had ended. Confusion arose over whether large numbers of absentee ballots should be counted, whether a recount should be permitted, and how such a recount should proceed. "Chads," hanging bits of paper left partially attached to paper punch card ballots after votes were cast (and which sometimes confused computer scanners used to tabulate votes), became the topic of lengthy news stories and the focus of much of the battle over which party would claim the White House. Both parties filed lawsuits and staged rallies as a partial recount ensued. The Florida Supreme Court, with a Democratic majority, overruled Harris, finding in Gore's favor. The Republican-controlled state legislature called a special session to certify Republican electors. Then on December 10, more than a month after the election, the U.S. Supreme Court voted 7–2 that the Florida recount was improper and voted 5–4 to prohibit other legal recounts. Though Democrats and some editors complained that a single vote from Supreme Court justice on a conservative court gave Bush the election, the official margin of victory in Florida ended up being 537 votes. Overall, Bush won the electoral count 271–267 while losing the popular vote by more than 500,000 votes.

Several media organizations later conducted their own Florida recounts, most concluding that Bush would have won the state if an official recount had been conducted based on legal votes, while Gore would have won if a count included "voter intent" (because apparently more Gore voters made errors that disallowed their ballots). "It would take the Almighty to really know who 'won' Florida," the *Pittsburgh Post-Gazette* editorialized. "The differing postmortem scenarios for winner and loser only underscore the point that an election this close could not be definitively decided given the deeply flawed process in place in Florida last November."[21] By the time election "ended" it had produced a peacetime record of twenty consecutive banner headlines for the *New York Times*.[22]

The election-night actions of the networks prompted widespread media criticism and a congressional investigation, and the networks promised they would change their forecasting methods for the 2004 presidential election. The news media probably would not have erred, however, if not for other election problems. Besides, whatever effect the networks may have had, other factors contributed far more to the closeness of the election. Other states besides Florida also reported lost votes and confusion among voters. Consumer activist Ralph Nader, the Green Party candidate, drew enough votes to shift the total in Florida and perhaps other states, and surveys showed that most of his support was pulled from Gore (leading many Democrats to express dismay when Nader ran again in 2004). Florida also would not have mattered in terms of the final result if Gore had won his home state of Tennessee or Clinton's home state of Arkansas.

Incidentally, though Democrats complained that Bush had unfairly and perhaps illegally won the election, another allegedly "stolen election" years earlier contributed to the Republican revolution that culminated in Bush's victory. A contested 1984 Indiana congressional election ended with the Democratic incumbent apparently leading, but then a recount gave the GOP challenger a thirty-four-vote victory certified by the state's Republican secretary of state. House Democrats refused to seat the Republican, however, and after a legal battle a congressional task force composed of two Democrats and a Republican voted to seat the incumbent. After the full House voted to seat the Democrat, Republicans marched out in protest. The incident provided a focus for those angry with the system and helped empower Gingrich: "It was essential to Newt and his success to drive home the point that . . . something corrupting had happened to Democratic rule and that it was not just not in our interest but really wrong to be in bed with the Democrats," one Republican congressman said after the stunning 1994 election.[23] The incident also contributed to an increasing tendency for legislators, who previously had worked largely in anonymity, to call media attention to congressional activities.

Despite his narrow margin of victory in 2000, Bush—who had declared during his campaign that he would be "a uniter, not a divider"—did little to sooth the feelings of his opponents, further angering Democrats by proceeding, in their view, as if he had a mandate. With Republicans controlling the House of Representatives (and the Senate, before Jeffords' switch and then again after the 2002 election) he pushed through tax cuts, relaxed environmental standards, an education reform bill, and deregulation of various industries. The news media paid little attention, focused largely on the election aftermath, terrorism and then war, with occasional diversions for celebrity trials.

Of course, the corporate media benefited from deregulation, as the Federal Communications Commission voted in 2003 to relax ownership rules even further than had the Telecommunications Act of 1996. After holding only one public hearing on the issue, and despite hundreds of thousands of e-mails and letters from concerned citizens opposing the change, the FCC voted 3–2 along strict party lines (Republicans on the commission for the changes, Democrats against) to allow ownership of three television stations, eight radio stations, a cable system, and a daily newspaper within a single city. The change would allow a single corporation to own stations that reached 45 percent of Americans, up from 35 percent before the change (though Viacom, which owned CBS and UPN, and News Corp, owner of the Fox networks, already were in violation of the lower figure). Perhaps the most vocal broadcast critic of the proposal was Bill Moyers, through his new politically liberal PBS newsmagazine program *Now*. He and others warned that the changes could drown out independent voices in many areas, though, as one writer complained, "The notion of free speech has been on life-support for nearly 15 years now. Corporate mergers and buy-outs of CNN, Warner Bros., Time-Life and Disney have slowly narrowed outspoken and uninhibited news reporting."[24]

Even before the FCC decision, protests came from consumer interest groups, some journalism organizations, and many others, ranging from the United Church of Christ to the National Association of Black Journalists, the Communication Workers of America, media magnate Ted Turner, and owners of small broadcast stations who feared being squeezed out of business. Those protests help prompt the House of Representatives to vote overwhelmingly to block the 10 percent increase in a network's potential national broadcast audience. Many criticized the FCC's apparent lack of concern for public opinion, with Republican Congressman George Nethercutt noting, "99.9 percent of the 750,000 comments to FCC on this issue expressed opposition to these regulations—the highest number of comments expressed ever on a single proceeding."[25] A federal court temporarily blocked implementation of the rule changes, and the Senate, despite a threatened Bush veto, also passed a resolution to overturn the FCC decision. Later, Bush and House Republicans agreed to a cap of 39 percent, or about what Fox and CBS already had. The maneuvering angered Democrats and provided a plot line for a popular White House-based fictional television show, *The West Wing*, but Congress passed the new limits in January 2004 as part of a large spending bill. The FCC ruling continued to face other legal and congressional challenges.[26]

Before the end of Bush's first year in office, the differences between political conservatives and liberals—and those between journalists and the people they sought to serve—often seemed as stark, as prominent and as unyielding as the giant skyline-defining twin towers of New York's World Trade Center. Yet tragedy, often portrayed through and explained by the news media, can bring unity. One of the highlights of American journalism throughout most of its history has been how often it has helped bring people together during difficult times. As noted by the editors of an academic journal devoted to news coverage of September 11, 2001, "Journalism, after all, is at its best when the world is at its worst."[27] That fact became obvious when the twin towers collapsed.

Sudden deadly violence was nothing new to the news media, of course. One of the most common criticisms of modern American journalism has been its frequent and sometimes sensationalistic focus on crime and bloodshed. Random violence provided headlines and editorial subject matter for newspapers around the country when a string of random sniper killings terrorized residents of the Washington, D.C., in 2002. On the day after Christmas 1996, in a case that highlighted tabloid media excesses, someone murdered 6-year-old beauty pageant contestant JonBenet Ramsey in her Colorado home. Suspicion immediately fell on her parents, and the story quickly became TV-movie fodder, but no one ever was charged in the case, and her father later ran for office in Michigan. In the same state just over two years later, two students in trench coats strode into Columbine High School and killed thirteen other people before committing suicide. News cameras captured images of frightened students running from the building and the case drew national attention, prompting a local newspaper columnist to write: "Why did this story become the school-kid shooting story, above all the others? Why is this the school-kid shooting story that defines the trend? Well, it has everything," including "outcast" killers who drove BMWs and spouted hatred on the Internet, and a "cultural divide—the left blames guns; the right blames video games/movies/Marilyn Manson."[28] The case led to a rash of news stories about school security, teen angst, youth violence, and media violence. News stories reported that the killers apparently "practiced" shooting by playing a video game, and a Kentucky couple later sued video game manufacturers, movie producers, and Internet companies after their son killed three people in his high school the year after the "Columbine massacre." Other social critics blamed television and heavy metal music for contributing to violence among teens.[29]

Three years before the Columbine killings, former Berkeley professor and "Unabomber" Ted Kaczynski was arrested and charged with making numerous bombs, several of which he mailed to university professors and others involved with technology. One of his bombs also killed a public relations professional who, according to a Unabomber letter, worked for a PR firm that "helped Exxon clean up its public image after the Exxon Valdez incident." In all, Kaczynski's bombs killed three people and injured more than twenty others during a seventeen-year period before he (calling himself "the terrorist group FC") sent a letter to the *New York Times* promising to stop the bombings if the *Times* or another national publication printed a 35,000-word anti-technology treatise he had written, titled "Industrial Society and Its Future."[30]

After consultation with the U.S. attorney general and the FBI, the *Times* and the *Washington Post* entered an agreement through which "for public safety reasons" both newspapers would fund the publication of an eight-page pull-out section in the *Post* that carried the full text of the "Unabomber Manifesto." (Perhaps ironically, considering the subject matter of the treatise, the *Post* printed the treatise because it had better technology than the *Times* for producing such a section.) Publishers of both newspapers apparently struggled with the decision, recognizing that they had little journalistic reason for yielding to a terrorist's demands and printing the manifesto. "Whether you like it or not, we're turning our pages over to a man who has murdered people," said *Times* publisher Arthur Sulzberger Jr. "But I'm convinced we're making the right choice between bad options."[31] He argued that the case was unlikely to become a journalistic precedent and that typically the newspaper would ignore such a demand but the Unabomber case "differs in the most obvious way. Here we are dealing with an individual with a 17-year record of violent actions."[32] The *Post* quoted him saying the issue "centers on the role of a newspaper as part of a community."[33] Most other editors and media ethicists agreed with the decision, though some disagreed. The *Washington Times* probably was the most adamant critic, and even U.S. Congressman James A. Traficant Jr. voiced an opinion. "Sometimes writers labor for years to get their manuscripts published and never get a chance," he argued. "But in America, if you blow up a few people and terrorize a nation, you become Ernest Hemingway overnight."[34] Most interested readers scanned the anti-technology screed not in the *Post* but via the Internet. The *Oakland Tribune* accessed it the same way and then reprinted it in a pull-out section. As events unfolded, the decision to publish the manifesto did more than save more lives. It also led to the capture and eventual life sentence of the Unabomber, whose brother recognized the phrasing and themes in the treatise and turned Kaczynski in to the FBI.

Journalism played a more clearly negative role in another bombing case the same year the Unabomber was captured. A pipe bomb at the Olympics in Atlanta killed one person and injured more than 100 others. Security guard Richard Jewell first was treated as a hero for discovering the bomb and preventing more potential victims, but then he found himself wrongly accused of being the bomber. Though several stories contained law officers' warnings not to focus on one suspect, the news media quickly spread Jewell's name and photo around the world, and implied that the FBI was working too slowly to arrest him. "Olympic security guard Richard Jewell is still on the spot in the Atlanta bomb investigation this morning, but he still hasn't been charged with anything, and the FBI refuses to even call him a suspect," a *CBS This Morning* anchor reported five days after the explosion.[35] The same day, CNBC suggested that the news media already might be going too far: "It's a good bet that many

Americans know more about Richard Jewell than they do about their next door neighbor. Anyone following the news the past two days could find out where Jewell went to school, where he's worked since 1983, why he was arrested in 1990, how much rent he pays for the apartment he shares with his mother. And for the last two nights we've even been able to show you live pictures from one of the many cameras stationed outside that apartment. All this for someone who is not even officially a suspect, who has not been arrested, not been charged, and even if charged is, of course, innocent until proven guilty."[36] Regardless, a CNN report three days later noted in a typical story, "Sources tell CNN that, although Richard Jewell has still not been arrested, he is investigators' leading suspect in the Centennial Park bombing."[37] That report came only about a week after the original bombing, but the media scrutiny of Jewell continued for almost three more months, until the Justice Department finally took the somewhat unusual step of officially clearing him as a suspect. "I felt like a hunted animal, followed constantly, waiting to be killed," Jewell said. "After 88 days of hell, it's hard to believe it is finally over."[38] He later received settlements from NBC, CNN, and a former employer who had offered negative information. He lost a suit against the *Atlanta Journal and Constitution*, which originally called him a suspect three days after the bombing with a banner headline stating, "FBI suspects 'hero' guard may have planted bomb."[39] The Georgia Supreme Court ruled that Jewell was a public figure (because of his early identification as a hero) by the time the newspaper identified him as a suspect, and the U.S. Supreme Court refused to hear his appeal. Officials later linked the Atlanta bombing to a self-proclaimed Christian activist accused of bombing a gay nightclub and at least two abortion clinics.

Americans who followed the cases of the Unabomber and the Olympics bombings had reason to be terrified of explosive devices. A year earlier, the worst terrorist attack on American soil had destroyed the Alfred P. Murrah Federal Building in Oklahoma City, killing 168 people. Timothy McVeigh, a former soldier who had fought in the Persian Gulf War before developing a deep distrust of the federal government, used fertilizer and a rented truck to blow up the building. He later was executed for the crime. The explosion came on the second anniversary of a televised stand-off between the FBI and a cult in Waco, Texas, which ended when the cult's compound burst into flames. The fire killed eighty people, including many children, angering many Americans.

Despite the date of the Oklahoma City bombing, first reports about the bombing suggested that Arab Muslims might be to blame, an assumption deemed logical because Islamic fundamentalists had used a car bomb to try to destroy the World Trade Center in 1993. The New York bombing did not topple the towers, as planned, but killed six people and shook many Americans. "We all have that feeling of being violated," New York

Governor Mario Cuomo said. "No foreign people or force has ever done this to us. Until now we were invulnerable."[40] Years later, some reporters questioned a government panel that officially blamed only McVeigh and another American, Terry Nichols, for the Oklahoma City blast. Some talk radio hosts and a former Oklahoma City television reporter (who also produced a book about the subject) continued to insist that Islamic terrorists were involved in destroying the federal building. Others, including Nichols's attorney, suggested that American white supremacists also contributed to the bombing plot.

None of the media blamed anyone other than foreign terrorists for the 2001 event that dwarfed the Oklahoma City blast. "Nine-eleven" became a term immediately identifiable as the date when Islamic terrorists hijacked four commercial airliners. The first plane crashed into the North Tower at 8:46 a.m. and was at first assumed to be a tragic accident—until a second plane slammed into the South Tower sixteen minutes later. A third airliner hit the Pentagon at 9:37 and about a half hour later the fourth plane crashed in Pennsylvania, apparently after passengers fought with the hijackers because relatives of those passengers had told them via cell phone about the earlier attacks.

Most Americans knew of the attacks within hours and many spent the day gathered around their televisions. They saw the horror of the original crashes compounded by the collapse of the South Tower at 10:05 a.m. and then of the North Tower eighteen minutes later. Stunned viewers repeatedly fell upon references appropriate to their mass media world to describe the indescribable. Perhaps the most common reaction among those queried by journalists, including among those who saw it in person and not just on television, was that the images were "like a movie" (a quote appearing in newspapers around the country and heard on every major network and that prompted some critics to launch new attacks on the entertainment industry). "Which was to say they had seen it before in countless disaster movies," noted one *New York Times* writer. "The explosion and fireball, the crumpling buildings, the dazed and panicked victims, even the grim presidential address assuring action would be taken—all were familiar, as if they had been lifted from some Hollywood blockbuster."[41]

Early reports estimated that the attacks might have killed more than 10,000 people, demonstrating a tendency typical of major disasters around the world. Officials and the news media typically have overestimated death tolls, which has the odd result of making the final totals seem less dramatic. In the case of September 11, that final total was just under 3,000.

Television networks covered the event around the clock. Much of the cable coverage ran without commercials, and thanks largely to years of consolidation owners of many of the entertainment networks found it easy to run news from other networks instead of their usual programming. Some simply ran messages referring viewers to news channels. More than 170 morning newspapers produced "extra" after-noon editions (probably helping explain why many neglected to update their Web sites very quickly—and far more users turned to television than to the Internet, anyway). Front pages became collectors' items, and read-ers later could compare them via various Web sites and a Poynter Insti-tute book. Newspapers long since accustomed to using large banner headlines for all sorts of stories tried various ways to portray the magni-tude of the event. Many filled most of the front page with a single large photo of one or both of the towers in flames, of the second plane about to hit the South Tower, of the destruction after the towers fell, or of panicked people trying to escape. Many used huge one-word or two-word banners, such as "Attack," "Terror," "Outrage," "Devastation," or "U.S. Attacked." Some added exclamation marks. Some relied on partial quotes from a speech given by President Bush after the attacks, such as "Evil Acts," "Act of War," or "Today Our Nation Saw Evil." Several hearkened back to the 1941 attack on Pearl Harbor, with banners stating, "A New Day of Infamy." The *San Francisco Chronicle* was most blunt with its single-word headline: "BASTARDS!" The *Chronicle* and many other newspapers used their covers in the fashion of tabloids or magazines, moving all stories inside the paper.[42]

The days to come brought more shocks as the scope of the terrorist attack unfolded, and editors and producers faced tough choices about what pictures to use. Besides the images of the towers and destruction, some of the photos showed corpses or people leaping to their deaths. Many newspapers ran those photos, placing them on inside pages. "Something like this, I think it's our duty to bring out the exclamation points and the visual sledgehammers so that we can tell this in the enor-mity of the story, as best as we possibly can," one editor said.[43] ABC and MSNBC refused to run video of the jumpers, but CBS, CNN, and Fox used them. NBC ran the footage once, but decided that doing so was a mistake. Some readers and viewers complained, but one oddity of the situation was that because many of the victims' could not be found or identified, some newspaper readers asked for blown-up versions of the photos so they could try to determine if the victims photographed were family members. Enlarging the photos made them too blurry to identify features, however. "We couldn't tell who anyone was," one photo editor said. "We tried different ways of opening the pictures in Photoshop and studying them and enlarging them and shrinking them. Other than bright colored clothing, there were no identifiable features that we could ascer-tain."[44] Some remains later were identified using DNA.

Television viewership and newspaper readership both increased as a result of the tragedy and especially for television stayed much higher than usual even weeks later. Though some readers and viewers tired of seeing the repeated images, the news media generally received positive reactions for their coverage. Concerned with the impact of repeat exposure, ABC announced eight days after the disaster that it would stop showing video of the planes hitting the buildings. (Video of the first crash appeared the day after the event; the second crash was filmed from multiple angles on the day of the attack.) The network began using still images for some stories. A number of wild rumors circulated on the Internet, most involving incredible escapes from the disaster, pending attacks, or the supposed involvement of various groups. CNN fell for one story, about five firefighters in a vehicle supposedly surviving under the rubble. Fox News reported a faked story about a woman who received a phone call from her husband, also trapped. Several media organizations reported incorrectly that airlines had foiled other attempted hijackings the same day, and many early reports included the names of "victims" who turned out not to have been anywhere close to the scene. In most cases the mistakes quickly were corrected. All in all, especially considering the pace and magnitude of events and the nature of around-the-clock coverage, journalists generally did a good job of separating fact from fiction.[45]

Much of the coverage in the weeks following the event focused on the victims and their families. Two days after the attack, *Newsday* began running a daily two-page spread profiling victims, publishing more than 1,300 profiles in all, and then continued to post profiles on an Internet database. The database also included more than 1,400 family photos, as well as links to profiles on other newspaper Web sites. Internet users accessed the site, which *Newsday* called "a commitment to our neighbors," approximately a million times during its first two weeks.[46] Emotion touched reporters like it did other Americans. CBS anchor Dan Rather drew praise for crying during an appearance on a late-night talk show. "The lost and the missing are chasing us now as we drive to work or put on our clean clothes and shiny shoes," wrote Stephanie McCrummen, one of the writers of the *Newsday* project. "They are chasing us in words and story after story on page after page, and they are catching up to us all."[47]

The September 11 attacks gave Americans and their president a new focus: retribution against Osama bin Laden, quickly identified as the primary suspect behind the destruction, and his terrorist organization known as al-Qaida. Three days after the attacks, Bush stood in the rubble of the World Trade Center and promised that the guilty would pay. A day later he told Americans to prepare for war. During the following weeks, the news media split much of their focus between ongoing cleanup activities at the World Trade Center and events leading up to the war in Afghanistan, a country charged with harboring bin Laden.

Demonstrating how terrorism had united the nation, Al Gore—giving his first political speech since conceding the controversial 2000 election— called Bush "my commander in chief" and pledged, "Regardless of party, regardless of ideology, there are no divisions in this country where our response to the war on terrorism is concerned."[48]

U.S. bombs began falling on Afghanistan on October 7, less than a month after the attacks in New York and Washington. American ground troops followed, quickly ousting the radical Taliban government, though bin Laden remained at large more than three years later. He occasionally managed to release audio or videotapes to the news media, and all of the major American television networks agreed to edit tapes that might inspire his followers or which might contain coded messages to other terrorists. "The decision, the first time in memory that the networks had agreed to a joint arrangement to limit their prospective news coverage, was described by one network executive as a 'patriotic' decision that grew out of a conference call between the nation's top television news executives and the White House national security adviser," the *New York Times* reported.[49] Some newspapers and letter writers agreed with the networks' decision; others criticized it, arguing that journalists should not promise to withhold information and pointing out that the tapes would run in full on the Arabic TV stations most likely to be watched by bin Laden's supporters. A *San Diego Union-Tribune* headline characterized the media as "stuck between a rock and the White House."[50]

The same month that the war began in Afghanistan, Congress overwhelmingly passed the Patriot Act (officially, the USA PATRIOT, or Uniting and Strengthening America by Providing Appropriate Tools Required to Intercept and Obstruct Terrorism, Act of 2001), 357–66 in the House, 98–1 in the Senate. The law gave the government greater powers to detain suspected terrorists, including allowing indefinite imprisonment without trial of any non-citizen deemed by the attorney general to be a national security threat. Defining who was a terrorist became an issue of legal contention. The bill also made it easier for federal law enforcement officials to search a suspect's home or computer, to eavesdrop on communications, and to counter money-laundering. In November, Bush signed a directive to try suspected terrorists in secret military tribunals rather than in the courts. Some critics expressed fears about the new laws, mindful that war often provided an excuse for governments to restrict civil liberties (including Abraham Lincoln's Civil War suspension of habeas corpus, press restrictions during World War I and the internment of Japanese-Americans during World War II) or to limit privacy, but the news media paid relatively little attention to the Patriot Act before it passed. Some newspapers offered weak objections after it became law, mostly protesting the speed with which it passed. Later more than 400 U.S. cities—including New York City and Washington,

D.C., the targets of the September 11 attacks—and the states of Alaska, Colorado, Hawaii, Idaho, Maine, Montana, and Vermont passed resolutions opposing parts of the act.[51]

Part of the reason that neither legislators nor journalists worried much about the Patriot Act was that a more viscerally frightening concern had appeared: anthrax. Within a few weeks of September 11, Democratic Senate Majority Leader Tom Daschle, ABC, CBS, NBC, and the *New York Post* all were mailed envelopes that contained spores of the disease. On October 5, the same day the letter to Daschle was postmarked in New Jersey (it was not opened until ten days later), an editor at a Florida tabloid became the first of five victims killed by anthrax. Officials blamed terrorists for the new form of "biological warfare" and said the mailings might be linked to bin Laden, though no one knew whether the terrorists were foreign or domestic and investigators failed to find the culprit. Three days later (one day after announcing the war on Afghanistan), Bush signed an executive order creating a new Office of Homeland Security, leading to a massive restructuring of federal law enforcement agencies. Congress passed the Patriot Act a week after the first anthrax death.

Some suggested almost immediately after the September 11 attacks that Iraq and its leader, Saddam Hussein, might be involved in the tragedy. CBS anchor Dan Rather asked a former defense secretary the day after the tragedy: "True or untrue that if we are to defeat terrorism, that sooner or later we have to deal and have to deal strongly with Saddam Hussein?"[52] A day later, MSNBC reported that Bush administration officials were "looking at the possibility that Iraq's Saddam Hussein may have lent some support to the terrorists, all potential targets now in this new war on terrorism, a war that will surely prove long and bloody."[53] A few days later, Secretary of State Colin Powell reported no apparent link: "We see no fingerprints between Iraq and what happened last Tuesday. But we are looking. We'll pull it up by its roots."[54]

Later, even as U.S. troops fought in Afghanistan, officials looked to expand its "war on terrorism." Iraq immediately became a possible target, identified in Bush's January 2002 State of the Union address as part of an "axis of evil." "The Iraqi regime has plotted to develop anthrax and nerve gas and nuclear weapons for over a decade," he said, promising that the United States would "not permit the world's most dangerous regimes to threaten us with the world's most destructive weapons."[55] In months to come, administration officials continued to maintain that Iraq possessed "weapons of mass destruction" that threatened America and that Hussein might be supporting al-Qaida. In a June speech at West Point, he introduced a new defense doctrine, asserting that the U.S. had the right to implement "pre-emptive action" to prevent a potential threat from growing. Congress authorized an attack on Iraq in October, and U.S. officials began trying to get international support for action. In his next

State of the Union address, weeks after sending troops to the region, Bush announced that he was ready to attack with or without support from the United Nations. Powell—at the time called by CBS "the most trusted man in America"—made an impassioned plea before the United Nations for assistance, insisting that Iraq had dangerous weapons and links to al-Qaida.[56] "Wielding dramatic satellite photos and intelligence intercepts, Secretary of State Powell cited 'irrefutable and undeniable' evidence yesterday that Iraq still conceals massive quantities of terror weapons," the *New York Daily News* reported.[57] The speech impressed most Americans, editorial writers, and even Democratic members of Congress, but the United Nations and most countries (including longtime U.S. allies Germany and France) remained unconvinced and refused to support the war effort. The United States began massive bombing of Iraq early in the morning on March 20, with a ground attack starting a few days later. Though Bush called the effort that of a multinational "coalition of the willing," only about thirty-five nations supported the U.S. action. Most provided few troops and for only limited roles. Great Britain did provide several thousand soldiers; however, considerably more than 80 percent of the coalition forces (and an even greater percentage of the coalition casualties) were Americans.[58]

Some newspapers questioned the relationship between Iraq and the war on terrorism before the war began, but few offered more than muted criticism. The news media made little effort to check administration officials' claims about either arms or terrorism, a fact that embarrassed some journalists after the war and a year-long search turned up none of the so-called weapons of mass destruction, nor meaningful links between Hussein and al-Qaida. Editorial writers for most newspapers "all essentially pronounced Powell right, though they couldn't possibly know for sure that he was," a *Columbia Journalism Review* critic complained. "The country could have profited from a much more searching examination of the so-called preemption doctrine."[59] Government officials later said "faulty intelligence" had misled them about the supposed weapons. Much of the incorrect information came from Iraqi exiles determined to aid in the overthrow of Hussein, and more than a year after the war ended, the *New York Times* publicly acknowledged that at least one of its reporters relied far too heavily on some of the same information while writing flawed reports about alleged Iraqi weapons programs and supposed terrorist training camps. "While many news organizations reported on WMD claims before the war, few did so as aggressively as the Times," wrote the *Washington Post* after the admission. "The failure to find such weapons has produced growing calls by critics . . . for the Times to own up to past errors."[60] Other journalists had questioned some of the *Times* reports before an editor's note admitted to "a number of instances of coverage that was not as rigorous as it should have been."[61] A *Columbia*

Journalism Review story almost a year earlier also had raised the issue, claiming that the even while the *Times* editorials and some stories avoided weapons claims, nearly a dozen other reports—all written by reporter Judith Miller—suggested "such weapons were just about to be found or had recently been destroyed."[62] Hundreds of U.S. newspapers carried those stories, distributed by the New York Times News Service. CBS reporter Leslie Stahl also said in a 2004 speech that she had erred with two pre-war stories from Iraq in which she implied Hussein had weapons.[63] *CJR* also had warned reporters about the possibility of faulty information even before the war began, pointing out that Powell's U.N. presentation "was nothing if not selective," and reminding readers of several previous instances in which intelligence failures had misled journalists and government officials.[64]

The war differed from any previous conflict for journalists and for their readers and viewers. Rather than immediately imposing the types of restrictions that had become common in every war after Vietnam, the Pentagon invited reporters along. Approximately 600 national and local "embedded" reporters joined troops as they entered Iraq, lived with the soldiers, and sometimes produced riveting reports from the front. The "embeds" had to sign contracts agreeing to the overview of military commanders, but most considered the tradeoff worthwhile. "The embedding process is the best single move the American military has ever made in its relations with the press," one reporter wrote. "The Pentagon went from one blunder after another—the 1991 gulf war, Grenada, Panama—to placing us inside the story."[65] Not everyone in the military was happy to have the press along, especially at first. "Most of the Alpha Company officers and senior NCOs initially acted as if having journalists along was like having snakes crawl into their tent; some were convinced that reporters were little better than spies," wrote newspaper columnist Gordon Dillow. "It took a couple of weeks of sharing their hardships and dangers before they realized that we weren't using our Iridium cell phones to alert the Iraqi army high command to the Marines' next move."[66] Digital cameras and lightweight equipment made airing television reports from Iraq a simple and relatively inexpensive process. Print reporters used laptop computers and satellite phones. Some TV reporters used traditional satellite equipment, but for most, the videophone was, in the words of *New York Daily News* technology reporter Michelle Megna, "almost as important as a chemical protection suit and gas mask. This $10,000 lunchbox-size device is powered by a camera or car battery and set up by one person."[67] Reporters also could use the equipment to keep personal war diaries or "war blogs" and to correspond with editors or family members via e-mail. Soldiers also used e-mail to stay in regular contact with family members, and many Americans used the Internet to read or watch news coverage offered by the media of other nations, including Arabic and European nations that sometimes carried more graphic footage of the destruction than could be seen in U.S. news reports.

Many in the American press focused coverage on their own technology and the reporters themselves. Former ABC executive Paul Friedman wrote that too many of the reports "were of the standing-in-front-of-the-camera, chest-thumping, look-where-I-am, and we're-ready-to-go-but-I-can't-tell-you-exactly-where-for-security-reasons variety, followed by the anchors back home warning the reporters to 'stay safe' and asking them to relay best wishes to the troops."[68] Little of the coverage was critical, and reporters became friends with the soldiers they covered. At home, many local and national anchors pinned American flags to their lapels, the news often came with a patriotic musical soundtrack, and at times the networks seemed to be competing to see which could have the most flag images on screen at one time. Even the embedded reporters riding across the desert on trucks and tanks sometimes felt like they were "cheerleaders on the team bus," noted National Public Radio reporter John Burnett.[69] Mostly, embedded journalists provided brief personal glimpses of the lives of soldiers, but they occasionally provided meaningful information that military briefing officers might otherwise have been tempted to ignore. One notable example came when *Washington Post* reporter William Branigin revealed that soldiers had mistakenly killed ten members of an Iraqi family at a checkpoint.[70]

For most reporters in the field, the work was dry, dirty, and sometimes difficult, but rarely dangerous. At least two American (and dozens of non-American) reporters were killed, however, and others encountered frightening experiences. "At one point a marine gave me a hand grenade to throw if the enemy started to overwhelm us," a journalist reported. "It had been more than thirty years since I'd held a grenade, and I knew that my having it violated written and unwritten rules. Still, it felt comforting in my hand. (I never had occasion to throw it.)"[71] Some reporters enjoyed their time with the troops. "This project is flat-out cool," said one longtime television reporter. "Because of the embed rules, I'm operating like a modern-day Ernie Pyle. No cumbersome crew with lights and assistants; just a single partner."[72] Some reporters did go to Iraq independently as "unilaterals" rather than "embeds," but most discovered they could cover little without military assistance. They also found that sometimes both the American military and the Iraqis considered them to be untrustworthy, and they wondered what would happened if they got into trouble. "Did we as unilaterals have the right to expect the military to rescue us?" pondered ABC correspondent John Donvan. "As one of us said, 'How are you going to explain to some marine's mother that he died trying to save an idiot journalist?' "[73]

The Iraqi army put up little resistance and the Americans roared into Baghdad. On May 1, just forty-three days after the war began, President Bush donned a flight suit and landed on the aircraft carrier *Abraham Lincoln*, which was returning from the Persian Gulf. With a huge banner stating "Mission Accomplished" hanging behind him, Bush declared major combat operations to be over. Hussein's sons were killed, and eventually the dictator was captured. Fighting continued, however, and by late 2005 more than 2,000 American soldiers and perhaps 100,000 Iraqis had died in the conflict. The U.S. media showed few images of death. The government drew criticism after releasing photos of Hussein's dead sons, both because of the graphic nature of the photos and because few other victims had been pictured. (The administration released the photos to prove the men were dead.) Some newspapers ran the photos, typically on inside pages. The government blocked photographers from taking photos of military funerals or flag-draped coffins, but hundreds of those photos ran on the Internet, and many were picked up by newspapers and television stations. Ted Koppel stirred some controversy by devoting an entire episode of *Nightline* to reading the names of the dead while showing their photos (some stations refused to run the *Nightline* episode), and *60 Minutes* and many newspapers published photos of the dead for Memorial Day. *The Newshour* on PBS and other news programs regularly closed their programs by listing names of the dead, as those names became available.

As the war went on, news coverage became more critical. Disturbed by their perception that "Iraq-based media focuses [sic] on catastrophic events such as car bombs and soldiers' deaths, while giving short shrift to U.S. rebuilding efforts," the Pentagon announced it would begin its own news service to send video, text, and photos directly to news organizations.[74] With the project, called Digital Video and Imagery Distribution System, Army teams could offer free pictures and stories to news outlets within hours of their arrival at battle zones or military bases. With civilian reporters denied similar access, "We have an unfair advantage," an Army spokesman admitted. "We're going to be able to get closer to the incident and provide better spokespeople to give the right information."[75]

Media images proved their power in April 2004 when photos on *60 Minutes II* and in newspapers around the world showed young American soldiers, including female soldiers, physically and sexually abusing Iraqi captives at Abu Ghraib prison, a former Hussein torture center. The photos prompted worldwide anti-American protests, and Bush appeared on two Arab television stations to condemn the abuse. Some soldiers were punished, and a congressional investigation tried to determine who was at fault.

Another series of 2004 committee hearings, many aired on live television, explored the reasons for the September 11, 2001, terrorist attacks in America. The committee's final report, which became an immediate best-seller in bookstores, criticized both the Clinton and Bush approaches to fighting terrorism, and recommended significant changes in U.S. intelligence agencies. A year later, after an interim Iraqi civilian government had officially taken over administration of the country and approved a constitution, more than 100,000 U.S. troops remained in Iraq.

NOTES

1. Kenneth J. Cooper and Helen Dewar, "For Most Republicans on Hill, Last Week was like No Other," *Washington Post*, November 20, 1994.

2. Howard Kurtz, "The Bad News about Clinton; Report Says Coverage Unfair to President," *Washington Post*, September 1, 1994.

3. Joseph Hayden, *Covering Clinton: The President and the Press in the 1990s* (Westport, Conn.: Praeger, 2001); William J. Hughes, "The 'Not-So-Genial' Conspiracy: The *New York Times* and Six Presidential 'Honeymoons,' 1953–1993," *Journalism & Mass Communication Quarterly* 72 (Winter 1995): 841–850.

4. Editorial, "The Republican 'Contract,'" *Washington Times*, September 14, 1994.

5. Dan Balz and Charles R. Babcock, "Gingrich, Allies Made Waves and Impression; Conservative Rebels Harassed the House," *Washington Post*, December 20, 1994.

6. Colleen Cason, "Kenneth Starr: How I Wonder Where You Are," *Ventura County* (California) *Star*, January 30, 1998. Also see David Maraniss, "First Lady Launches Counterattack," *Washington Post*, January 28, 1998; Warren P. Strobel, "Hillary Slams 'Vast Right Wing Conspiracy,'" *Washington Times*, 8 January 28, 1998.

7. "Sex, Lies and Impeachment," BBC News Online, accessed at http://news.bbc.co.uk/1/hi/specialreport/1998/12/98/reviewof98/themes/208715.stm (accessed March 5, 2006).

8. Committee of Concerned Journalists, "The Clinton Crisis and the Press: A Second Look," Committee of Concerned Journalists/ Project for Excellence in Journalism Web site: http://www.journalism.org. Also see Michael D. Murray, "The Contemporary Media, 1974–Present," in Wm. David Sloan, ed., *The Media in America: A History*, 5th ed. (Northport, Ala.: Vision Press, 2002); Kenton Bird, "White House Sex Scandal Absorbs the News Media," in Sloan, *The Media in America*.

9. Ben Wattenberg, "Refer, Impeach, Endure," *Washington Times*, December 16, 1998.

10. Richard Sisk, "Rehnquist to Grant Leeway, Experts Say," *New York Times*, January 7, 1999; Jules Witcover, "Where We Went Wrong," *Columbia Journalism Review*, March/April 1998.

11. Michael Powell, "Buffalo Bill's Wild Road Show," *Washington Post*, January 22, 1999.

12. Thomas V. DiBacco, "Clinton's Majority...Uneven Justice," *Washington Times*, February 15, 1999.

13. Michael Kramer, "Bush Set to Fight Electoral College Loss," *New York Post*, November 1, 2000.

14. Ibid.

15. *ABC News Special Report* transcript, November 7, 2000. Also see Neil Hickey, "The Big Mistake," *Columbia Journalism Review*, January/February 2001, 32–35.

16. NBC News, *Decision 2000* transcript, November 7, 2000.

17. Rather's statement almost immediately became one of the most-widely quoted examples of media wrongdoing in articles, books, and Web sites.

18. Howard Kurtz, "Bush Cousin Made Florida Vote Call for Fox News," *Washington Post*, November 14, 2000.

19. John Ellis, "Why I Won't Write Anymore about the 2000 Campaign," *Boston Globe*, July 3, 2000. Ellis announced his resignation from the newspaper later that month: John Ellis, "Thank You for Reading," *Boston Globe*, July 29, 2000.

20. Hickey, "The Big Mistake."

21. Editorial, "More on the Recount: Did Bush Really Win? Yes and Maybe," *Pittsburgh Post-Gazette*, April 7, 2001. Also see "Ballot Recount Supports Bush Win," *St. Petersburg* (Florida) *Times*, November 12, 2001; John F. Harris, "A Symbolic, but Muddled, Victory," *Washington Post*, November 12, 2001; Editorial, "Bush Wins Again," *New York Post*, February 27, 2001; John M. Broder, "Counties Can't Account for All Ballots Reported in 2000," New York Times, April 5, 2001; Douglas Kellner, *Grand Theft 2000*: Media Spectacle and a Stolen Election (Lanham, Md.: Rowman & Littlefield, 2001).

22. Timeline, *New York Times* Web site, accessed at http://www.nytco.com (accessed March 5, 2006).

23. Balz and Babcock, "Gingrich, Allies Made Waves."

24. News release, "Green Light for Mergers Could Result in Media Giants Dominating 100 Local Markets," Consumer Federation of American Web site, May 21, 2003, accessed at http://www.consumerfed.org/releases2.cfm?filename=mediamergers05.22.03.txt (accessed March 5, 2006); Barbara J. McKee, "Thanks FCC: Dough, not Truth, Drives Media," *Albuquerque Tribune* online edition, June 17, 2003, accessed at http://www.chairgrrl.com/Trib2003/ABQTrib061703.htm (accessed March 5, 2006).

25. George Nethercutt, "Nethercutt Votes for Congressional Oversight on FCC Media Ownership Rule," George Nethercutt Web site, http://www.house.gov/nethercutt/news/030716.html (accessed July 16, 2003). Also see *Democracy Now!* radio transcript, "Diverse Organizations Around the Country Testify Against Media Consolidation," June 2, 2003.

26. *The West Wing*, NBC, aired on April 21, 2004; media regulation timeline, PBS Web site, http://www.pbs.org/now/politics/mediatimeline.html (accessed March 5, 2006).

27. Dana Scott Rosengard, Elinor Kelley Gusin, and Sandra H. Utt, "Editor's Comments: Reflections on An American Tragedy: Media Studies of September 11, 2001," *Newspaper Research Journal* 24 (Winter 2003): 1.

28. Mike Littwin, "A Story that, Sadly, Invites Excess," *Rocky Mountain News*, May 2, 1999.

29. Erica Scharrer, Lisa M. Weidman, and Kimberly L. Bissell, "Pointing the Finger of Blame: News Media Coverage of Popular-Culture Culpability," *Journalism & Mass Communication Monographs* 5 (Summer 2003).

30. Text of letter to New York Times, 'Lectric Law Library Web site, http://www.lectlaw.com/files/cur55.htm (accessed March 5, 2006). The test of the letter also is available through numerous other Web sites.

31. Robert D. McFadden, "Times and The Washington Post Grant Mail Bomber's Demand," *New York Times*, September 19, 1995. Actually the manifesto was not quite complete. A typist inadvertently left out 72 words, which ran a few days later in the *Post*.

32. Ibid.

33. Howard Kurtz, "Unabomber Manuscript is Published," *Washington Post*, September 19, 1995. Also see Howard Kurtz, "Unabomber Publication Draws Criticism, Support," *Washington Post*, September 20, 1995.

34. John McCaslin, "Inside the Beltway," *Washington Times*, September 20, 1995. Also see William Glaberson, "Publication of Unabomber's Tract Draws Mixed Response," *New York Times*, September 20, 1995; David M. Rubin, "Unabomber's Tract: Two Newspapers Set Terrible Precedent," *Syracuse Post-Standard*, September 22, 1995; Rowan Scarborough, "Papers Criticized for Capitulation," *Washington Times*, September 20, 1995; William Serrin, "The Papers Submitted to Blackmail by a Killer," *Washington Times*, September 24, 1995; John McCaslin, "Inside the Beltway," *Washington Times*, September 21, 1995.

35. Comments by anchor Sharyl Attkisson, *CBS This Morning*, CBS News transcript, August 1, 1996.

36. Comments by host John Gibson, *Rivera Live*, CNBC News transcript, August 1, 1996.

37. Art Harris, "Though Still Free, Richard Jewell is Leading Suspect," CNN transcript, August 4, 1996.

38. Frank LoMonte, "A Tearful Richard Jewell Lashes Out," *Augusta Chronicle* Web site, http://www.augustachronicle.com/headlines/102996/jewel.html (accessed March 5, 2006).

39. Bill Rankin, "Olympic Bombing Aftermath," *Atlanta Journal and Constitution*, October 29, 1996.

40. "1993: World Trade Center Bomb Terrorises New York," BBC Web site, http://news.bbc.co.uk/onthisday/hi/dates/stories/february/26/newsid2516000/2516469.stm (accessed March 5, 2006).

41. Neal Gabler, "This Time the Scene was Real," *New York Times*, September 16, 2001. Also see Stacey Frank Kanihan, and Kendra L. Gale, "Within 3 Hours, 97 Percent Learn About 9/11 Attacks," *Newspaper Research Journal* 24 (Winter 2003): 78–91; "Aftermath of the Terrorist Attacks in New York and Washington, D.C.," *CBS News Special Report*, CBS News transcript, September 11, 2001; "Planes Crash into World Trade Center," *Today*, NBC News transcript, September 11, 2001; *NPR News Special*, National Public Radio transcript, September 11, 2001; *NBC News Special Report: Attack on America*, NBC News transcript, September 11, 2001; "American Under Attack," *ABC News Special Report*, ABC News transcript, September 12, 2001; "Attack on America," Fox News transcript, September 16, 2001; "America's New War," CNN transcript, September 17, 2001.

42. The Poynter Institute Web site offers galleries of front pages from the day after the attacks and from the "extra" editions published the same day: http://poynteronline.org/column.asp?id=49&aid=3401 (accessed March 5, 2006). Also see September 11 News Web site, http://www.september11news.com/USANewspapers.htm (accessed March 5, 2006); Poynter Institute (ed.): *September 11, 2001* (Kansas City, Mo.: Andrews McMeel Publishing, 2001); Murray, "The Contemporary Media"; Quint Randle, Lucinda D. Davenport, and Howard Bossen, "Newspapers Slow to Use Web Sites for 9/11 Coverage," *Newspaper Research Journal* 24 (Winter 2003): 58–71.

43. Quoted in Renee Martin Kratzer and Brian Kratzer, "How Newspapers Decided to Run Disturbing 9/11 Photos," *Newspaper Research Journal* 24 (Winter 2003): 34–47.

44. Ibid. Also see Allison Gilbert, Phil Hirshkorn, Melinda Murphy, Robyn Walensky, and Mitchell Stephens, eds., *Covering Catastrophe: Broadcast Journalists Report September 11* (Chicago: Bonus Books, 2002); Jim Rutenberg and Felicity Barringer, "After the Attacks: The Ethics," *New York Times*, September 13, 2001.

45. Guido H. Stempel III and Thomas Hargrove, "Newspapers Played Major Role in Terrorism Coverage," *Newspaper Research Journal* 24 (Winter 2003): 55–57; Paula M. Poindexter and Mike Conway, "Local, Network TV News Shows Significant Gains," *Newspaper Research Journal* 24 (Winter 2003): 114–127; Dominic Lasorsa, "News Media Perpetuate Few Rumors About 9/11 Crisis," *Newspaper Research Journal* 24 (Winter 2003): 10–21.

46. "Remembering the Lost," *Newsday* Internet database, http://www.newsday.com/news/ny-victimsdatabase.framedurl.

47. Quoted by Alex Martin, "*Newsday*," *Newspaper Research Journal* 24 (Winter 2003): 75–77. Also see Jennifer Harper, "Media Take Steps toward Sensitivity," *Washington Times*, September 19, 2001.

48. Dan Balz, "Gore Pledges to Back Bush, Calls for Unity," *Washington Post*, September 30, 2001.

49. Bill Carter and Felicity Barringer, "Networks Agree to U.S. Request to Edit Future bin Laden Tapes," *New York Times*, October 11, 2001.

50. Robert P. Laurence, "News Media Stuck Between a Rock and the White House," *San Diego Union-Tribune*, October 19, 2001. Also see Changho Lee, "*Post, Times* Highlight Government's War Efforts," *Newspaper Research Journal* 24 (Winter 2003): 190–203.

51. A list of communities opposing the act can be seen on the American Civil Liberties Union Web site, http://www.aclu.org/SafeandFree/SafeandFree.cfm?ID=11294&c=207 (accessed March 5, 2006). Also see David Enrich, "In Senate, Feingold is Anti-Terrorism Bill's Lone Opponent," States News Service, October 25, 2001; Editorial, "Stampeded in the House," *Washington Post*, October 16, 2001; Bill Fein, "Trust . . . but Verify," *Washington Times*, October 30, 2001.

52. *CBS News Special Report*, CBS News transcript, September 12, 2001. Also see "Rescue Efforts Move Slowly; FBI Follows Up Leads," CNN News transcript, September 12, 2001.

53. *News with Brian Williams*, MSNBC news transcript, September 13, 2001.

54. *Face the Nation*, CBS News transcript, September 16, 2001.

55. George W. Bush, "State of the Union Address," *New York Times*, January 30, 2002.

56. Martin Plissner, "The Most Trusted Man in America," CBS Web site, February 4, 2003, http://www.cbsnews.com/stories/2003/02/04/opinion/main539298.shtml (accessed March 5, 2006).

57. Thomas M. DeFrank, "Powell Pounds Iraq at UN Show and Tell," *New York Daily News*, February 6, 2003.

58. Celeste Katz, "72 in Poll Applaud Powell's Pitch," *New York Daily News*, February 10, 2003.

59. Chris Mooney, "The Editorial Pages and the Case for War," *Columbia Journalism Review*, March/April 2004.

60. Howard Kurtz, "N.Y. Times Cites Defects in Its Reports on Iraq," *Washington Post*, May 26, 2004.

61. Editor's note, *New York Times*, May 26, 2004. Also see Keith J. Kelly, "NYT Whispers Apology for WMD Stories," *New York Post*, May 27, 2004.

62. Liza Featherstone, "Parallel Universe at the *Times*," *Columbia Journalism Review*, March/April 2003.

63. Kate Wiltrout, "Stahl of '60 Minutes' Says She Regrets Iraq WMD Stories," April 22, 2004, *Virginian*-Pilot article online at http://home.hamptonroads.com (accessed April 23, 2004).

64. Ted Gup, "Useful Secrets," *Columbia Journalism Review*, March/April 2003.

65. Bob Arnot, "Embedded/Unembedded," *Columbia Journalism Review*, May/June 2003.

66. Gordon Dillow, "Grunts and Pogues: The Embedded Life," *Columbia Journalism Review*, May/June 2003.

67. Michelle Megna, "Embedded in Technology," *New York Daily News*, April 6, 2003.

68. Paul Freidman, "TV: A Missed Opportunity," *Columbia Journalism Review*, May/June 2003.

69. John Burnett, "Embedded/Unembedded II," *Columbia Journalism Review*, May/June 2003. Also see Nicholas Engstrom, "The Soundtrack for War," *Columbia Journalism Review*, May/June 2003.

70. William Branigin, "A Gruesome Scene on Highway 9," *Washington Post*, April 1, 2003.

71. Dillow, "Grunts and Pogues."

72. Chuck Stevenson, "A TV Producer's 'Best Assignment,'" *Columbia Journalism Review*, May/June 2003.

73. John Donvan, "For the Unilaterals, No Neutral Ground," *Columbia Journalism Review*, May/June 2003.

74. Jim Crane, "Pentagon Starts Its Own News Service in Iraq," Associated Press, March 1, 2004, story online at http://www.mediainfo.com/eandp/departments/newsroom/articledisplay.jsp?vnucontentid=1000448218, accessed March 5, 2006.

75. Ibid.

CHAPTER 9

Reflections on American Journalism, 1965–2005

In 1964, America went to war after an alleged North Vietnamese attack on a U.S. gunboat. The French, traditional U.S. allies victimized by their own earlier Vietnam struggles, opposed the American effort. The North Vietnamese attack later was found to have been exaggerated, and Johnson apparently had been victimized by faulty intelligence. During the Vietnam War, the news media used a combination of almost-unprecedented access and new technology to bring disturbing wartime images into American homes. In 2003, America went to war in Iraq after that nation allegedly harbored a stockpile of weapons that threatened the United States. The French drew considerable U.S. criticism for their unwillingness to join in the American effort. The Iraqi weapons threat later was found to have been exaggerated, and Bush may have been victimized by faulty intelligence. During the war, the news media used a combination of new kinds of access and new technology to bring disturbing wartime images into American homes. As French writer Alphonse Karr wrote more than 150 years ago, *"Plus ça change, plus c'est la même chose* [The more things change, the more they are the same]."

Despite the similarities between 1964 and 2003, of course, Americans saw their nation and their news change in dramatic ways during and after the 1960s. Ever-expanding media brought frightening new realities of a broader, more confusing world. Americans saw their news presented by new faces, as women and people of color made inroads into journalism. Americans saw their news via different media. Though television had been around for two decades, network TV news went to its current half-hour format in the 1960s, and local stations soon began changing their formats to reflect entertainment trends. Newspaper journalists reacted slowly and negatively to the new competition, even as their publishing bosses sought increasing involvement with television. Thanks to satellite technology, Americans also saw their news more quickly than they could previously. Soon they also saw more of it. Only three television networks existed in 1965. New cable stations showed hints in the 1970s of what would come, and the first national 24-hour news network debuted in 1980. Images—and "image"—became increasingly important, not just for the glowing electric box but also for newspapers. Computers and then the Internet led to more dramatic changes in news content, style and access.

The Vietnam War helped define the nation and its journalism during the 1960s and 1970s, as the first television war brought previously unseen images into American homes. It also brought new opportunities for reporters, including women, who were willing to expose themselves to hardship and danger. Journalists revealed during the war that Americans could not always trust their government, even in matters of life and death. The war ended, but distrust remained. The government would never again allow reporters the kind of wartime access that they enjoyed in Vietnam, and the government never fully regained its credibility. Oddly, perhaps, Americans typically trusted their leaders most, and sometimes trusted the media least, during times of war. After the graphic nature of the Vietnam coverage, politicians recognized the difficulty of maintaining support for a war in which Americans could see their sons and brothers and fathers and husbands—and with the second Iraq war, their daughters and sisters and mothers and wives—killing and dying. Though perhaps no American reporter in any twentieth-century war actually aided an enemy with his or her work, and journalists often withheld information at the request of military or government officials, patriotic Americans tended to believe leaders who complained that the news media would hinder military efforts by getting in the way or perhaps providing the enemy with valuable information. Eventually journalists gained access to the most recent American war, signing restrictive contracts and tagging along with the military as "embedded" reporters.

In some ways, the Vietnam War never ended, becoming a touchstone against which Americans measured politicians and journalists. While Lyndon Johnson chose not to run for re-election because of the war, and Richard Nixon won the presidency saying he had a secret plan to end the conflict, more than fifteen years after the fighting stopped Democratic presidential candidate Bill Clinton drew criticism because he avoided fighting in Vietnam. A dozen years later, in 2004, the same war again became a presidential election issue when Democrats questioned incumbent George W. Bush's service, while calling their candidate, John Kerry, a hero because of the medals he won there. Republicans questioned Kerry's patriotism because he publicly protested the war after leaving Vietnam. Both sides used television footage of antiwar testimony Kerry had offered before the Senate Foreign Relations Committee in 1971. In a presidential election in which each side raised more than $200 million, a relatively small group calling itself "Swift Boat Veterans for Truth" drew considerable attention for its actions in questioning Kerry's actions during the war. Despite producing no evidence that Kerry had misrepresented his service, the group provided a major focus for the news for several weeks during the campaign. One media organization, the Sinclair Broadcasting Group, announced that just before the election it would require its 62 television stations to show a prime-time documentary highly critical of Kerry's antiwar activities. After considerable protest from viewers, advertisers, and others, Sinclair decided to air a more balanced program that excerpted the documentary.

By the 2004 campaign, a new war in Iraq was calling forth phrases commonly used in Vietnam: For supporters, Americans were "winning hearts and minds" in Iraq, though the hearts and minds in question belonged to people oppressed by fundamentalist Muslim terrorists rather than by Communists. For opponents, the Iraq War was becoming a "quagmire." Journalists in Iraq had more access than with any war since Vietnam, as government officials found that embedding journalists with troops proved a more effective way to generate war support than did trying to keep the news media away. Also in 2004, the *Toledo Blade* won the Pulitzer Prize for investigative reporting for a four-part series about an Army platoon that killed unarmed Vietnamese civilians in 1967. The story made Americans remember 1969 stories and photos in the *Cleveland Plain Dealer* and *Life* magazine about the massacre at My Lai, in which American soldiers killed scores of Vietnamese civilians.

During the 1960s and 1970s, on the heels of the civil rights movement and with racial violence shaking several American cities, women and members of minorities gained increasing access to newsrooms and to the news. Newspapers and television stations hired more nonwhites of both genders, though white men continued to dominate management and leadership positions in the news business. Minority women perhaps benefited the most, as some news organizations sought to cover two affirmative action bases, race and gender, with one new employee. With a couple of brief exceptions, white men continued to occupy the news desks of the three major networks throughout the period. Dan Rather, Peter Jennings, and Tom Brokaw all moved into network anchor seats in the early 1980s. Brokaw became the first of the three to step down, replaced by Brian Williams, another middle-aged white man, in late 2004. That same year, Dan Rather announced he would leave his anchor post in March 2005. At the time, the former "Tiffany Network" nightly news program typically finished behind ABC and NBC in the ratings, and

Rather had been forced to apologize after CBS rushed a story critical of Bush's military service onto the air before the election. The story used supporting documents that apparently had been forged. Less than a month after Rather left the anchor desk, the last of the "big three" anchors, Peter Jennings of ABC, hoarsely announced during a broadcast that he had lung cancer: " 'Yes, I was a smoker until about 20 years ago, and I was weak and I smoked over 9/11.' " Jennings's announcement came just days after another ABC icon, Ted Koppel, announced that he would be leaving *Nightline*, the late-night news show he had made famous. Jennings died in August 2005 of the same disease that had killed Edward R. Murrow forty years earlier.

After Jennings's 2005 death, Elizabeth Vargas became an ABC co-anchor with Bob Woodruff, and in 2006 NBC *Today* morning personality Katie Couric was named as Dan Rather's replacement at CBS, though throughout most of the period women failed to establish a national anchor presence. (Soon after being named a co-anchor, Woodruff suffered serious injuries from a roadside bomb in Iraq.) In addition, with both local and national television, women were more subject than men to job security issues based on their physical appearance. Still, they did advance even on the national scene. Barbara Walters became the first news person to make $1 million per year in 1976. Fourteen years later, then 68 and a 22-year veteran of ABC's *20/20* newsmagazine, she signed a $12 million annual contract making her again the highest paid "news personality" (though she was virtually the only network newswoman who had been allowed to age). A year later, Couric signed a 4.5-year, $65 million contract to continue her job as co-host of NBC's *Today*, making her the highest-paid news personality.

Throughout the period, journalists worked to understand and report issues affecting groups of Americans once largely excluded from the news. "Women's issues" and diversity concerns became important, especially after journalists began to recognize how much those issues also affected white men. Societal divisions lingered, however, erupting in cases such as the Clarence Thomas vs. Anita Hill nationally televised controversy during Clarence Thomas's 1991 confirmation hears, the 1991–1992 Rodney King case and ensuing riots, the 1994–1995 O.J. Simpson murder trial, and the 1998 Texas murder of a black man dragged to death behind a pickup. Television images of stranded New Orleans hurricane victims, most of them poor and black, in 2005 raised new questions about racial equality in American—and administrative missteps in response to the hurricane (coupled with the ongoing Iraq War) even seemed to prompt a renewed vigor among journalists.

Homosexuality, which in 1965 was considered a mental illness and largely invisible to mainstream America, "came out" in the late 1960s and then drew more attention with the unfolding of the AIDS crisis in the 1980s. By the following decade gay characters were commonplace on entertainment television and in American politics, and editorial writers and social critics debated whether homosexuals should be allowed to adopt children or marry. Like the race-based Texas murder the same year, the 1998 "hate crime" murder of a gay Wyoming college student drew national condemnation and widespread media attention. President Bill Clinton approved a "don't ask, don't tell" homosexuality policy for the military in 1993, and three years later signed a bill denying federal recognition of gay marriages. After some states began performing those marriages, President George W. Bush in 2004 called for a constitutional amendment banning them. That same year, voters in eleven states passed measures prohibiting gay marriages. Much of the news coverage of the election revolved around "values."

New groups made it into the news in part because of new modes of journalism. Alternative newspapers of the 1960s and 1970s provided a voice for many who could not make themselves heard through traditional news media. Most of those publications did not last long, but mainstream newspapers also began seeking broader representation of sources. News media of all types became more conscious of customer concerns. They used surveys, focus groups, and eventually "civic" (or "public") journalism to discover and cover citizens' concerns. Some critics complained that the changes meant the news media sometimes gave readers and viewers more of what consumers wanted than what citizens needed. Some types of news, including international news, largely disappeared, meaning that historical and political context could be lost. As the world became more complex, much of the news became more simplistic. Often it focused on dramatic stories about crime, sex, or celebrity, typically stories of little relevance to most people's lives. Some of those stories sparked feeding frenzies among journalistic packs.

In the years after terrorists destroyed the World Trade Center, network news became more serious and local television began to offer a bit more international coverage, though much of it was related to U.S. military operations. To make room for that coverage, stations cut coverage of everything else except crime and disaster. More than a quarter of local TV stories were devoted to crime and legal issues, the most since 1998. New 24-hour news stations offered the possibility of letting Americans see more of their world, in greater context, but largely fell short. The hours of extra time all too often were devoted to repeated rehashing of old information, while the competitive deadline nature of a 24-hour news cycle sometimes pushed producers into airing rumors or mistakes that in an earlier era would never have made the news. Tragedies around the world, including genocide in Rwanda, Sudan, and the Balkans, often went largely unreported, especially if no American interests could easily be tied to the story. Financial journalism had become increasingly important, yet most of the news media seemed to be caught off guard by giant corporate scandals involving telecommunications goliath WorldCom and energy giant Enron—the largest corporate contributor to President Bush's campaign—both in 2001. The securities fraud case of homemaking media maven Martha Stewart affected far fewer Americans than either case, yet drew more media attention, undoubtedly because of the celebrity aspects involved in her case.[1]

Newspaper readership declined throughout the period discussed in this book, and many questioned the long-term viability of the print media that once comprised the heart of "the press." Single-newspaper cities became the norm. Circulations generally increased, but by far less than population growth (and in the first half of 2005 actually decreased). Competition from other media, budget considerations, and shifting readership patterns prompted distinct pessimism about the future of newspapers even among print journalists. While most people relied on television for most of their news—allowing one network to say for years, "More Americans get their news from ABC news than from any other source"—throughout the period, by the end of the 1990s most people could turn to the Internet for information. The new medium created new difficulties in determining the credibility of information, and rumors and hoaxes became easier to spread and tougher to eradicate. At the same time, careful readers could now access news media around the world, reading their morning newspaper and any of thousands of other newspapers online. They could read news sites produced in other nations, including America's allies and enemies. Readers could even bypass the news media in many cases, for example going directly to the White House Web site to read a president's address in his own words or to the congressional Web site to follow the progress of a tax bill. Many Web sites combined the written aspects of newspapers with the sound and visuals of television.[2]

Entertainment values also came to the news media in a multitude of other ways. Newspaper writing became more literary, boosted by the "new journalism" of the 1970s. The 1982 arrival of USA Today became the most obvious and dramatic symbol of a move among most newspapers toward shorter stories, more and larger photos, flashy infographics, and splashes of color. Even before USA Today, newspapers turned to computer "pagination," taking the composition of pages out of the back shop (eliminating some jobs, while adding to the duties of editors). Layout editors skilled with computer software such as QuarkXPress, PageMaker, or InDesign worked with writers, photographers, and artists to craft pages as creative as those found in magazines. Television news saw the arrival of image consultants, music soundtracks, and "happy talk" among on-camera "talent." Television documentaries that provided lengthier looks at issues mostly disappeared, replaced by pseudo-documentary "newsmagazines" that offered fifteen-minute stories driven by emotional close-ups, ambush interviews, dramatic film-style editing, mood music, and sometimes hidden cameras.

Alternative newspapers and tabloids blurred the lines between news and entertainment in print, and tabloid television programs with their own "reporters" and "anchors" made it even more difficult to separate news from entertainment. Talk radio, popularized most notably by Rush Limbaugh and other political conservatives during and after the 1980s, offered a lively mix of news, commentary, and entertainment. In later years many Americans admitted learning much of their news from late-night talk show monologues and comedy sketch shows. Documentary films continued to provide context, but most aired in small "art house" movies theaters or on PBS and were seen by few viewers. The rare exceptions were far different in style and tone from Edward R. Murrow's famed 1960 television documentary, *Harvest of Shame*. Michael Moore used interesting details, feature film techniques, and his own quirky personality to attract large audiences (and numerous admirers and critics) with his Academy Award-winning 2002 film *Bowling for Columbine* about the Colorado high school killings, and *Fahrenheit 9/11*, a film critical of President Bush that in 2004 became the first documentary in fifty years to win the top award at the famed Cannes Film Festival and the first ever to take in more than $100 million at the box office. "Instant books," some written by reporters and some by participants, began to appear after every significant news event, letting those involved and outside critics offer their own perspectives. Some of those books became television movies. One thinly veiled fictional account of Bill Clinton's 1996 presidential campaign drew attention in part because of its author, listed as "Anonymous." *Newsweek* columnist Joe Klein first denied, then admitted, writing *Primary Colors*, which also became a popular movie. Limbaugh, Moore, and others on both ends of the political spectrum also offered popular books lambasting their opponents in take-no-prisoners language, including such titles as Molly Ivins's *Bushwacked: Life in George W. Bush's America*, Al Franken's *Lies and the Lying Liars Who Tell Them*, Sean Hannity's *Deliver Us from Evil*, and Ann Coulter's *Slander: Liberal Lies About the American Right*.[3]

Those flame-throwing books might be viewed as the bastardized descendents of another journalistic trend that began to expand in the 1960s and 1970s—that of journalists not only relaying the news, but also interpreting it. Sometimes the trend proved useful, as in the best of circumstances those who read or watched the news might learn not only what happened, but why it happened. The always-problematic ideal of "objectivity" faded, replaced by "fairness." Reporters no longer merely relied on letting two sides tell their own stories, leaving it to readers to determine which side might be lying. At the same time, those in the news media found that they and news consumers liked interpretation, and eventually commentary became a customary part of most political news. When they did not do their own analysis, the news media relied on experts such as academics, military officers, or attorneys. The arrival of CNN and other 24-hour news stations gave broadcasters more airtime to fill, adding to the use of interpretation (and entire shows devoted to that interpretation). Despite the additional time, however, even cable television journalists took the words out of newsmakers' mouths, as officials' "sound bites" steadily decreased in length. Stuck with their half hour of nightly news, ABC, CBS, and NBC slashed sound bites to a few seconds each. Actually, of course, they offered far less than thirty minutes. As the writers of one 2004 study noted: "The nightly newscasts used to be described as 22 minutes of news in a 30-minute program. That is no longer the case. ... The amount of news on the three commercial nightly newscasts, after teases, promotional announcements and commercials were removed, was closer to 18 minutes, 48 seconds."[4]

Despite the "civic journalism" that arose during the 1990s, the high point of American journalism in terms of its civic potential may have come two decades earlier when investigative journalism hit its peak. The Pentagon Papers case and Watergate both illustrated the value of a watchdog press. Key court cases and new laws regarding open meetings and open records helped loosen strictures on what information journalists could obtain and publish. Computers, and more-educated reporters, made it easier to compile and use meaningful databases to uncover problems in government or industry. New technology ranging from copy machines and tape recorders to laptop computers and cell phones allowed journalists and their sources to work faster and more efficiently. Sometimes, as when television sometimes turned to hidden cameras to glamorize stories, the technology became too important. The resulting footage made for entertaining television but often focused on relatively small targets. The big targets, particularly those in government, sometimes were overlooked, especially as budgetary concerns meant fewer reporters had less time to pursue complicated stories, and as government officials vastly improved their media savvy and their use of public relations.

Starting primarily with positive coverage of President John Kennedy and then more negatively with Lyndon Johnson and especially Richard Nixon, coverage of government officials often focused on personalities. Even election coverage increasingly shied away from political issues, turning to poll results and other technical "horse race" elements of the electoral process. Beginning in the 1970s, much of the political coverage also focused on personal scandal, especially involving sex. Revelations about Bill Clinton's affair with White House intern Monica Lewinsky damaged his presidency and, after a bitterly contested election, in 2000 helped give Republicans control of every branch of the federal government for the first time in almost five decades. The first "journalist" to report the Clinton/Lewinsky affair was Internet gossip Matt Drudge, who opened the floodgates for other media. During the 2004 presidential campaign, the same Internet site reported rumors of a similar affair involving Democratic candidate John Kerry. Mainstream journalists found that story, like many of the fanciful tales flooding the Internet, to be considerably less credible, though not until the woman's name had flashed around the globe and she was forced to call a news conference—an event now used far more often by celebrities and by media victims than by leading political figures—to dispute the rumors.

For their part, during the 2004 campaign the mainstream media spent weeks covering the allegations of the Swift Boat Veterans for Truth, Bush's Vietnam record, and similar stories. A regular question for reporters became "Why is John Kerry having so much trouble defining himself for the voters?" Those reporters apparently saw little role for themselves in providing that definition for voters, despite a climate in which millions of dollars in misleading television advertising targeted and tried to redefine each candidate. Bush, who defined himself as a "war president" and who held fewer news conferences than any other president of the television age, also largely managed to bypass negative publicity during his campaign. Those who refused to voice support for the president were blocked from Bush campaign appearances, and sometimes arrested if they managed to get in, despite the fact that the rallies typically were held in public settings. As a result, when each network news program produced a short nightly news segment on each candidate's activities, viewers saw the president—who almost never spoke directly to the news media—addressing crowds of cheering followers. Few stories in the mainstream media pointed out or questioned the remoteness of the president. Stories occasionally pointed out the lies—typically called "inaccuracies" or "exaggerations"—by both candidates' campaigns in their advertising and public addresses, but the lies continued unabated. As with the election of four years earlier, the final result came down to the electoral votes of one state (Ohio, this time, instead of Florida). In 2004, however, Bush carried the deciding state relatively easily, avoiding the controversy and recriminations of 2000. On election night, the networks showed far more caution in their projections than they had four years earlier, though Fox again was first to declare Bush the apparent winner.

During the Bush administration, government institutions probably worked harder than during any other recent period to maintain official secrecy. After the *New York Times* revealed in 2005 (after withholding the information for several months at the government's request) that the president had approved a secret National Security Agency surveillance program within the United States, the FBI investigated various leaks, going so far as to question reporters about stories based on supposedly secret documents. The administration warned journalists that they could be prosecuted under espionage laws. Meanwhile, a Republican-controlled Congress—a body that often provided reporters with leaked information—considered passing laws to increase the penalties for revealing official secrets. At the same time, those secrets were becoming increasingly numerous. Also in 2005, journalists uncovered another secret program that began under the Clinton administration and continued under Bush, through which thousands of previously declassified documents were withdrawn from public access at the National Archives. Some of those documents dated back to the 1940s and 1950s, some had already been published elsewhere, and some seemed to pose no risk other than that of potential embarrassment. One example was a CIA memo to President Harry Truman—dated about six weeks before China invaded Korea in November 1950—suggesting that Chinese intervention in the Korean War was possible but unlikely.

Access to the Web meant many more Americans also could produce their own news, continuing another trend seen with the alternative publications of the 1960s when offset printing made publishing much easier and cheaper than printing with hot lead type. The technology especially suited smaller publications, including college newspapers. A decade or so later, computers and desktop publishing simplified the process even further, allowing any organization or individual with a computer and a printer to produce a newsletter. Some early Internet users produced electronic magazines, or "e-zines," predecessors to the interactive Web logs or "blogs" that came later. Inexpensive computer equipment, combined with simple copy-and-paste technology and access to millions of stories and images via the Web, allowed almost anyone with a strong opinion to become a reporter of sorts. "Anyone with no training or credentials, like Drudge, who works on his laptop in Los Angeles, can deliver the news of the world to a global audience," former NBC president Lawrence Grossman noted.[5] In 1999, more reputable Web journalists founded the Online News Organization, made up primarily of journalists who worked on the Web sites of mainstream newspapers and broadcast companies. The organization's mission statement calls for ethical journalistic behavior, while calling the Internet "the most powerful communications medium to arise since the dawn of television."[6]

Digital photo technology made it easier for producers of all news media to use and to manipulate photos. The *Los Angeles Times*, for example, was forced during the 2003 Iraq War to apologize for a front-page photo (which also ran in other newspapers around the country) in which a photographer had digitally enlarged a crowd of Iraqi civilians. Newspapers commended the justifiable firing of the photographer. Yet few of those newspapers, and perhaps none of the networks, noted a far more common version of photo manipulation that occurred earlier in the war. Television viewers around the world saw what seemed to be a large crowd of Iraqis, helped by American soldiers, pulling down a large statue of Saddam Hussein. Television reporters and administration officials breathlessly compared the destruction of the statue to the fall of the Berlin Wall. Newspaper front pages solidified the images the following day. News programs repeated the images throughout the following year, even after some newspaper and Internet reports revealed that perhaps fewer than 200 Iraqis took part in the destruction of the statue. At the time of the event, even print journalists generally failed to provide crowd size estimates for their next-day stories. "The crowd was small, but the square quickly filled with journalists anxious to capture the iconic images of victory," the PBS program *Frontline* noted almost in passing a year later.[7] News cameras "enlarged" the crowd for viewers by focusing tightly on the scene (and even inexperienced public events planners know that close proximity to cameras increases the apparent size and energy of an event). Other critics later noted the availability of American equipment used to destroy the statue and suggested that the "spontaneous" event, which occurred directly in front of a hotel occupied by journalists from around the world, may have been almost entirely staged. An American military officer later admitted coming up with the idea.

Aside from the obviously prejudiced perspectives of some modern Internet "journalists" and their predecessors, government complaints about bias among mainstream journalists dated back at least to the Nixon administration and played a part in declining news media credibility among Americans. Several other factors (not all avoidable, nor the fault of journalists) also contributed. Good investigative reporting contributed to societal distrust of institutions, and American corporate journalism came to be viewed as one of those institutions. In the 1970s, many in the news media became more willing to openly discuss the problems of journalism via ombudsmen or media reporters, and a number of journalism reviews arose. By the 1990s, many newspapers had implemented a "media beat" with reporters who covered the news business. Some media organizations, ranging from liberal alternative newspapers of the 1960s to more recent conservative talk radio hosts and Fox News, sought to enhance their own credibility by openly attacking other journalists for errors, alleged biases, and perceived arrogance. Well-organized and well-funded new critics also came from outside of journalism with the arrival of organizations such as the politically conservative Accuracy in Media in 1969 and the politically liberal Fairness and Accuracy in Reporting in 1986. Later, numerous Web editors devoted their efforts to media criticism. While the criticism from all fronts probably made the news media more careful and more accountable, the exposure of the problems made journalists look bad. Between the criticism and the perceived negativity of good investigative journalism, in effect, the better the news media did their job, the worse they looked. Even PBS came under attack, after conservatives complained that a Bill Moyers program, *Now*, exemplified a network that had become riddled with bias. Kenneth Tomlinson, the staunchly conservative chairman of the Corporation for Public Broadcasting, secretly hired a consultant to monitor *Now* and other programs. He resigned in 2005 just before the release of a report critical of his activities.[8]

Still, journalists contributed to their problems in obvious ways. Throughout the period beginning in the 1960s, reporters relied more and more upon unnamed or unattributed sources, even in cases where doing so seemed to be less to protect sources than for journalistic convenience—or worse, to cover up journalistic ineptitude or dishonesty. A *Washington Post* reporter led to industry-wide hand wringing by fabricating a Pulitzer Prize-winning story in 1980, but other reporters later committed similar sins. Several reporters and columnists plagiarized the work of others, an act that became both easier to commit and easier to verify in an Internet world. In 1998, a *Cincinnati Enquirer* reporter admitted stealing e-mails for a story about corporate misdeeds. The same year, editors caught a *New Republic* reporter making up stories; he later profited from a book and a movie based on his dishonesty. A few years later, reporters for two of the nation's three national newspapers, the *New York Times* and *USA Today*, were fired (along with editors) for fabricating stories. Judith Miller, another *New York Times* reporter, came under fire for pre-war stories suggesting that Saddam Hussein had chemical or biological weapons, and then spent eighty-five days in jail in 2005 for refusing to tell a grand jury the name of a White House source who may illegally have revealed the name of a covert U.S. agent. Oddly, Miller was jailed despite the fact that she had never revealed the name of the agent in print, and a White House staffer was indicted on charges related to the case, while conservative columnist Robert Novak did publish the agent's name but apparently never faced the possibility of jail. (Novak refused to publicly discuss whether he had testified before the grand jury.) Miller then drew criticism from editors at her own newspaper, which supported her refusal to give up a source while finding fault with the closeness of her relationship with administration officials. In late 2005, she left the *New York Times* under a cloud, saying she was retiring because she had "become the news."

Perhaps no individual journalist better illustrated the highs and lows of recent decades in American journalism than did Peter Arnett, who while with the Associated Press won a 1966 Pulitzer Prize for his coverage of the Vietnam War. Twenty-five years later, he stayed in Baghdad during the

Persian Gulf War, interviewing Saddam Hussein and offering CNN viewers dramatic narration during the first hours of U.S. bombing. He drew both praise and criticism for his broadcasts from behind enemy lines. A 1998 story drew only criticism, however. The "Operation Tailwind" story claimed that U.S. forces used poison nerve gas during illegal operations in Laos during the Vietnam War. CNN and *Time* combined efforts for the story, with the network offering a rare documentary narrated by Arnett, and *Time* producing a print version (which carried Arnett's byline, along with that of another reporter). After an internal CNN investigation both news organizations were forced to apologize for the story. Arnett later blamed the problems in part on "producer-driven" magazine-style stories that relied on second-hand information gathered by producers rather than on eyewitness accounts by reporters. In doing so, he admitted that he had contributed little to the story other than his name and face. Reprimanded, he soon left the network. Five years later, during the Iraq War, he again stayed in Baghdad, reporting for NBC and *National Geographic*. Interviewed there by a state-run Iraqi television station, he offered his opinion that the initial U.S. military plan "failed because of Iraqi resistance." Arnett's comments met with an immediate uproar from U.S. officials and listeners, and NBC and *National Geographic* quickly fired him. He apologized for the comments, and a British tabloid newspaper that opposed the war hired him the same day.[9]

Corporate consolidation made possible the joint operations between CNN and *Time* (both then owned by Time Warner) and between NBC and *National Geographic* (both owned by General Electric). Probably nothing changed and defined U.S. journalism more after 1965 than the business aspects involved. It was during this period that for many Americans, including many reporters, journalism shifted from an honorable change-the-world, comfort-the-afflicted-and-afflict-the-comfortable "calling"—the "Fourth Estate," or the "fourth branch of government"—to just another business. Such characterizations are somewhat naïve. After all, newspapers that failed to make money have never succeeded, "the press" never has been a unified whole, and perceived evils such as chains have existed for more than a century. Even so, business trends did change the news media in significant ways during the past forty years.

Media consolidation continued unabated throughout the period. Media companies grew, traded properties, and swallowed one another. Newspaper publishers were among the earliest investors in television. After the arrival of the Internet, newspapers and broadcasters quickly established Web presences. An obvious problem came from conflicts of interests, or at least the appearance of such conflicts, especially when journalists appeared to ignore stories that might negatively affect the bottom line of the corporate owner. Even within the media, conscientious reporters sometimes found themselves having to report potential conflicts while maintaining that the conflicts made no difference. On more than one occasion, for example, an author interviewed on *60 Minutes* wrote a book published by another subsidiary of CBS parent Viacom. Sometimes consolidation created strange bedfellows, because the many interests represented by corporate owners ranged from military contracts to snack foods to pornography. Aside from those ethical issues, many critics worried about the loss of editorial competition—the diminishing number of meaningful voices that might contribute to the "marketplace of ideas"—that resulted from consolidation. Ben Bagdikian's 1983 book *The Media Monopoly*, which worried about fifty corporations controlling most major American media, quickly proved outdated. Twenty years later, those fifty corporations had become a half-dozen. Aided by deregulation, Clear Channel Communications grew from one Texas radio station in 1972 to almost 1,400 stations in 2004. Its holdings in sixty-five countries included control of 700,000 billboards and more concert venues than any other company.[10]

Particularly from a short-term profit-oriented perspective, the consolidation and corporatization of the news media often helped with the bottom line. Companies could benefit from cross-promotion among various news and entertainment properties, such as ABC's promotion of Disney movies, and a network might find it easier to land interviews with top stars from elsewhere in the corporate fold. Media "convergence" meant that a reporter might write for a company's newspaper, its Web site, its radio station, and its television station. In other cases, different media organizations, such as the various newspapers and television stations involved in civic journalism, pooled their talents. A chain of newspapers could share columnists and advertising personnel, or even reporters, and advertising sales went up even as readership declined. Despite occasional dips, newspapers enjoyed ad revenues 250 percent higher in 2000 than fifty years earlier, in part because costs for newspaper readers stayed remarkably consistent and low compared to other goods. (Some newspapers began to charge fees to access their Internet news, especially for archived stories.)[11]

Sometimes media organizations obviously went too far in their business pursuits. A notable example came in 1999 when the *Los Angeles Times* devoted one issue of its entire Sunday magazine to the new Staples Center arena. Other publications first revealed that the *Times* shared advertising revenues from the insert with Staples in exchange for the newspaper gaining special advertising privileges in the arena, a fact that had been hidden from its readers and from reporters who wrote stories in the issue (and who later were enraged at the damage to their reputations).

Because of standardization and cost "benefits of scale," chain ownership sometimes improved quality, especially if quality was measured in terms of consistency of overall appearance or the number of visible errors that appeared in the newspaper. Errors of omission, however, were more difficult to qualify. Corporate media managers encouraged editors and producers to cut costs and increase profits. News staffs shrunk, sometimes even as the number of ad salespeople and managers increased, and fewer reporters did more work. Investigative journalism often went by the wayside largely because of at least three financial concerns: It could be expensive to do well, it was time-consuming (taking away time that reporters could devote to other stories), and it was more likely than other forms of journalism to lead to lawsuits.[12]

Corporate influence may have affected television journalism more than it did newspapers, but the problems of newspapers may have most troubled longtime press watchers. As a relatively new medium that from the beginning was intended more for entertainment than for news, television brought far less history and fewer expectations than did the print media. Television and Internet forms of news have changed quickly and regularly throughout their history. In addition, the Internet added new sources of information virtually every minute, while expanding cable and satellite network possibilities gave at least the appearance that television, too, provided viewers with an increasing number of news choices. The explosion of powerful newspaper chains had the opposite effect for newspapers, however. Strong newspapers have always worked to put weaker ones out of business, but they succeeded at an increasing rate after 1965. Only recently have one-newspaper cities become the norm in most of America, and afternoon newspapers, typically the least profitable, were the first to go. As newspapers disappeared, so did readers—especially the working-class readers of afternoon papers, who now could watch ninety minutes of local news in the afternoon and another thirty minutes in the evening before going to bed. The 1970 Newspaper Preservation Act, designed to save failing newspapers through joint operating agreements, further hastened the demise of many (sometimes while enhancing the profits of their owners).

Still, not all the competitive media news was bad, even for newspapers. Joint operating agreements in San Francisco and Honolulu ended without the demise of any of the newspapers involved. In both cases, new buyers for the weaker papers offered the promise of new competition. A dozen JOAs remain, with expiration dates ranging from 2007 in Cincinnati to 2090 in York, Pennsylvania (In 2006 a three-year *Seattle Times* legal battle to dissolve its JOA with the *Seattle Post-Intelligencer* continued.). Other new news sources also arose. Among the most promising new media options, despite their small audiences, were new regional 24-hour news stations that in some cases began offering a kind of news different from anything else. Regional stations typically drew stories from local stations, but unlike those local stations tended to focus on news related only to the region. Some regional stations ignored most of the largely irrelevant crime, fire, and animal stories from afar that often entertained local news viewers, and generally skipped the lifestyle stories and political commentary that pervaded national television news.

Other new options also appeared. In the mid-1990s, C-SPAN added a Web site that viewers could use to watch Congress in action, and added its third network for live coverage of public affairs. In 2000, the Rev. Sun Myung Moon's Unification Church, which already owned and operated the politically conservative *Washington Times*, bought the news wire service United Press International. Air America, a politically liberal radio network intended to combat conservative talk radio, began programming in 2004. A year later, former Vice President Al Gore and others launched Current TV, an independent youth-oriented cable/satellite news network for which much of the content came via Internet submissions from amateur journalists.

By the early years of the so-called New Millennium, Americans had a multitude of news options from which to choose. For both better and worse, most still relied heavily on mainstream news media, even though many had largely abandoned the traditional "press" format in favor of television or the Internet. Dramatic changes in the news media and in U.S. society since 1965 left many inside and outside of journalism disillusioned.

As they had in 1965, journalists in 2004 joined the rest of America in remaining decidedly split about whether the profession was on the right track. Recent years had seen the journalistic job market diminish, workloads increase, and newsroom salaries decrease. Even so, after a brief decline, journalism schools saw significant enrollment increases in those same years. Still, that did not necessarily mean the number of potential journalists had increased, as many journalism schools had incorporated public relations and sometimes advertising or other disciplines into their curriculums. The 2002–2003 school year saw the largest enrollments ever, almost two-thirds of them women. The percentage of African American students enrolled in undergraduate journalism and mass communication programs in that year was 13.7 percent, the highest ever. In addition, 6.4 percent were Hispanic, 3.2 percent Asian American, 2 percent Native American and 2.3 percent classified as "other." The face of the news media obviously would continue to change.[13]

Despite the many problems and contradictions associated with evolving journalism standards and practices, most Americans continued to see their news media as a vibrant force, a singular "it" rather than a plural "they." Especially in troubled times, many still looked to the press to make sense of events and to play an important role in safeguarding the future of the nation as a whole—assuming journalists managed to save the most important elements of what supporters and critics alike had come to recognize as the American press.

NOTES

1. Wally Dean and Lee Ann Brady, "After 9/11, Has Anything Changed?" Project for Excellence in Journalism Web site, http://www.journalism.org/ resources/research/reports/localTV/2002/postsept11.asp; Samantha Power, *A Problem from Hell: America and the Age of Genocide* (New York: Basic Books, 2002).

2. Tanjev Schultz and Paul S. Voakes, "Prophets of Gloom: Why Do Newspaper Journalists Have So Little Faith in the Future of Newspapers?" *Newspaper Research Journal* 20 (Spring 1999): 23–40.

3. Oceanic explorer Jacques Cousteau's film *The Silent World* won at Cannes in 1956.

4. "State of the News Media" survey results, Project for Excellence in Journalism Web site, http://www.stateofthenewsmedia.org (accessed March 5, 2006).

5. Lawrence K. Grossman, "From Marconi to Murrow to—Drudge?" *Columbia Journalism Review*, July/August 1999.

6. Online News Association Web site, http://www.journalists.org.

7. "Inside the Story of the Invasion of Iraq," *Frontline*, Federal News Service transcript, March 1, 2004. Also see Katie Couric, "In Some Parts of Baghdad, Residents Cheered and Danced in Streets When U.S. Forces Came In," *Dateline*, NBC News transcript, April 9, 2003.

8. Susanne Fengler, "Holding the News Media Accountable: A Study of Media Reporters and Media Critics in the United States," *Journalism & Mass Communication Quarterly* 80 (Winter 2003): 818–832.

9. Arnett's "Operation Tailwind" comments can be heard via audio streaming on the Newseum Web site, http://www.newseum.org/warstories/interviews/ mp3/journalists/bio.asp?ID=24.

10. Frank Rich, "Finally Porn Does Prime Time," *New York Times*, July 27, 2003; Clear Channel Communications Web site, http://www.clearchannel.com (accessed March 5, 2006).

11. Robert G. Picard, "U.S. Newspaper Ad Revenue Shows Consistent Growth," *Newspaper Research Journal* 23 (Fall 2002): 21–33.

12. Marilyn Greenwald and Joseph Bernt, eds., *The Big Chill: Investigative Reporting in the Current Media Environment* (Ames, Iowa: Iowa State University, 2000).

13. "State of the News Media" survey results; Lee B. Becker, Tudor Vlad, Jisu Huh, and Nancy R. Macy, "Annual Enrollment Report: Graduate and Undergraduate Enrollments Increase Sharply," *Journalism & Mass Communication Educator* 58 (Autumn 2003): 273–300.

Bibliographic Essay

Like American journalism, the study of American history changed in significant ways in the 1960s and 1970s. An influx of women and minorities into both professions, combined with a society in turmoil and a growing distrust of established institutions, meant that both journalism and history became more complicated, and in some respects more fragmented. "New journalism" and various forms of "new history" helped redefine what topics were worth discussing, and how to discuss them. Radical journalists and "radical historians" pushed the boundaries further and faster than either discipline had seen before. More historians began to devote their studies to smaller pieces of history, such as individual groups or communities or newspapers. At the same time, historians and journalists alike continued to try to understand an increasingly complicated world (either the world of the past or that of the present), and then to try to use uncomplicated ways to enlighten the unsettled masses. A desire among members of both groups for simple prose, and even for simple answers, is understandable. After all, their readers also wanted straightforward answers, as demonstrated by one frustrated book reviewer: "One can't read the book and not come away with a deep sense of how much our sense of the past has been hopelessly muddled by the internal imperatives of the profession. It is by endless cycles of cutting and slashing, revising and revisioning, 'neo'ing and 'post'ing, interrogating and all the rest of the tedious professional jargon, that reputations are made, empires are built, careers are jumpstarted, and—not to put too fine a point on it—tenure is won and promotion secured. The dynamic of revisionism, a dynamic of churning, incessant

novelty, serves the cause of academic careerism even more than it does
the cause of political correctness. And such careerism and specialization
has the effect of stamping out an appreciative sense of the past."[1]

Still, if Americans outside of academia lost any of their appreciation of
the past, probably they did so more because of changes in journalism,
which they saw every day, than because of changes in historiography
(other facts such as television, education, fascinating technological
advances, and other societal changes likely also contributed to any
such loss). Far more than historians, journalists showed most Americans
that the "great men" of society were not necessarily great in all ways.
Both journalism and history began showing more often that people
worth writing about were not necessarily men, either. In fact, historiographical changes probably expanded the potential audience. More than
ever before, women and members of various minorities saw their own
stories being told, giving them a stronger connection with the discipline.
Of course, outside of the academy probably few readers consciously
noticed the shifting nature of historiography, a shift perhaps best regis-
tered through the new topics apparent in journal articles and conference
papers. Besides, neither more traditional forms of historiography nor
more traditional forms of journalism disappeared, and readers continued to find broad, readable histories. Most historians recognized an
increasing diversity of perspectives in historical scholarship to be
healthy for the profession as a whole, and that, as historian Lawrence
Levine has pointed out, new areas of study should expand knowledge
rather than restricting it.[2]

Shorter time periods, individual communities, or previously unknown
people may have interested fewer mainstream readers than did broader
histories. If so, those readers may have read fewer works by academic
historians and turned more often to popular historians such as celebrity
biographers, or even to novelists in some cases. Increasingly they also
could turn to other media. Television became a force for news in the
1960s, and soon it also provided Americans with much of their non-
academic historical information. Public television provided informative
history programming, and later the cable explosion brought the History
Channel and the Biography Channel and numerous other networks that
devoted at least part of their time to history. Later, the Internet offered an
ever-expanding multitude of choices, however wildly inconsistent in
their reliability.

Those various non-academic choices did not necessarily decrease
Americans' overall interest in history. What less-scholarly historians
lacked in academic rigor, they sometimes made up for in enthusiasm
and accessibility—becoming recent descendants of the nineteenth-
century "amateur" historians, who, as historian James Startt has noted,
offered writing with "a powerful appeal that later professional historians

would seldom, if ever, match. ...Nor did they neglect the 'story' in 'history.' "[3] Sometimes professional historians have lost themselves in academic minutia or debates about the right way to present information. That may have become more common during the 1970s, apparently prompting one-time *Journalism History* editor Tom Reilly to comment, "Ironically, it seems that many productive people have spent more time on discussing how to write history than on writing history."[4]

In trying to deal with the new complications of their respective worlds, both historians and journalists sometimes fell into the trap of offering overly simplistic answers, despite the unfortunate truth that neither ever could be entirely sure they were right. "It would be unrealistic for any audience to expect the full truth about a segment of the past from historians and arrogant of them to think they had discovered it," states a leading manual of communication history.[5] Faced with complex issues when researching and telling their stories, both historians and journalists sometimes fall back on customary artificial structures such as story "frames" or academic theories. For academics, the theories may be relatively narrow, often stemming from theories of contemporary mass communication developed for such areas as media management or sociology, or they may develop into broadly recognized "schools." American historical research has gone through a number of such schools, discussed by many writers including the authors of earlier volumes in this *History of American Journalism* series. James Startt and David Sloan identify six major schools of interpretation (with more recent subgroups), beginning with the nineteenth-century Nationalist School and ending with the Cultural School, which became noteworthy in the mid-twentieth century. Michael Emery and others also included a "New Left School" that began in the 1960s. Typically a group of historians who worked in similar ways became identified with one of the historical schools that persisted for a time and then to some degree (though not always entirely) faded away as another school gained credibility. In fact, looking back at such phenomena as the rise and fall of various schools of historical interpretation, or at the willingness with which historians and journalists leapt into the production of propaganda during World War I, one might well conclude that historical "synthesis," or substantial agreement of any kind, has been achieved more often when a group of writers was temporarily wrong, rather than when they were right.[6]

Historians associated with each of the various historical schools wrote histories that covered most of the time periods covered by the *History of American Journalism* series. Most of the schools largely have faded and have less relevance to the period covered by this volume, but a brief discussion of them here might give the reader a sense of how the study and telling of history arrived at its current state (for a more comprehensive view, see Startt and Sloan's *Historical Methods in Mass*

Communication, which provided the basis for this discussion). The eighteenth-century Nationalist School reflected the national Enlightenment ideas about natural rights and progress, and often contained patriotic themes. By the 1830s, Romantic School historians (typically amateur historians who thought of history as a literary art) emphasized narration to tell moving stories about individuals in and outside of the press. Their more recent descendents can be seen with such books as William Shawcross's *Murdock: The Making of a Media Empire* (1992), Porter Bibb's *Ted Turner: It Ain't as Easy as it Looks* (1993), and Bob Edwards's *Edward R. Murrow and the Birth of Broadcast Journalism* (2004). Women drew more attention than in previous years with such books as Marilyn S. Greenwald's *A Woman of the Times: Journalism, Feminism, and the Career of Charlotte Curtis* (1999), Deborah Davis's *Katharine the Great: Katharine Graham and the Washington Post Company* (1987), and Roberta Ostroff's *Fire in the Wind: The Life of Dickey Chapelle* (1991). Killed by a land mine in Vietnam, Chapelle was the first woman war correspondent killed in battle. Innumerable national and local journalists have written autobiographies that also lean toward the romantic (especially, as historian William Huntzicker has pointed out, with war stories). They include Liz Trotta's *Fighting for Air: In the Trenches with Television News* (1991), Peter Arnett's *Live from the Battlefield: From Vietnam to Baghdad—35 Years in the World's War Zones* (1994), Al Neuharth's *Confessions of an S.O.B.* (1989), and Walter Cronkite's *A Reporter's Life* (1996). Other recent tales that might be viewed as related to the Romantic school involve individual incidents in the news, such as *All the President's Men* (1974) by Watergate reporters Carl Bernstein and Bob Woodward or a 2003 discussion of the Enron energy scandal, *24 Days: How Two Wall Street Journal Reporters Uncovered the Lies that Destroyed Faith in Corporate America* by Rebecca Smith and John R. Emshwiller.[7]

The most important historical school of interpretation, because it "has provided the underlying assumptions of most histories of American mass media and continues today as one of the most commonly held perspectives," was the Developmental School.[8] The most important characteristic of this school is its association with the professional development of the press. Studies of this type tended to focus on the evolution of the media, but sometimes separated the press from society and often led to a "whiggish" view that previous events naturally led up to an ever-improving future. Generally positive in their portrayals of the press, they also often reinforced the positive aspects of the journalism as a government watchdog or other social instrument. Startt and Sloan note that many journalism history texts have tended to rely on developmental interpretations. The focus on development can contribute significantly to an understanding of the evolution of press practices, and can remind readers that what seems new may in fact have distant roots. An excellent modern example of the appropriate use of developmental history is John Hartsock's *A History of American Literary Journalism* (2000).

The arrival of the twentieth century brought with it the Progressive School, which typically highlighted struggles between and among various elements in society such as the rich versus the poor. Some histories that clearly hearken back to this approach include *The New Muckrakers* by Leonard Downie Jr. (1976), David Halberstam's *The Powers that Be* (1979), and former underground newspaper editor Abe Peck's *Discovering the Sixties: The Life and Times of the Underground Press* (1991). Progressive historians also often relied on more sociology, quantification, and statistical methods than did their predecessors.

A later but perhaps less enduring approach arrived during the mid-twentieth century with the Consensus School. Like Progressive historians, Consensus writers recognized that events tended to result from a number of complicating factors. Unlike their Progressive counterparts, Consensus historians tended to view those events in positive terms, focusing on factors that unified the media and the nation. Journalists and newspapers were viewed in terms of how they contributed to the American experience, rather than how they may have hindered it. Startt and Sloan point out that Consensus views have been more popular during wartime and other difficult periods for America, with those historians believing "that the media should aid in defeating the threats and solving the problems faced by the nation. To them, history revealed that the media had performed best when they contributed to national unity." In addition, "the enormity of the threat from America's and democracy's enemies fully justified media support of the war effort."[9]

That perspective may be worth more consideration in light of the events of September 11, 2001, and the resulting American "war on terror." Americans, whose opinions of the media had steadily declined since the 1970s, viewed journalists in more positive terms during the 2003 Iraq War—despite the fact that the news media as a whole did a poor job of covering events leading up to the Iraq War and tended to portray the government and the military in overly positive terms while engaging in their own flag-waving. It will be interesting to see if future historians follow the lead of those cheerleading journalists, though more recent journalistic criticisms of the war and the events that led up to it suggest that a more complicated picture will develop.

Most recent American journalism histories probably would be classified as belonging to the Cultural School, which recognized that the news media cannot be separated from the rest of society. Most importantly, those historians see journalism as a part of the society, not as the major societal force. Journalism both reflects and shapes society, though Cultural historians may disagree on how much it reflects and how much it shapes. In short, the world is complicated. One of the effects of this type of history was a decreasing focus on "great men" in major population centers. From Cultural history evolved various splinter areas such as women's history, black history, gay history, and others that previous historians often had considered insignificant or irrelevant.

In most cases placing a history or a writer into a school of interpretation creates a less-than-perfect fit, especially with modern historians. Some might question the need for classification, but especially when dealing with earlier periods recognizing those categories can help modern historians understand their predecessors' relationships to the periods in which they worked, and to help identify potential biases. Most historians now recognize that they and their predecessors were influenced greatly by societal factors of the times in which they wrote. The same was true of the "New Left School" that arrived in the 1960s (or which might be viewed as a harsher, more modern form of Progressivism). Despite constant (and ongoing) concerns among historians about "presentism"—the application of current values to past events—the historical approaches of the period inevitably reflected the turbulence, increased inclusiveness and fragmentation seen elsewhere during those years. Ideological battles were occurring in twentieth-century America, and ideological conflict became a central focus of some histories. As women and various groups gained more power in American society, they also appeared more frequently and more favorably in histories of virtually every period. As society increasingly sought measurable "proof" of claims, and especially as university administrators and some historians became enamored with the so-called social sciences, applied theoretical approaches and quantification became increasingly common in historical research (sometimes contributing to concerns such as the one cited in the opening paragraph of this essay). For the period of American history beginning in 1965, the vast majority of the most modern approaches to history have appeared in journal articles, particularly in *American Journalism, Journalism History*, and sometimes *Journalism & Mass Communication Quarterly*. Many books critical of the recent press that incorporate an ideological perspective also have appeared, with some of those noted below.[10]

One should not assume that a shift from one period or interpretive school to another necessarily improved or devalued the histories that came before, that all recent histories were limited in historical scope, or that they met with widespread approval. Some of the new professional historians, despite new methods and a wider variety of potential source material, were as careless as any of their amateur predecessors. Some went beyond the recognition of bias to seemingly revel in it. Like many of the old histories, many of the new histories still covered wide periods of time or broad terrain and interpreted events with highly readable prose. Going even more broadly than journalism, two relatively recent views of America—Ronald Takaki's *A Different Mirror: A History of Multicultural America* (1993) and especially "radical historian" Howard Zinn's *A People's History of the United States 1492–Present* (1980)—provide well-known and sometimes well-regarded examples. Both looked at now-common events and times with a fresh and controversial eye. For new broad-ranging journalism histories, readers could turn to the Cultural approach of Mitchell Stephens's *A History of News from the Drum to the Satellite* (1988), Hiley H. Ward's *Mainstreams of American Media History* (1997), or *Voices of a Nation: A History of Mass Media in the United States*, a fairly standard 1989 textbook in which authors Jean Folkerts and Dwight L. Teeter Jr. tried to give more emphasis to women and minorities.

Besides a willingness to take on jobs they can never hope to perfect, good historians and good journalists tend to share a number of other characteristics, perhaps chief among them innate curiosity, healthy skepticism, and a love of language. Both historians and journalists recognize and sometimes agonize over the fact that no story is as complete as it might be if only the writer had more time, more resources, more pages or inches for more words, or more depth of understanding. Members of the press and historians both try to tell stories in interesting ways, recognizing that most readers care less about the issue than does the writer, and perhaps less than they should. Journalists and historians publish their work proudly and put their names (and sometimes their faces) on it, despite the fact that they are bound to make potentially embarrassing mistakes. Some of the more egregious errors immediately are recognized as humiliating folly, while others help perpetuate myth and falsehood by going undiscovered for long periods. Cut-and-paste Web versions of those errors fly around the world in seconds, thanks to the Internet. In that ethereal world, the errors multiply like the heads of Hydra and never completely die. Despite their inevitability, the errors may harm the reputation of not just the writer, but of the writer's profession as a whole.

Historians and oftentimes members of the press increase the likelihood for error because they do much more than simply report random events. They try to interpret those events in a way that makes sense for readers, identifying and exploring trends and noteworthy events. By focusing on the most interesting rather than on the typical, both may distort the larger picture, while at the same time normalizing the sensational. In becoming a specialist, the writer may conflate the importance of his or her own topic area, whether a historical period, a social movement, or a journalistic beat. Those who study and write about things important to them personally (and one might wonder why, given a choice, they would write about anything else) face accusations of further bias, often from others in the same profession whose biases lie elsewhere. That is something historians and journalists have shared in recent years: an increased willingness to examine the perceived problems of their professions, and to air disparagements to the world at large. Especially when considered from outside the profession, the criticism may increase perceptions of weakness within the discipline. Yet criticism undoubtedly makes both professions stronger in the long run, and is absolutely necessary. As James Startt has noted, "As historians we think seriously about history more than most people do, but not more than we should."[11]

Despite occasional departures into pseudo-science or propaganda, both disciplines generally have shifted from believing in a mythical ideal of objectivity (what historian Peter Novick called "that noble dream") to recent desires for fairness, balance, and plausibility—aims perhaps less satisfying at some level than final and complete objective truth, but goals that seem more attainable. Meanwhile, criticisms from outside persist, aggravated by the fact that neither journalists nor historians have been particularly good at explaining their professions to readers. Political conservatives complain about liberal bias in the news media and in academia, citing polls in which journalists and professors tend to identify themselves as more liberal than most other Americans. Political liberals complain about a conservative bias, pointing out that most sources and "the bosses" (publishers and university administrators) still tend to be more conservative middle-aged white males, and arguing that powerful political, corporate, and financial influences force media and academic institutions to help maintain a conservative societal status quo.[12]

In addition to the problems common to those who study history from other perspectives, journalism historians face other concerns. "Communication" departments have supplanted journalism programs, bringing different priorities and different kinds of students. News professionals and students alike want journalism degrees to be "practical" in an immediately obvious sense, emphasizing technical skills over liberal arts courses. New technology has become increasingly important, and many departments have de-emphasized or eliminated history courses. A loss of history classes leads to a decreasing number of historians in both the short term and the long term: Academics end up having to devote their efforts to areas more appreciated by administrators, and potential future historians fail to get the exposure to history that would trigger their own interest. Where history classes remain, the increasing complexity of the discipline complicates decisions about what to cover, and how best to do so.

Some might argue that students interested in history have another obvious option if media history courses are cut, in that those students can take classes from what some refer to as "the real historians." However, traditional historians have their own complexities and biases to deal with, and many historians seem to have little use for the media (just as, equally unfortunately, many journalists seem to have little regard for history). Aware that the press of the past often fails miserably as a reliable source of the truth, some historians seem to shy away from it altogether. In doing so, they fail to consider related issues. For example, if newspapers made mistakes or even overtly lied, readers may have believed the faulty information and acted as if it were true. Journalists and their readers obviously had reasons for their actions, and those reasons and actions influenced history. A number of writers have demonstrated obvious cases in which the media had a social impact. "Mainstream American history is often simplistic, even naïve in its understanding and portrayal of mass communication. In fact, few historians look at the *process* at all," journalism historian David Paul Nord wrote more than two decades ago. Problems still exist, though the interaction among various types of historians has improved considerably. Richard Kielbowicz notes several noteworthy examples of "real" historians taking journalism seriously.[13]

On the other hand, the history of journalism is unique and worthy of study for its own sake, and for how it relates to other parts of the discipline of mass communication. Anyone who would suggest that communication students should turn to the history department for a deeper understanding of their own discipline also should be prepared, it seems, to see other communication-related topics handled elsewhere: perhaps writing and editing in the English department, research from the social sciences, media management and advertising in the business school, photography and page design from the art department, interviewing from the counseling program and new technology in the computer science department.

Admittedly, even some of its most noteworthy practitioners have complained that journalism historians sometimes excessively credit or blame the media. Though most cultural historians recognized that one cannot understand the journalism of a period without social and political context, critics complain that too many journalism historians unjustifiably assume, or let their readers assume, that the media significantly affected their society or accurately reflected it. "The importance of journalism, relative to other factors in human affairs, is to be demonstrated, not assumed," argues media historian Michael Schudson. "It is all too common to find this forgotten and the premise of the research becomes its conclusions."[14] The more journalism historians know about American history at large, the stronger their own histories are likely to be. Still, it seems that some of those who complain about media-centered history overlook how much America has become a media-centered society, and how the news and entertainment media overlap. That interaction and pervasiveness may be relatively recent, but they definitely factor into the years discussed by this book. The variations in media and new examinations of the societal effects should be considered by historians working since at least the 1960s and definitely by any historian working after the arrival of cable television and the Internet. Any prospective historian who intends to study the late twentieth century would benefit from studying media literacy and media criticism in addition to the usual history, historiography, and writing classes (in fact, many social critics suggest that democracy would benefit if all Americans studied media literacy).

Of course, not every historian agrees that the period involved with this volume, starting in the 1960s, even constitutes "history." Admittedly, most of the events involved occurred too recently for much of the reflection that should go into the "social construction" that comprises any history. One advantage, however, may be the opportunity to construct some of the history while the pieces are still in place. Not surprisingly, fewer histories of this period are available than with earlier years, and the vast majority of the recent histories come in small pieces such as journal articles, essays, reflections in trade publications, and book chapters. In some circumstances, each of those may prove useful for the historian seeking to put the late-twentieth-century news media in context. Many other sources also exist. While the period may so far be the least-studied by American historians, improvements in education and media technology contribute to the fact that the late twentieth century probably is the one most studied by social critics of all stripes (including the press, which at times attempted to critically study itself). The sources of information now available range from serious sociological and historical research journals to trade journals and magazines to "instant books" and frothy popular "blogs" that combine self-centered navel-gazing, voyeurism, and an exhibitionistic desire for attention.

Television news transcripts are available through Lexis/Nexis and through the Vanderbilt Television News Archive. The Vanderbilt archive boasts a collection of more than 30,000 individual network broadcasts available for loan, and institutional subscribers can access broadcasts online. The Internet has made available a wealth of useful information, along with a deluge of misleading and useless material. It becomes increasingly important for researchers to learn to evaluate Web information, and, because errors frequently spread quickly to other Internet sources, to carefully verify that information. The latest edition of Startt and Sloan's *Historical Methods in Mass Communication* devotes a chapter to Internet history sources and their use, and provides an excellent bibliography of Internet and traditional sources for the student learning to "do history" or for historians seeking various sources. The Poynter Institute and some universities also maintain regularly updated online bibliographies of journalism history sources.[15]

Technological advances have made oral histories a valuable resource. Several universities and historical societies now maintain media-related oral history collections. An invaluable resource for anyone wanting to hear the voices of journalists and former journalists is a list developed by James Startt for the American Journalism Historians Association. One notable oral history source, particularly relevant to some of the key issues discussed in this volume, is the Washington Press Club Foundation's "Women in Journalism" project. More than sixty women journalists were interviewed for the project, and transcripts of most of those interviews can be accessed via the Internet.[16]

More women and minorities also appeared in history books, some of which focused on their struggles and gains. Those books included Judith Marlane's *Women in Television News Revisited* (1999), Marion Marzolf's *Up From the Footnote: A History of Women Journalists* (1977) and *Taking Their Place: A Documentary History of Women and Journalism* by Maurine Beasley and Sheila J. Gibbons (1993), Carolyn Martindale's *The White Press and Black America* (1986), and J. Fred MacDonald's *Blacks and White TV: African Americans in Television Since 1948* (1992).

The historian who wanted to know more about individual journalists had numerous biographies from which to choose, and in 1986 William H. Taft offered his *Encyclopedia of Twentieth-Century Journalists*, which included brief sketches of hundreds of reporters and editors.

Other works discussed various specific types of media, such as Robert J. Glessing's *The Underground Press in America* (from 1971 and not overly historical because the movement was still underway), Michael D. Murray's *Encyclopedia of Television News* (1999), Lauren Kessler's *The Press: Alternative Journalism in American History* (1994), *The Conservative Press in Twentieth-Century America* by Ronald Lora and William Henry Longton (1999), and Wm. David Sloan's *Media and Religion in American History* (2000) (though the latter three works are devoted largely to events before 1965).

Many of the journalism histories related to the brief period since 1965 have been stories about news organizations or their product. They include Kevin Michael McAuliffe's *The Great American Newspaper: The Rise and Fall of the Village Voice* (1978), Howard Bray's *The Pillars of the Post: The Making of a News Empire in Washington* (1980), Robert F. Keeler's *Newsday: A Candid History of the Respectable Tabloid* (1990), Hank Whittemore's *CNN: The Inside Story* (1990), and *Nightline: History in the Making and the Making of Television* by Ted Koppel and Kyle Gibson (1996). Several television news histories have appeared, including *Stay Tuned: A Concise History of American Broadcasting* by Christopher Sterling and John M. Kittross (1978), Erik Barnouw's *Tube of Plenty: The Evolution of American Television* (1975, later revised at least twice), and J. Fred MacDonald's *One Nation Under Television: The Rise and Decline of Network TV* (1990).

Business aspects played a huge role in the story of journalism since 1965 and many books (most of them not histories, but of value to historians studying the period) discussed pluses and minuses of consolidation and corporatization, beginning with Ben H. Bagdikian's important 1983 book *The Media Monopoly*. Others include David Demers's *The Menace of the Corporate Newspaper: Fact or Fiction?* (1996), Erik Barnow's *Conglomerates and the Media* (1997), James D. Squires's *Read All About It! The Corporate Takeover of America's Newspapers* (1993), Richard McCord's *The Chain Gang: One Newspaper versus the Gannett Empire* (2001), *The Business of Media: Corporate Media and the Public Interest* by David Croteau and William Hoynes (2001), and *Joint Operating Agreements: The Newspaper Preservation Act and Its Application* by John C. Busterna and Robert G. Picard (1993), which includes a history of the act and of JOAs.

Political leaders and wars from Vietnam to Iraq redefined the relationship between journalists and the government. Histories that focused on the relationship between the press and presidents, especially Richard Nixon and Ronald Reagan, included William Porter's *Assault on the Media: The Nixon Years* (1976), Louis W. Liebovich's *Richard Nixon, Watergate, and the Press: A Historical Perspective* (2003) and *The Press and the Presidency: Myths and Mindsets from Kennedy to Election 2000* (2001), Richard Curry's *Freedom at Risk: Secrecy, Censorship, and Repression in the 1980s* (1988), Mark Hertsgaard's *On Bended Knee: The Press and the Reagan Presidency* (1988), and *The Press and the Presidency: From George Washington to Ronald Reagan* by John Tebbel and Sarah Miles Watts (1985). Later came Joseph Hayden's *Covering Clinton: The President and the Press in the 1990s* (2001). War examples include Peter Braestrup's *Battle Lines: Report of the Twentieth Century Fund Task Force on the Military and the Media* (1985), which discusses press coverage and press-military relationship of all U.S. wars through Grenada, Daniel C. Hallin's, *The "Uncensored War": The Media and Vietnam* (1989), William M. Hammond's *Reporting Vietnam: Media & Military at War* (1998), John R. MacArthur's, *Second Front: Censorship and Propaganda in the Gulf War* (1992), Hedrick Smith's *The Media and the Gulf War: The Press and Democracy in Wartime* (1992), and *The Iraq War Reader: History, Documents, Opinions* by Micah L. Sifry and Christopher Cerf (2003).

The rise and partial fall of two key movements, investigative journalism and civic journalism, provided some writers with subject matter, though both seem to provide ripe possibilities for future historians. Among the books related to investigative journalism are *Custodians of Conscience: Investigative Journalism and Public Virtue* by James S. Ettema and Theodore L. Glasser (1998), which includes investigative reporters' "tales from the front," and Margaret H. DeFleur's *Computer-Assisted Investigative Reporting: Development and Methodology* (1997). Occasionally the histories essentially are book-length reprints of what a newspaper published, such as The Pentagon Papers from the *New York Times* (1971) or

America: What Went Wrong by Pulitzer Prize-winning reporters Donald L. Barlett and James B. Steele (1992). Works about civic journalism include Don H. Corrigan's *The Public Journalism Movement in America: Evangelists in the Newsroom* (1999) and *Twilight of Press Freedom: The Rise of People's Journalism* by John C. Merrill, Peter J. Gade, and Frederick R. Blevens (2001).

As noted in this volume, many authors have criticized the press for its failures. Besides the books that focus on more specific problems such as business aspects of the media, those criticisms include James Fallows's *Breaking the News: How the Media Undermine American Democracy* (1997), Michael Janeway's *Republic of Denial: Press, Politics, and Public Life* (1999), Thomas Patterson's *Out of Order* (1994), Lance Bennett's *News: The Politics of Illusion* (1988), Richard Davis's *The Press and American Politics: The New Mediator* (1996), and Jack Fuller's *News Values: Ideas for an Information Age* (1996).

Some of the most exciting recent histories of American journalism examine the ideas that drive the press. Many of the works mentioned above at least touch on those ideas. Others that in interesting ways explore those philosophical aspects and how they relate to society include Michael Schudson's *The Power of News* (1995) and *The Significance of the Media in American History* (1994) by Startt and Sloan. It is unfortunate that as journalism historians have worked more diligently to consider culture and society in their analyses, the people who make up society often have become more separated from historians and from American journalism. The news media have drawn a great deal of criticism since 1965, much of it warranted, more from political and sociological perspectives than from historians. Praise for the press—some of which also is well-deserved—has been less common, with even many working journalists losing faith in their profession. Perhaps a deeper examination by historians of the roles and ideas of journalism, combined with intriguing stories and writing styles that appeal even to those outside of academia, will help both journalists and historians gain stature within the American society they try to serve.

NOTES

1. Review by anonymous reviewer listed as "a reader from the library," critiquing Peter Novick's *That Noble Dream: The "Objectivity Question" and the American Historical Profession*, for Amazon.com, posted October 26, 2003, accessed at http://www.amazon.com/exec/obidos/tg/detail/-/0521343283/102-0259578-7809731?v=glance&vi=customer-reviews (accessed March 5, 2006). Also see Jean Folkerts and Stephen Lacy, "Journalism History Writing, 1975–1983," Journalism Quarterly 62 (Autumn 1985): 585-588; Jonathon Wiener, "Radical Historians and the Crisis in American History, 1959-1980," *Journal of American History* 76 (September 1989): 399–434; Ronald Takaki, *A Different*

Mirror: A History of Multicultural America (Boston: Little, Brown and Company, 1993).

2. Lawrence Levine, *The Unpredictable Past: Explorations in American Cultural History.* (New York: Oxford University, 1993).

3. James Startt, "Historiography and the Media Historian," *American Journalism* 10 (Summer/Fall 1993): 17–25.

4. Quoted in Michael Emery, "The Writing of American Journalism History," *Journalism History* 10 (Autumn/Winter 1983): 38–43.

5. James Startt and Wm. David Sloan, *Historical Methods in Mass Communication* (Northport, Ala.: Vision Press, 2003).

6. Ibid.; Emery, "The Writing of American Journalism History"; Wm. David Sloan and Julie Hedgepeth Williams, *The Early American Press, 1690–1783* (Westport, Conn.: Greenwood, 1994); Carol Sue Humphrey, *The Press of the Young Republic, 1783–1833* (Westport, Conn.: Greenwood, 1996); William E. Huntzicker, *The Popular Press, 1833–1865* (Westport, Conn.: Greenwood, 1999).

7. Startt and Sloan, *Historical Methods*; Huntzicker, *The Popular Press.*

8. Startt and Sloan, *Historical Methods.*

9. Ibid.

10. Sloan and Williams, *The Early American Press*; Emery, "The Writing of American Journalism History"; Huntzicker, *The Popular Press.*

11. James Startt, "The Historiographical Tradition in 20th Century America," 1998 American Journalism Historians Association presidential address printed in *American Journalism* 16 (Winter 1999): 105–131.

12. Peter Novick, *That Noble Dream: The "Objectivity Question" and the American Historical Profession* (New York: Cambridge University Press, 1988).

13. Richard B. Kielbowicz, "On Making Connections with Outside Subfields," *American Journalism* 10 (Summer/Fall 1993): 30–37.

14. Michael Schudson, "Toward a Troubleshooting Manual for Journalism History," a*Journalism & Mass Communication Quarterly* 74 (Autumn 1997): 463–476.

15. Vanderbilt Television News Archive Web site, http://tvnews.vanderbilt. edu; Startt and Sloan, *Historical Methods*; Poynter Institute Web page, http:// www.poynter.org/content/content_view.asp?id=1199.

16. James Startt, *Oral Histories Relating to Journalism History*, 2nd ed. American Journalism Historians Association, available online at http://www.elon.edu/ dcopeland/ajha/oralhistory.htm (accessed March 5, 2006); Washington Press Club Foundation, Women in Journalism Oral History Project, Washington Press Club Foundation, Washington, D.C., transcripts available online at http://npc.press.org/wpforal/ohhome.htm (accessed March 5, 2006).

Sources

UNPUBLISHED PAPERS AND DOCUMENTS

ABC News transcripts, via LexisNexis™.

American Society of Newspaper Editors convention proceedings, State Historical Society of Wisconsin, Madison.

Associated Press Managing Editors Association records, State Historical Society of Wisconsin, Madison.

California journalists' oral histories, from the California State University, Fullerton, Oral History Program.

California journalists' oral histories, from the Southern California Journalism Oral History Project, California State University, Northridge.

CBS News transcripts, via LexisNexis™.

Centers for Disease Control and Prevention *HIV/AIDS Surveillance Report 2002*.

CNBC News transcripts, via LexisNexis™.

CNN News transcripts, via LexisNexis™.

Day, Samuel H. Interviews by author.

Federal Information Systems Corporation transcripts, via LexisNexis™.

Federal News Service transcripts, via LexisNexis™.

MSNBC news transcripts, via LexisNexis™.

National Public Radio transcripts, via LexisNexis™.

NBC New transcripts, via LexisNexis™.

Samuel H. Day papers, State Historical Society of Wisconsin, Madison.

States News Service, via LexisNexis™.

Vanderbilt News Archives, Vanderbilt University, Nashville.

Washington Press Club Foundation, Women in Journalism Oral History Project, Washington Press Club Foundation, Washington, D.C.

PUBLISHED PAPERS, MEMOIRS, DIARIES, AND DOCUMENTS

Arnett, Peter. *Live from the Battlefield: From Vietnam to Baghdad—35 Years in the World's War Zones*. New York: Simon & Schuster, 1994.

Bernstein, Carl and Bob Woodward. *All the President's Men*. New York: Simon & Schuster, 1974.

Braestrup, Peter. *Battle Lines: Report of the Twentieth Century Fund Task Force on the Military and the Media*. New York: Priority Press, 1985.

Buzenberg, Susan, and Bill Buzenberg, eds., *Salant, CBS, and the Battle for the Soul of Broadcast Journalism: The Memoirs of Richard S. Salant*. Boulder, Colo.: Westview, 1999.

Chase, Harold W. and Allen H. Lerman, eds., *Kennedy and the Press: The News Conferences*. New York: Thomas Y. Crowell, 1965.

Cronkite, Walter. *A Reporter's Life*. New York: Alfred A. Knopf, 1996.

DeVolpi, A., G.E. Marsh, T.A. Postol, and G.S. Stanford. *Born Secret: The H-Bomb, the* Progressive *Case, and National Security*. New York: Pergamon, 1981.

Editorials on File. New York: Facts on File, various years.

Edwards, Lee, ed., *Our Times: The Washington Times 1982–2002*. Washington, D.C.: Regnery Publishing, 2002.

Ellerbee, Linda. *And So It Goes: Adventure in Television News*. New York: G.P. Putnam's Sons, 1986.

Gilbert, Allison, Phil Hirshkorn, Melinda Murphy, Robyn Walensky, and Mitchell Stephens, eds., *Covering Catastrophe: Broadcast Journalists Report September 11*. Chicago: Bonus Books, 2002.

Hunter-Gault, Charlayne. *In My Place*. New York: Farrar, Straus & Giroux, 1992.

King, Larry, and Mark Stencel. *On the Line: The New Road to the White House*. New York: Harcourt Brace & Company, 1993.

Koppel, Ted and Kyle Gibson. *Nightline: History in the Making and the Making of Television*. New York: Times Books, 1996.

Laurence, John. *The Cat from Hue: A Vietnam War Story*. New York: Public Affairs, 2002.

Library of America. *Reporting Vietnam: American Journalism 1959–1975*. New York: Library of America, 1998.

McCord, Richard. *The Chain Gang: One Newspaper versus the Gannett Empire*. Columbia, Mo.: University of Missouri, 2001.

McDonald, Lucile, with Richard McDonald. *A Foot in the Door: The Reminiscences of Lucile McDonald*. Pullman, Wash.: Washington State University Press, 1995.

Morland, Howard. *The Secret That Exploded*. New York: Random House, 1981.

National News Council. *An Open Press*. New York: National News Council, 1977.

Neuharth, Al. *Confessions of an S.O.B.* New York: Doubleday, 1989.

New York Times. The Pentagon Papers. New York: Bantam, 1971.

Poynter Institute, ed., *September 11, 2001*. Kansas City, Mo.: Andrews McMeel Publishing, 2001.

Rather, Dan. *The Camera Never Blinks: Adventures of a TV Journalist*. New York: William Morrow, 1977.

Sifry, Micah L. and Christopher Cerf, eds., *The Iraq War Reader: History, Documents, Opinions*. New York: Touchstone, 2003.

Sims, Norman, ed., *The Literary Journalists*. New York: Ballantine, 1984.

Trotta, Liz. *Fighting for Air: In the Trenches with Television News*. New York: Simon & Schuster, 1991.

Twentieth Century Fund Task Force. *A Free and Responsive Press*. New York: Twentieth Century Fund, 1973.

Wolfe, Tom. *The New Journalism*. New York: Harper & Row, 1973.

Woodward, Bob and Carl Bernstein. *The Final Days*. New York: Avon Books, 1976.

NEWSPAPERS AND MAGAZINES

Albuquerque Tribune
Atlanta Journal and Constitution
Berkeley Barb
Boise (Idaho) *Intermountain Express*
Boston Globe
Business Week
Cape Cod (Massachusetts*) Times*
Chicago Tribune
Christian Science Monitor
Helping Hand (Mountain Home Air Force Base, Idaho)
Lewiston (Idaho) *Morning Tribune*
Life
Los Angeles Free Press
Los Angeles Times
Ms.
New Republic
New York Daily News
New York Post
New York Times
Newsweek
Nieman Reports
Palm Beach (Florida) *Post*
Pittsburgh Post-Gazette
Playboy
Portland Oregonian
The Progressive
Rocky Mountain News (Denver)
San Diego Union-Tribune
San Francisco Bay Guardian
San Francisco Chronicle
St. Louis Post-Dispatch
St. Petersburg (Florida) *Times*
Seattle Post-Intelligencer
Seattle Times
Spokane (Washington) *Spokesman-Review*
Syracuse Post-Standard
Texas Observer
Time
Toledo Blade

USA Today
U.S. News and World Report
Ventura County (California) *Star*
Village Voice
Wall Street Journal
Washington Post
Washington Times

TRADE PUBLICATIONS AND JOURNALS

American Journalism
American Journalism Review
Brill's Content
Broadcasting
Columbia Journalism Review
Editor & Publisher
Electronic Journal of the U.S. Information Agency
Gannett Center Journal
Journal of Mass Media Ethics
Journalism History
Journalism & Mass Communication Educator
Journalism & Mass Communication Monographs
Journalism & Mass Communication Quarterly
Mass Comm Review
Masthead
Media Studies Journal
News Media and the Law
Newspaper Research Journal
Online Journalism Review
Quill

INTERNET SOURCES

Accuracy in Media Web site, http://www.aim.org.
Advanced Television Systems Committee Web site, http://www.atsc.org/
    memberpr/WRALDVCP.htm.
American Civil Liberties Union Web site, http://www.aclu.org.
American Society of Newspaper Editors Web site, http://www.asne.org.
Associated Press Web site, http://www.ap.org.
Association Women in Communications Web site, http://www.womcom.org.
Augusta Chronicle Web site, http://www.augustachronicle.com.
BBC Online Network, http://news.bbc.co.uk.
Bureau of Labor Statistics Web site, http://www.bls.gov.
CBS News Web site, http://www.cbsnews.com.
Center for Media and Public Affairs Web site, http://www.cmpa.com.
Clear Channel Communications Web site, http://www.clearchannel.com.
CNN Web site, http://cnn.com.
Committee of Concerned Journalists/Project for Excellence in Journalism Web
    site, http://www.journalism.org.

Consumer Federation of American Web site, http://www.consumerfed.org.

Drudge Report Web site, http://www.drudgereport.com.

Fairness and Accuracy in Reporting Web site, http://www.fair.org.

Howe, Walt. "A Brief History of the Internet," http://www.walthowe.com/navnet/history.html.

International Media and Democracy Project Web site, http://www.imdp.org.

Investigative Reporters and Editors Web site, http://www.ire.org.

'Lectric Law Library Web site, http://www.lectlaw.com.

Media History Project Web site, University of Minnesota, http://www.mediahistory.umn.edu/index2.html.

Media Research Center Web site, http://www.mediaresearch.org.

National Press Photographers Association Web site, http://www.nppa.org.

Newseum Web site, http://www.newseum.org.

off our backs Web site, http://www.igc.org/oob.

Online News Association Web site, http://www.journalists.org.

Pew Center for Public Journalism Web site, http://www.pewcenter.org.

Poynter Intitute Web site, http://poynter.org.

Project Censored Web site, http://www.projectcensored.org.

Public Broadcasting System Web site, http://www.pbs.org.

Public Journalism Network Web site, http://www.pjnet.org.

Pulitzer Prize Web site, http://www.pulitzer.org.

"Remembering the Lost." *Newsday* Internet database, http://www.newsday.com/news/ny-victimsdatabase.framedurl.

Robert C. Maynard Institute for Journalism Education Web site, http://www.maynardije.org.

September 11 News Web site, http://www.september11news.com.

Village Voice Web site, http://www.villagevoice.com.

We the People Wisconsin Web site, http://www.wtpeople.com.

Winston Churchill Home Page, maintained by the Churchill Centre and Societies, http://www.winstonchurchill.org.

World Wide Web Consortium Web site, http://www.w3.org.

SELECTED SECONDARY SOURCES

Abelman, Robert. "News on The 700 Club: The Cycle of Religious Activism," *Journalism Quarterly* 71 (Winter 1994): 887–892.

Adler, Ruth, ed., *The Working Press.* New York: Bantam, 1970.

Alterman, Eric. *What Liberal Media? The Truth about Bias and the News.* New York: Basic Books, 2003.

Altschull, J. Herbert. *From Milton to McLuhan: The Ideas behind American Journalism.* New York: Longman, 1990.

Anderson, Douglas A., and Marianne Murdock. "Effects of Communication Law Decisions on Daily Newspaper Editors," *Journalism Quarterly* 58 (Winter 1981): 525–528, 534.

Anderson, Douglas A., Joe W. Milner, and Mary-Lou Galician. "How Editors View Legal Issues and the Rehnquist Court," *Journalism Quarterly* 65 (Summer 1988): 294–298.

Ashley, Laura, and Beth Olson. "Constructing Reality: Print Media's Framing of the Women's Movement, 1966 to 1986," *Journalism & Mass Communication Quarterly* 75 (Summer 1998): 263–277.

Associated Press. *The Associated Press Stylebook and Libel Manual*. New York: Associated Press, 1977.

Atwater, Tony, and Norma F. Green. "News Sources in Network Coverage of International Terrorism," *Journalism Quarterly* 65 (Winter 1988): 967–971.

Aucoin, James. "The Early Years of IRE: The Evolution of Modern Investigative Journalism," *American Journalism* 12 (Winter 1995): 425–443.

———. "The Re-emergence of American Investigative Journalism 1960–1975," *Journalism History* 21 (1995): 3–15.

Auman, Ann. "Design Desks: Why are More and More Newspapers Adopting Them?" *Newspaper Research Journal* 15 (Spring 1994): 116–127.

Bagdikian, Ben H. *The Media Monopoly*. Boston: Beacon, 1983.

Bain, Chic, and David H. Weaver. "Readers' Reactions to Newspaper Design," *Newspaper Research Journal* 1 (November 1979): 48–59.

Baldwin, Thomas F., Marianne Barrett, and Benjamin Bates. "Influence of Cable on Television News Audiences," *Journalism Quarterly* 69 (Fall 1992): 651–658.

Barlett, Donald L., and James B. Steele. *America: What Went Wrong?* Kansas City: Andrews and McMeel, 1992.

Barnouw, Erik. *Tube of Plenty: The Evolution of American Television, 2nd Rev. ed.* New York: Oxford University, 1990.

Barnouw, Erik, et al. *Conglomerates and the Media*. New York: New Press, 1997.

Beasley, Maurine H., and Sheila J. Gibbons. *Taking Their Place: A Documentary History of Women and Journalism*. Washington, D.C.: American University Press, 1993.

Becker, Lee B., Vernon A. Stone, and Joseph D. Graf. "Journalism Labor Force Supply and Demand: Is Oversupply an Explanation for Low Wages?" *Journalism and Mass Communication Quarterly* 73 (Autumn 1996): 519–533.

Becker, Lee B., Tudor Vlad, Jisu Huh, and Nancy R. Macy. "Annual Enrollment Report: Graduate and Undergraduate Enrollments Increase Sharply," *Journalism & Mass Communication Educator* 58 (Autumn 2003): 273–300.

Bennett, W. Lance. *News: The Politics of Illusion*, 2nd ed. New York: Longman, 1988.

Bernt, Joseph P., Frank E. Fee, Jacqueline Gifford, and Guido H. Stempel III. "How Well Can Editors Predict Reader Interest in News?" *Newspaper Research Journal* 21 (Spring 2000): 2–10.

Bibb, Porter. *Ted Turner: It Ain't as Easy as it Looks*. New York: Crown, 1993.

Bird, S. Elizabeth. "Newspaper Editors' Attitudes Reflect Ethical Doubt on Surreptitious Reporting," *Journalism Quarterly* 62 (Summer 1985): 284–288.

Blanchard, Robert. *Images of a Free Press*. Chicago: University of Chicago, 1991.

Blankenburg, William B. "Predicting Newspaper Circulation after Consolidation," *Journalism Quarterly* 64 (Summer/Autumn 1987): 585–587;

Bogart, Leo. *Press and Public: Who Reads What, When, Where, and Why in American Newspapers*, 2nd ed. Hillsdale, N.J.: Lawrence Erlbaum Associates, 1989.

Bowles, Dorothy. "Missed Opportunity: Educating Newspaper Readers About First Amendment Values." *Newspaper Research Journal* 10 (Winter 1989): 39–53.

Bowman, Karlyn. "Knowing the Public Mind," *Wilson Quarterly* online edition (Autumn 2001): http://wwics.si.edu/OUTREACH/WQ/WQSELECT/BOWMAN.HTM.

Brasch, Walter. *Forerunners of Revolution: Muckrakers and the American Social Conscience.* Lanham, Md.: University Press of America, 1990.

Bray, Howard. *The Pillars of the Post: The Making of a News Empire in Washington.* New York: W.W. Norton & Company, 1980.

Brown, Jane Delano, Carl R. Bybee, Stanley T. Wearden, and Dulcie Murdock Straughan. "Invisible Power: Newspaper News Sources and the Limits of Diversity." *Journalism Quarterly* 64 (Spring 1987): 44–54.

Bunker, Matthew D. "Have it Your Way? Public Records Law and Computerized Government Information." *Journalism & Mass Communication Quarterly* 73 (Spring 1996): 90–101.

Bunker, Matthew D., and Sigman L. Splichal. "Legally Enforceable Reporter-Source Agreements: Chilling News Gathering at the Source?" *Journalism Quarterly* 70 (Winter 1993): 939–946.

Bush, Larry. "Journalists aren't Asking the Tough Questions," *Newspaper Research Journal* 11 (Summer 1990): 50–52.

Busterna, John C. "Trends in Daily Newspaper Ownership." *Journalism Quarterly* 65 (Winter 1988): 831–838.

———. "National Advertising Pricing: Chain vs. Independent Newspapers," *Journalism Quarterly* 65 (Summer 1988): 307–312, 334.

———. "Price Discrimination as Evidence of Newspaper Chain Market Power." *Journalism Quarterly* 68 (Spring/Summer 1991): 5–14.

Busterna, John C., and Robert G. Picard. *Joint Operating Agreements: The Newspaper Preservation Act and Its Application.* Norwood, N.J.: Ablix Pulishing, 1993.

Cameron, Glen T. and David Blount. "VNRs and Air Checks: A Content Analysis of the Video News Release in Television Newscasts." *Journalism & Mass Communication Quarterly* 73 (Winter 1996): 890–904.

Cameron, Glen T., Kuen-Hee Hu-Pak, and Bong-Hyun Kim. "Advertorials in Magazines: Current Use and Compliance with Industry Standards," *Journalism & Mass Communication Quarterly* 73 (Autumn 1996): 722–733.

Carey, James. "The Problem of Journalism History," *Journalism History* 1 (Spring 1974): 3–5, 27.

———. "Journalism and Technology," *American Journalism* 17 (Fall 2000): 129–135.

Carroll, Raymond C. "Content Values in TV News Programs in Small and Large Markets," *Journalism Quarterly* 62 (Winter 1985): 877–882, 938.

Cassady, David. "Press Councils—Why Journalists Won't Participate," *Newspaper Research Journal* 5 (Summer 1984): 19–25.

Chambers, Stan. *News at Ten: Fifty Years with Stan Chambers.* Santa Barbara, Calif.: Capra Press, 1994.

Chyi, Hsiang Iris, and Dominic Lasorsa. "Access, Use and Preferences for Online Newspapers," *Newspaper Research Journal* 20 (Fall 1999): 2–13.

Clor, Harry M., ed., *The Mass Media and Modern Democracy*. Chicago: Rand McNally, 1974.

Corrigan, Don H. *The Public Journalism Movement in America: Evangelists in the Newsroom*. Westport, Conn.: Praeger, 1999.

Coulson, David C. "Editors' Attitudes and Behavior toward Journalism Awards," *Journalism Quarterly* 66 (Spring 1989): 143–147.

———. "Impact of Ownership on Newspaper Quality." *Journalism Quarterly* 71 (Summer 1994): 403–410.

———. "Impact of JOAs on Newspaper Competition and Editorial Performance," *Mass Comm Review* 21 (1994): 236–249.

Coulson, David C., and Stephen Lacy. "Journalists' Perceptions of How Newspaper and Broadcast News Competition Affects Newspaper Content." *Journalism Quarterly* 73 (Summer 1996): 354–363.

Coulter, Ann. *Slander: Liberal Lies about the American Right*. New York: Crown, 2002.

Cremedas, Michael E. "Corrections Policy in Local Television News: A Survey." *Journalism Quarterly* 69 (Spring 1992): 166–172.

Croteau, David and William Hoynes. *The Business of Media: Corporate Media and the Public Interest*. Thousand Oaks, Calif.: Pine Oaks Press, 2001.

Crouse, Timothy. *The Boys on the Bus*. New York: Ballantine, 1972.

Curry, Richard, et al. *Freedom at Risk: Secrecy, Censorship, and Repression in the 1980s*. Philadelphia: Temple University, 1988.

Davie, William R., and Jung-Sook Lee. "Sex, Violence, and Consonance/Differentiation: An Analysis of Local TV News Values," *Journalism & Mass Communication Quarterly* 72 (Spring 1995): 128–138.

Davies, David R. *An Industry in Transition: Major Trends in American Daily Newspapers, 1945–1965*. Doctoral dissertation, University of Alabama, 1997.

Davis, Deborah. *Katharine the Great: Katharine Graham and the Washington Post*. 2nd ed. Bethesda, Md.: National Press, 1987.

Davis, Richard. *The Press and American Politics: The New Mediator*, 2nd ed. Upper Saddle River, N.J.: Prentice Hall, 1996.

DeFleur, Margaret H. *Computer-Assisted Investigative Reporting: Development and Methodology*. Mahwah, N.J.: Lawrence Erlbaum, 1997.

Demers, David. *The Menace of the Corporate Newspaper: Fact or Fiction?* Ames, Iowa: Iowa State University, 1996.

Dennis, Everette, Donald Gillmor, and Theodore Glasser, eds., *Media Freedom and Accountability*. New York: Greenwood, 1989.

Dickson, Tom, Wanda Brandon, and Elizabeth Topping. "Editors, Educators Agree on Outcomes but Not Goal." *Newspaper Research Journal* 22 (Fall 2001): 44–56.

Dionne, E.J. *Why Americans Hate Politics*. New York: Simon & Schuster, 1991.

Dominick, Joseph R. "Impact of Budget Cuts on CBS News," *Journalism Quarterly* 65 (Summer 1988): 469–473.

Dominick, Joseph R., Alan Wurtzel, and Guy Lometti. "Television Journalism vs. Show Business: A Content Analysis of Eyewitness News." *Journalism Quarterly* 52 (Summer 1975): 213–218.

Downie, Leonard Jr. *The New Muckrakers*. New York: New American Library, 1976.

Edgerton, Gary R., and Peter C. Collins, eds., *Television Histories: Shaping Collective Memory in the Media Age*. Lexington, Ky.: University Press of Kentucky, 2001.

Edwards, Bob. *Edward R. Murrow and the Birth of Broadcast Journalism*. Hoboken, N.J.: John Wiley & Sons, 2004.

Ehrlich, Matthew G. "The Journalism of Outrageousness: Tabloid Television News vs. Investigative News," *Journalism & Mass Communication Monographs* 155 (February 1996).

Emery, Edwin, and Michael Emery. *The Press and America: An Interpretive History of the Mass Media*, 4th ed. Englewood Cliffs, N.J.: Prentice-Hall, 1978.

Emery, Michael. "The Writing of American Journalism History," *Journalism History* 10 (Autumn/Winter 1983): 38–43.

Engstrom, Erika, and Anthony J. Ferri. "From Barriers to Challenges: Career Perceptions of Women TV News Anchors," *Journalism & Mass Communication Quarterly* 75 (Winter 1998): 789–802.

Entman, Robert. *News from Nowhere: Television and the News*. New York: Random House, 1973.

———. *Democracy without Citizens: Media and the Decay of American Politics*. New York: Oxford University, 1989.

———. "Blacks in the News: Television, Modern Racism and Cultural Change." *Journalism Quarterly* 69 (Summer 1992): 341–361.

Esrock, Stuart L., and Greg B. Leichty. "Corporate World Wide Web Pages: Serving the News Media and Other Publics," *Journalism & Mass Communication Quarterly* 76 (Autumn 1999): 456–467.

Ettema, James S., and Theodore L. Glasser. *Custodians of Conscience: Investigative Journalism and Public Virtue*. New York: Columbia University, 1998.

Evensen, Bruce. "Surrogate State Department? *Times* Coverage of Palestine, 1948." *Journalism Quarterly* 67 (Autumn 1990): 391–400.

Everett, Stephen E. "Financial Services Advertising Before and After the Crash of 1987," *Journalism Quarterly* 65 (Winter 1988): 920–924, 980.

Fahmy, Shahira, and C. Zoe Smith. "Photographers Note Digital's Advantages, Disadvantages," *Newspaper Research Journal* 24 (Spring 2003): 82–96.

Fallows, James. *Breaking the News: How the Media Undermine American Democracy*. New York: Vintage, 1997.

Farrar, Ronald. "News Councils and Libel Actions," *Journalism Quarterly* 63 (Autumn 1986): 509–516.

Fengler, Susanne. "Holding the News Media Accountable: A Study of Media Reporters and Media Critics in the United States," *Journalism & Mass Communication Quarterly* 80 (Winter 2003): 818–832.

Ferri, Anthony J., and Jo E. Keller. "Perceived Career Barriers for Female Television News Anchors," *Journalism Quarterly* 63 (Autumn 1986): 463–467.

Fialka, John J. *Hotel Warriors: Covering the Gulf War*. Washington, D.C.: Woodrow Wilson Center Press and Johns Hopkins University Press, 1992.

Flanagin, Andrew J., and Miriam J. Metzger. "Perceptions of Internet Information Credibility," *Journalism & Mass Communication Quarterly* 77 (Autumn 2000): 515–540.

Folkerts, Jean, and Stephen Lacy. "Journalism History Writing, 1975–1983," *Journalism Quarterly* 62 (Autumn 1985): 585–588.

Foote, Joe S., ed., *Live from the Trenches: The Changing Role of the Television News Correspondent*. Carbondale, Ill.: Southern Illinois University Press, 1998.

Franck, Thomas, and Edward Weisband, eds., *Secrecy and Foreign Policy*. New York: Oxford University, 1974.

Franken, Al. *Rush Limbaugh is a Big Fat Idiot and Other Observations*. New York: Delacorte Press, 1996.

Frazier, Lowell D. "The Fax News Flood: Editors Grapple with Technology's Benefits, Burdens," *Newspaper Research Journal* 13 (Winter/Spring 1992): 100–111.

Fredin, Eric S. "Rethinking the News Story for the Internet: Hyperstory Prototypes and a Model of the User," *Journalism & Mass Communication Monographs* 163 (September 1997).

Fuller, Jack. *News Values: Ideas for an Information Age*. Chicago: University of Chicago, 1996.

Gade, Peter J., and Earnest L. Perry. "Changing the Newsroom Culture: A Four-Year Case Study of Organizational Development at the St. Louis Post-Dispatch," *Journalism & Mass Communication Quarterly* 80 (Summer 2003): 327–347.

Gans, Herbert. *Deciding What's News: A Study of CBS Evening News, NBC Nightly News, Newsweek and Time*, Vintage Books ed. New York: Vintage, 1980.

Garrison, Bruce. "Online Services, Internet in 1995 Newsrooms," *Newspaper Research Journal* 18 (Summer/Fall 1997): 79–93.

———. "Journalists' Perceptions of Online Information-Gathering Problems," *Journalism & Mass Communication Quarterly* 77 (Autumn 2000): 500–514.

———. "Computer-assisted Reporting Near Complete Adoption," *Newspaper Research Journal* 22 (Winter 2001): 65–79.

Gaunt, Philip. *Choosing the News: The Profit Factor in News Selection*. New York: Greenwood, 1990.

Gaziano, Cecelie. "How Credible is the Credibility Crisis?" *Journalism Quarterly* 65 (Summer 1988): 267–278, 375.

Geraci, Philip C. "Comparison of Graphic Design and Illustration Use in Three Washington, D.C., Newspapers," *Newspaper Research Journal* 5 (Winter 1983): 29–39.

Gibbs, Cheryl, ed., *Public Journalism, Theory and Practice*. Dayton, Ohio: Kettering Foundation, 1997.

Gillmor, Donald M., Jerome A. Barron, Todd F. Simon and Herbert A. Terry. *Mass Communication Law: Cases and Comment*, 5th ed. St. Paul, Minn.: West Publishing, 1990.

Gitlin, Todd. *The Sixties: Years of Hope, Days of Rage*. New York: Bantam, 1987.

Gladney, George Albert. "The McPaper Revolution? *USA Today*-style Innovation at Large U.S. Dailies," *Newspaper Research Journal* 13 (Winter/Spring 1992): 54–71.

Glassner, Barry. *The Culture of Fear: Why Americans are Afraid of the Wrong Things.* New York: Basic Books, 1999.

Glessing, Robert J. *The Underground Press in America.* Bloomington, Ind.: Midland, 1971.

Goldstein, Tom. *The News at Any Cost: How Journalists Compromise their Ethics to Shape the News.* New York: Simon and Schuster, 1985.

Grabe, Maria Elizabeth. "Tabloid and Traditional News Magazine Crime Stories: Crime Lessons and Reaffirmation of Social Class Distinctions," *Journalism & Mass Communication Quarterly* 73 (Winter 1996): 926–946.

Graber, Doris A. "News and Democracy: Are Their Paths Diverging?" Roy W. Howard Public Lecture. Bloomington, Ind.: Indiana School of Journalism, 1992.

———. *Mass Media and American Politics,* 4th ed. Washington, D.C.: Congressional Quarterly Press, 1993.

Greenwald, Marilyn S. *A Woman of the Times: Journalism, Feminism, and the Career of Charlotte Curtis.* Athens, Ohio: Ohio University, 1999.

Greenwald, Marilyn, and Joseph Bernt, eds., *The Big Chill: Investigative Reporting in the Current Media Environment.* Ames, Iowa: Iowa State University, 2000.

Griffin, Michael, and Jongsoo Lee. "Picturing the Gulf War: Constructing an Image in Time, Newsweek, and U.S. News & World Report," *Journalism & Mass Communication Quarterly* 72 (Winter 1995): 813–825.

Grossman, Lawrence K. *The Electronic Republic: Reshaping Democracy in the Information Age.* New York: Penguin, 1996.

Gwin, Louis. "Prospective Reporters Face Writing/Editing Tests at Many Dailies," *Newspaper Research Journal* 9 (Winter 1988): 101–111.

Halberstam, David. *The Powers that Be.* New York: Dell, 1979.

Hale, Gary A., and Richard C. Vincent. "Locally Produced Programming on Independent Television Stations," *Journalism Quarterly* 63 (Autumn 1986): 562–567, 599.

Hallin, Daniel C. *The "Uncensored War": The Media and Vietnam,* paperback ed. Berkeley: University of California Press, 1989.

Halsuk, Martin E., and Bill F. Chamberlin. "Open Government in the Digital Age: The Legislative History of How Congress Established a Right of Public Access to Electronic Information Held by Federal Agencies," *Journalism & Mass Communication Quarterly* 78 (Spring 2001): 45–64.

Hamill, Pete. *News is a Verb: Journalism at the End of the Twentieth Century.* New York: Ballantine, 1998.

Hammond, Scott C., Daniel Petersen, and Steven Thomsen. "Print, Broadcast and Online Convergence in the Newsroom," *Journalism & Mass Communication Educator* 55 (Summer 2000): 16–26.

Hammond, William M. *Reporting Vietnam: Media & Military at War.* Lawrence, Kan.: University Press of Kansas, 1998.

Hansen, Kathleen A., Mark Nuezil, and Jean Ward. "Newsroom Topic Teams: Journalists' Assessments of Effects on News Routines and Newspaper Quality," *Journalism & Mass Communication Quarterly* 75 (Winter 1998): 803–821.

Harrower, Tim. *The Newspaper Designer's Handbook,* 5th ed. Boston: McGraw-Hill, 2002.

Hartman, John K. "*USA Today* and Young-Adult Readers: Can a New-Style Newspaper Win Them Back?" *Newspaper Research Journal* 8 (Winter 1987): 1–14.

Hartsock, John C. *A History of American Literary Journalism: The Emergence of a Modern Narrative Form*. Amherst, Mass.: University of Massachusetts, 2000.

Haskins, Jack B., and M. Mark Miller. "The Effects of Bad News and Good News on a Newspaper's Image," *Journalism Quarterly* 61 (Spring 1984): 3–13, 65.

Hayden, Joseph. *Covering Clinton: The President and the Press in the 1990s*. Westport, Conn.: Praeger, 2001.

Hemmer, Joseph Jr. *The Supreme Court and the First Amendment*. New York: Praeger, 1986.

Hertsgaard, Mark. *On Bended Knee: The Press and the Reagan Presidency*. New York: Farrar Straus Giroux, 1988.

Hindman, Elizabeth Blanks. "'Lynch-Mob Journalism' vs. 'Compelling Human Drama': Editorial Responses to Coverage of the Pretrial Phase of the O.J. Simpson Case," *Journalism & Mass Communication Quarterly* 76 (Autumn 1999): 499–515.

Hipsman, Barbara J., and Stanley T. Wearden. "Skills Testing at American Newspapers," *Newspaper Research Journal* 11 (Winter 1990): 75–89.

Holsworth, Robert D., and J. Harry Wray. *American Politics and Everyday Life*, 2nd ed. New York: Macmillan, 1987.

Howard, Herbert H. "An Update on Cable TV Ownership: 1985," *Journalism Quarterly* 63 (Winter 1986): 706–709, 781.

———. "Group and Cross-Media Ownership of TV Stations: A 1989 Update," *Journalism Quarterly* 66 (Winter 1989): 785–792.

———. "Group and Cross-Media Ownership of TV Stations: A 1995 Update," *Journalism & Mass Communication Quarterly* 72 (Summer 1995): 390–401.

Hubbard, J.T.W. "Newspaper Business News Staffs Increase Markedly in Last Decade," *Journalism Quarterly* 63 (Spring 1987): 171–177.

Huesca, Robert. "Reinventing Journalism Curricula for the Electronic Environment," *Journalism & Mass Communication Educator* 55 (Summer 2000): 4–15.

Hughes, William J. "The 'Not-So-Genial' Conspiracy: The *New York Times* and Six Presidential 'Honeymoons,' 1953–1993," *Journalism & Mass Communication Quarterly* 72 (Winter 1995): 841–850.

Humphrey, Carol Sue. *The Press of the Young Republic, 1783–1833*. Westport, Conn.: Greenwood, 1996.

Huntington, Samuel P. *American Politics: The Promise of Disharmony*. Cambridge, Mass.: Belknap, 1981.

Huntzicker, William E. *The Popular Press, 1833–1865*. Westport, Conn.: Greenwood, 1999.

Husselbee, L. Paul. "Media's Coverage of Itself: How Eight Newspapers Covered the Telecommunications Act of 1996," conference paper for Association for Education in Journalism and Mass Communication 1997 Convention; accessed at http://list.msu.edu/cgi-bin/wa?A2=ind9710a&L=aejmc&F=&S=&P=6953.

Hynds, Ernest C. *American Newspapers in the 1980s*. New York: Hastings House, 1980.

———. "Editorials, Opinion Pages Still Have Vital Roles at Most Newspapers," *Journalism Quarterly* 61 (Autumn 1984): 634–639.

———. "Editors at Most U.S. Dailies See Vital Roles for Editorial Page," *Journalism Quarterly* 71 (Autumn 1994): 573–582.

Iorio, Sharon Hartin. "How State Open Meetings Laws Now Compare with Those of 1974," *Journalism Quarterly* 62 (Winter 1985): 741–749.

Jacobson, Thomas L., and John Ullman. "Commercial Databases and Reporting: Opinions of Newspaper Journalists and Librarians," *Newspaper Research Journal* 10 (Winter 1989): 15–25.

James, Doug. *Walter Cronkite: His Life and Times*. Brentwood, Tenn.: 1991.

Janeway, Michael. *Republic of Denial: Press, Politics, and Public Life*. New Haven, Conn.: Yale University, 1999.

Jensen, Jay. "The New Journalism in Historical Perspective," *Journalism History* 1 (Summer 1974): 37, 66.

Johnson, Haynes. *Sleepwalking Through History: America in the Reagan Years*. New York: Anchor, 1991.

Johnson, Michael L. *The New Journalism: The Underground Press, the Artists of Non-fiction, and Changes in the Established Media*. Lawrence, Kan.: University Press of Kansas, 1971.

Johnson, Thomas J. "Exploring Media Credibility: How Media and Nonmedia Workers Judged Media Performance in Iran/Contra," *Journalism Quarterly* 70 (Spring 1993): 87–97.

Johnson, Thomas J., and Barbara K. Kaye. "Cruising is Believing?: Comparing Internet and Traditional Sources on Media Credibility Measures," *Journalism & Mass Communication Quarterly* 76 (Summer 1998): 325–340.

———. "A Boost or Bust for Democracy?: How the Web Influenced Political Attitudes and Behaviors in the 1996 and 2000 Presidential Elections," *Harvard International Journal of Press/Politics* 8 (July 2003): 9–34.

Johnson, Thomas J., Mahmoud A.M. Braima, and Jayanthi Sothirajah. "Doing the Traditional Media Sidestep: Comparing the Effects of the Internet and Other Nontraditional Media with Traditional Media in the 1996 Presidential Campaign," *Journalism & Mass Communication Quarterly* 76 (Spring 1999): 99–123.

Kamhawi, Rasha, and David Weaver. "Mass Communication Research Trends from 1980 to 1999," *Journalism & Mass Communication Quarterly* 80 (Spring 2001): 7–27.

Kanihan, Stacey Frank, and Kendra L. Gale. "Within 3 Hours, 97 Percent Learn About 9/11 Attacks," *Newspaper Research Journal* 24 (Winter 2003): 78–91.

Keeler, Robert F. *Newsday: A Candid History of the Respectable Tabloid*. New York: William Morrow, 1990.

Kellner, Douglas. *Grand Theft 2000: Media Spectacle and a Stolen Election*. Lanham, Md.: Rowman & Littlefield, 2001.

Kenney, Keith, and Stephen Lacy. "Economic Forces behind Newspapers' Increasing Use of Color and Graphics," *Newspaper Research Journal* 8 (Spring 1987): 33–41.

Kenney, Keith and Chris Simpson. "Was Coverage of the 1988 Presidential Race by Washington's Two Major Dailies Biased?" *Journalism Quarterly* 70 (Summer 1993): 345–355.

Keogh, James. *President Nixon and the Press*. New York: Funk & Wagnells, 1972.

Kerr, Peter A. and Patricia Moy. "Newspaper Coverage of Fundamentalist Christians, 1980–2000," *Journalism & Mass Communication Quarterly* 79 (Spring 2002): 54–72.

Kessler, Lauren. *The Press: Alternative Journalism in American History*. Beverly Hills, Calif.: Sage, 1984.

Ketterer, Stan. "Oklahoma Small Dailies, Weeklies Use Internet as Reporting Tool," *Newspaper Research Journal* 24 (Spring 2003): 107–113.

Kielbowicz, Richard B. "On Making Connections with Outside Subfields," *American Journalism* 10 (Summer/Fall 1993): 30–37.

King, Erika G. "The Flawed Characters in the Campaign: Prestige Newspaper Assessments of the 1992 Presidential Candidates' Integrity and Competence," *Journalism & Mass Communication* Quarterly 72 (Spring 1995): 84–97.

Kinnick, Katherine N., Dean M. Krugman, and Glen T. Cameron. "Compassion Fatigue: Communication and Burnout Toward Social Problems," *Journalism & Mass Communication Quarterly* 73 (Autumn 1996): 687–707.

Kintz, Linda, and Julia Lesage, eds., *Media, Culture, and the Religious Right*. Minneapolis: University of Minnesota, 1998.

Klein, Joseph (as "Anonymous"). *Primary Colors: A Novel of Politics*. New York: Random House, 1996.

Knightley, Philip. *The First Casualty: From the Crimea to Vietnam: The War Correspondent as Hero, Propagandist, and Myth Maker*. New York: Harcourt Brace Jovanovich, 1975.

Knowlton, Steven, and Patrick Parsons, eds., *The Journalist's Moral Compass: Basic Principles*. Westport, Conn.: Praeger, 1995.

Kostyu, Paul E. "Nothing More, Nothing Less: Case Law Leading to the Freedom of Information Act," *American Journalism* 12 (Fall 1995): 462–476.

Kratzer, Renee Martin and Brian Kratzer. "How Newspapers Decided to Run Disturbing 9/11 Photos," *Newspaper Research Journal* 24 (Winter 2003): 34–47.

Kraus, Michael and Joyce Davis. *The Writing of American History*, Rev. Ed. Norman, Okla.: University of Oklahoma, 1985.

Kreger, Donald S. "Press Opinion in the Eagleton Affair," *Journalism Monographs* 35 (August 1974).

Kurpius, David D. "Sources and Civic Journalism: Changing Patterns of Reporting?" *Journalism & Mass Communication Quarterly* 79 (Winter 2002): 853–866.

Kurtz, Howard. *The Trouble with America's Newspapers*. New York: Times Books, 1993.

———. *Hot Air: All Talk All the Time: An Inside Look at the Performers and the Pundits*. New York: Times Books, 1996.

Laakaniemi, Ray. "An Analysis of Writing Coach Programs on Daily American Newspapers," *Journalism Quarterly* 64 (Summer/Autumn 1987): 569–575.

Lacy, Stephen. "The Effects of Intracity Competition on Daily Newspaper Content," *Journalism Quarterly* 64 (Summer/Autumn 1987): 281–290.

Lacy, Stephen, and Alan Blanchard. "The Impact of Public Ownership, Profits, and Competition on Number of Newsroom Employees and Starting Salaries in Mid-Sized Newspapers," *Journalism & Mass Communication Quarterly* 80 (Winter 2003): 949–968.

Lacy, Stephen, Tony Atwater, and Angela Powers. "Use of Satellite Technology in Local Television News," *Journalism Quarterly* 65 (Winter 1988): 925–929, 966.

Lambeth, Edmund B., Philip E. Meyer, and Esther Thorson, eds., *Assessing Public Journalism.* Columbia, Mo.: University of Missouri Press, 1998.

Landers, James. "Specter of Stalemate: Vietnam War Perspectives in *Newsweek, Time,* and *U.S. News & World Report,* 1965–1968," *Journalism History* 19 (Summer 2002): 13–38.

Lasorsa, Dominic. "News Media Perpetuate Few Rumors About 9/11 Crisis," *Newspaper Research Journal* 24 (Winter 2003): 10–21.

Lee, Changho. "*Post, Times* Highlight Government's War Efforts," *Newspaper Research Journal* 24 (Winter 2003): 190–203.

Lee, Martin A., and Norman Solomon. *Unreliable Sources: A Guide to Detecting Bias in News Media.* New York: Carol Publishing, 1991.

Lee, Richard W., ed., *Politics & the Press.* Washington, D.C.: Acropolis, 1970.

Len-Rios, Maria E. "The Bush and Gore Presidential Campaign Web Sites: Identifying with Hispanic Voters during the 2000 Iowa Caucuses and New Hampshire Primary," *Journalism & Mass Communication Quarterly* 76 (Winter 2002): 887–904.

Levine, Lawrence. *The Unpredictable Past: Explorations in American Cultural History.* New York: Oxford University, 1993.

Lewis, Anthony. *Make No Law: The Sullivan Case and the First Amendment.* New York: Random House, 1991.

Li, Xigen. "Web Page Design and Graphic Use in Three U.S. Newspapers," *Journalism & Mass Communication Quarterly* 75 (Summer 1998): 353–365.

Lichtenberg, Judith, ed., *Democracy and the Mass Media.* New York: Cambridge University Press, 1990.

Liebovich, Louis W. *The Press and the Presidency: Myths and Mindsets from Kennedy to Election 2000,* Rev. 2nd ed. Westport, Conn.: Praeger, 2001.

———. *Richard Nixon, Watergate, and the Press: A Historical Perspective.* Westport, Conn.: Praeger, 2003.

Lin, Carolyn A. "Audience Selectivity of Local Television Newscasts," *Journalism Quarterly* 69 (Summer 1992): 373–382.

Lin, Carolyn A., and Leo W. Jeffres. "Comparing Distinctions and Similarities across Websites of Newspapers, Radio Stations, and Television Stations," *Journalism & Mass Communication Quarterly* 78 (Autumn 2001): 555–573.

Lindley, William R. "From Hot Type to Video Screens: Editors Evaluate New Technology," *Journalism Quarterly* 65 (Summer 1988): 486–489.

Lipschultz, Jeremy, and Michael L. Hilt. *Crime and Local Television News: Dramatic, Breaking and Live from the Scene.* Mahwah, N.J.: Lawrence Erlbaum, 2002.

Lofton, John. *The Press as Guardian of the First Amendment.* Columbus, S.C.: University of South Carolina, 1980.

Lora, Ronald, and William Henry Longton. *The Conservative Press in Twentieth-Century America*. Westport, Conn.: Greenwood, 1999

Lowry, Dennis T., and Jon A. Shidler. "The Sound Bites, the Biters, and the Bitten: An Analysis of Network News Bias in Campaign '92," *Journalism & Mass Communication Quarterly* 72 (Spring 1995): 33–44.

MacArthur, John R. *Second Front: Censorship and Propaganda in the Gulf War*. Berkeley, Calif.: University of California Press, 1992.

MacDonald, J. Fred. *One Nation Under Television: The Rise and Decline of Network TV*. Chicago: Nelson-Hall, 1990.

———. *Blacks and White TV: African Americans in Television since 1948*, 2nd ed. Chicago: Nelson-Hall, 1992.

Maier, Scott R. "Digital Diffusion in Newsrooms: The Uneven Advance of Computer-assisted Reporting," *Newspaper Research Journal* 21 (Spring 2000): 95–110

———. "The Digital Watchdog's First Byte: Journalism's First Computer Analysis of Public Records," *American Journalism* 17 (Fall 2000): 75–91.

Malcolm, Janet. *The Journalist and the Murderer*. New York: Alfred A. Knopf, 1990.

Marlane, Judith. *Women in Television News Revisited*. Austin, Texas: University of Texas, 1999.

Marron, Maria B. "The Founding of Investigative Reporters and Editors, Inc. and the Arizona Project: The Most Significant Post-Watergate Development in U.S. Investigative Journalism," *American Journalism* 14 (Winter 1997): 54–75.

Martin, Christine. "War Stories: Women Correspondents Battle to Cover the Vietnam Conflict," paper presented at 1997 American Journalism Historians Association Conference.

Martindale, Carolyn. *The White Press and Black America*. New York: Greenwood, 1986.

———. "Selected Newspaper Coverage of Causes of Black Protest," *Journalism Quarterly* 66 (Winter 1989): 920–923, 964.

———. "Coverage of Black Americans in Four Major Newspapers," *Newspaper Research Journal* 11 (Summer 1990): 96–112.

———. "Significant Silence: Newspaper Coverage of Problems Facing Black Americans," *Newspaper Research Journal* 15 (Spring 1994): 102–115.

Marzolf, Marion. *Up from the Footnote: A History of Women Journalists*. New York: Hastings House, 1977.

Massachusetts Institute of Technology Center for Reflective Community Practice and the Leadership Conference Education Fund. *Successes and Failures of the 1996 Telecommunications Act*. Cambridge, Mass.: Massachusetts Institute of Technology Center for Reflective Community Practice and the Leadership Conference Education Fund, 2002; accessed at http://www. civilrights.org/publications/reports/1996telecommunications/telecom. html#PageLinks.

Massey, Brian L., and Tanni Haas. "Does Making Journalism More Public Make a Difference? A Critical Review of Evaluative Research on Public Journalism," *Journalism & Mass Communication Quarterly* 79 (Autumn 2002): 559–586.

Mathes, Rainer, and Barbara Pfetsch. "The Role of the Alternative Press in the Agenda-Building Process: Spill-Over Effects and Media Opinion Leadership," *European Journal of Communication* 6 (March 1991): 33–62.

Matthews, Martha N. "How Public Ownership Affects Publisher Autonomy," *Journalism Quarterly* 73 (Summer 1996): 343–353.

McAuliffe, Kevin Michael. *The Great American Newspaper: The Rise and Fall of the Village Voice*. New York: Charles Scribner's Sons, 1978.

McGrath, Kristin, and Cecilie Gaziano. "Dimensions of Media Credibility: Highlights of the 1985 ASNE Survey," *Newspaper Research Journal* 7 (Winter 1986): 55–67.

McKean, Michael L., and Vernon A. Stone. "Deregulation and Competition: Explaining the Absence of Local Broadcast News Operations," *Journalism Quarterly* 69 (Autumn 1992): 713–723.

McLean, Deckle. "Press May Find Justice Scalia Frequent Foe but Impressive Adversary," *Journalism Quarterly* 65 (Spring 1988): 152–156.

McLeod, Douglas M., William P. Eveland, Jr., and Nancy Signorielli. "Conflict and Public Opinion: Rallying Effects of the Persian Gulf War," *Journalism Quarterly* 71 (Spring 1994): 20–31.

McPherson, James B. "Government Watchdogs: How Four Newspapers Expressed Their First Amendment Responsibilities in Editorials." Master's thesis, Washington State University, May 1993.

———. "Crosses Before a Government Vampire: How Four Newspapers Addressed the First Amendment in Editorials, 1962–1991," *American Journalism* 13 (Summer 1996): 304–317.

———. "Reasoned Protest and Personal Journalism: The Liberty and Death of *The Intermountain Observer*," paper presented at the 1996 American Journalism Historians National Convention, London, Ontario.

———. "From 'Military Propagandist' to The Progressive: The Editorial Evolution of H-Bomb Battler Samuel H. Day, Jr." Doctoral dissertation, Washington State University, August 1998.

Merrill, John C., and Harold A. Fisher. *The World's Great Dailies: Profiles of Fifty Newspapers*. New York: Hastings House, 1980.

Merrill, John C., Peter J. Gade, and Frederick R. Blevens. *Twilight of Press Freedom: The Rise of People's Journalism*. Mahwah, N.J.: Lawrence Erlbaum, 2001.

Merritt, Davis. *Public Journalism and Public Life: Why Telling the Truth is Not Enough*, 2nd ed. Hillsdale, N.J.: Lawrence Erlbaum, 1997.

Meyer, Philip. *Precision Journalism*. Bloomington, Ind.: Indiana University Press, 1973.

Moisy, Claude. "The Foreign News Flow in the Information Age." Discussion Paper D-23, the Joan Shorenstein Center of Press, Politics and Public Policy, Harvard University, November 1996.

Monmonier, Mark, and Val Pipps. "Weather Maps and Newspaper Design: Response to *USA Today*?" *Newspaper Research Journal* 8 (Summer 1987): 31–42.

Murray, Michael D., ed., *Encyclopedia of Television News*. Phoenix: Oryx Press, 1999.

Newhagen, John E. "The Relationship between Censorship and the Emotional and Critical Tone of Television News Coverage of the Persian Gulf," *Journalism Quarterly* 71 (Spring 1994): 32–42.

Nord, David Paul. "A Diverse Field Needs a Diversity of Approaches," *Journalism History* 9 (Summer 1982): 56–60.

———. "What We Can Do for Them: Journalism History and the History Profession," *American Journalism* 10 (Summer/Fall 1993): 26–30.

Novick, Peter. *That Noble Dream: The "Objectivity Question" and the American Historical Profession.* New York: Cambridge University Press, 1988.

O'Brien, David. *The Public's Right to Know: The Supreme Court and the First Amendment.* New York: Praeger, 1981.

Overholser, Geneva. "Good Journalism and Business: An Industry Perspective," *Newspaper Research Journal* 25 (Winter 2004): 8–17.

Patterson, Oscar III. "Television's Living Room War in Print: Vietnam in the News Magazines," *Journalism Quarterly* 61 (Spring 1984): 35–39, 136.

Patterson, Thomas E. *Out of Order.* New York: Vintage Books, 1994.

Pearson, Drew, and Jack Anderson. *The Case Against Congress.* New York: Simon and Schuster, 1968.

Pease, Ted. "Blaming the Boss: Newsroom Professionals See Managers as Public Enemy No. 1," *Newspaper Research Journal* 12 (Spring 1991): 2–21.

Peck, Abe. *Uncovering the Sixties: The Life and Times of the Underground Press.* New York: Citadel Underground, 1991.

Pell, Eve. *The Big Chill: How the Reagan Administration, Corporate America, and Religious Conservatives Are Subverting Free Speech and the Public's Right to Know.* Boston: Beacon Press, 1984.

Peng, Foo Yeuh, Naphtali Irene Tham, and Hao Ziaoming. "Trends in Online Newspapers: A Look at the U.S. Web," *Newspaper Research Journal* 20 (Spring 1999): 52–63.

Picard, Robert G. "U.S. Newspaper Ad Revenue Shows Consistent Growth," *Newspaper Research Journal* 23 (Fall 2002): 21–33.

Poindexter, Paula M., and Mike Conway. "Local, Network TV News Shows Significant Gains," *Newspaper Research Journal* 24 (Winter 2003): 114–127.

Porter, William. *Assault on the Media: The Nixon Years.* Ann Arbor, Mich.: University of Michigan, 1976.

Postman, Neil. *Amusing Ourselves to Death: Public Discourse in the Age of Show Business.* New York: Penguin, 1985.

Power, Samantha. *A Problem from Hell: America and the Age of Genocide.* New York: Basic Books, 2002.

Pritchard, David. "The Impact of Newspaper Ombudsmen on Journalists' Attitudes," *Journalism Quarterly* 70 (Spring 1993): 77–86.

Rajecki, D.W., Cheryl Halter, Andrew Everts, and Chris Feghali. "Documentation of Media Reflections of the Patriotic Revival in the United States in the 1980s," *The Journal of Social Psychology* 131 (1991): 401–411.

Ramaprasad, Jyotika. "Information Graphics in Newspapers," *Newspaper Research Journal* 12 (Summer 1991): 92–103.

Randall, Starr D. "How Editing and Typesetting Technology Affects Typographical Error Rate," *Journalism Quarterly* 63 (Winter 1986): 763–770.

Randle, Quint, Lucinda D. Davenport, and Howard Bossen. "Newspapers Slow to Use Web Sites for 9/11 Coverage," *Newspaper Research Journal* 24 (Winter 2003): 58–71.

Reese, Stephen D., John A. Daly, and Andrew P. Hardy. "Economic News on Network Television," *Journalism Quarterly* 63 (Spring 1987): 137–144.

Riffe, Daniel, and Alan Freitag. "A Content Analysis of Content Analysis: Twenty-Five Years of *Journalism Quarterly*," *Journalism and Mass Communication Quarterly* 74 (Autumn 1997): 515–524.

Roberts, Eugene, and Thomas Kunkel, eds., *Breach of Faith: A Crisis of Coverage in the Age of Corporate Newspapering*. Fayetteville, Ark.: University of Arkansas, 2002.

Roberts, Eugene, Thomas Kunkel, and Charles Layton, eds., *Leaving Readers Behind: The Age of Corporate Newspapering*. Fayetteville, Ark.: University of Arkansas, 2001.

Robinson, Piers. *The CNN Effect: The Myth of News, Foreign Policy and Intervention*. London: Routledge, 2002.

Rosensteil, Tom, and Bill Kovach. *The Elements of Journalism: What Newspeople Should Know and the Public Should Expect*. New York: Three Rivers Press, 2001.

Rothenberg, Elliot C. *The Taming of the Press: Cohen v. Cowles Media Company*. Westport, Conn.: Praeger, 1999.

Russial, John. "Pagination and the Newsroom: A Question of Time," *Newspaper Research Journal* 15 (Winter 1994): 91–101.

———. "How Digital Imaging Changes Work of Photojournalists," *Newspaper Research Journal* 21 (Spring 2000): 67–83.

St. Dizier, Byron. "Republican Endorsements, Democratic Positions: An Editorial Page Contradiction," *Journalism Quarterly* 63 (Autumn 1986): 581–586.

Sanders, Marlene, and Marcia Rock. *Waiting for Prime Time: The Women of Television News*. Urbana, Ill.: University of Illinois, 1988.

Scharrer, Erica, Lisa M. Weidman, and Kimberly L. Bissell. "Pointing the Finger of Blame: News Media Coverage of Popular-Culture Culpability," *Journalism & Mass Communication Monographs* 5 (Summer 2003).

Schartz, Bertnard. *Freedom of the Press*. New York: Facts on File, 1992.

Schmuhl, Robert, ed., *The Responsibilities of Journalism*. Notre Dame, Ind.: University of Notre Dame, 1984.

Schudson, Michael. *The Power of News*. Cambridge: Harvard University Press, 1995.

———. "Toward a Troubleshooting Manual for Journalism History," *Journalism & Mass Communication Quarterly* 74 (Autumn 1997): 463–476.

Schultz, Tanjev, and Paul S. Voakes. "Prophets of Gloom: Why Do Newspaper Journalists Have So Little Faith in the Future of Newspapers?" *Newspaper Research Journal* 20 (Spring 1999): 23–40.

Scott, David K., and Robert H. Gobetz. "Hard News/Soft News Content of the National Broadcast Networks, 1972–1987," *Journalism Quarterly* 69 (Summer 1992): 406–412.

Selnow, Gary W. *Electronic Whistle-Stops: The Impact of the Internet on American Politics.* Westport, Conn.: Praeger, 1998.

Semati, Mehdi. "Reflections on the Politics of the Global 'Rolling-News' Television Genre," *Transnational Broadcasting Archives* 6 (Spring/Summer 2001): http://www.tbsjournal.com.

Shaw, David. *Journalism Today: A Changing Press for a Changing America.* New York: Harper's College, 1977.

————. *Press Watch: A Provocative Look at How Newspapers Report the News.* New York: Macmillan, 1984.

Shaw, Eugene F., and Daniel Riffe. "NIS and Radio's All-News Predicament," *Journalism Monographs* 69 (August 1980).

Shawcross, William. *Murdoch: the Making of a Media Empire.* New York: Simon & Schuster, 1992.

Sherer, Michael D. "Vietnam War Photos and Public Opinion," *Journalism Quarterly* 66 (Summer 1989): 391–394, 530.

Singer, Jane B. "Changes and Consistencies: Newspaper Journalists Contemplate Online Future," *Newspaper Research Journal* 18 (Winter/Spring 1997): 2–18.

————. "Campaign Contributions: Online Newspaper Coverage of Election 2000," *Journalism & Mass Communication Quarterly* 80 (Spring 2003): 39–56.

Singletary, Michael W., and Chris Lamb. "News Values in Award-Winning Photos," *Journalism Quarterly* 61 (Spring 1984): 104–108, 233.

Sloan, Wm. David, ed., *Media and Religion in American History.* Northport, Ala.: Vision Press, 2000.

————, ed., *The Media in America: A History*, 5th ed. Northport, Ala.: Vision Press, 2002.

Sloan, Wm. David, and Julie Hedgepeth Williams. *The Early American Press, 1690–1783.* Westport, Conn.: Greenwood, 1994.

Sloan, Wm. David, and Lisa Mullikin Parcell, eds., *American Journalism: History Principles, Practices.* Jefferson, N.C.: McFarland & Company, 2002.

Slotnick, Elliot E., and Jennifer A. Segal. *Television News and the Supreme Court: All the News That's Fit to Air?* Cambridge: Cambridge University Press, 1998.

Small, William J. "Exxon Valdez: How to Spend Billions and Still Get a Black Eye," *Public Relations Review* 17 (1991): 9–25.

Smith, Conrad, and Lee B. Becker. "Comparison of Journalistic Values of Television Reporters and Producers," *Journalism Quarterly* 66 (Winter 1989): 793–800.

Smith, Hedrick, ed., *The Media and the Gulf War: The Press and Democracy in Wartime.* Washington, D.C.: Seven Locks Press, 1992.

Smith, Rebecca, and John R. Emshwiller, *24 Days: How Two Wall Street Journal Reporters Uncovered the Lies that Destroyed Faith in Corporate America.* New York: HarperBusiness, 2003.

Soley, Lawrence C. "Pundits in Print: 'Experts' and Their Use in Newspaper Stories," *Newspaper Research Journal* 15 (Spring 1994): 65–75.

Spellman, Robert L. "Tort Liability of the News Media for Surreptitious Reporting," *Journalism Quarterly* 62 (Summer 1985): 289–295.

Splichal, Sigman L., and Bill F. Chamberlin. "The Fight for Access to Government Records Round Two: Enter the Computer," *Journalism Quarterly* 71 (Autumn 1994): 550–560.

Spragens, William C. *Electronic Magazines: Soft News Programs on Network Television.* Westport, Conn.: Praeger, 1995.

Squires, James D. *Read All About It! The Corporate Takeover of America's Newspapers.* New York: Times Books, 1993.

Stamm, Keith, and Doug Underwood. "The Relationship of Job Satisfaction to Newsroom Policy Changes," *Journalism Quarterly* 70 (Autumn 1993): 528–541.

Starck, Kenneth, and Julie Eisele. "Newspaper Ombudsmanship as Viewed by Ombudsmen and Their Editors," *Newspaper Research Journal* 20 (Fall 1999): 37–49.

Startt, James. "Historiography and the Media Historian," *American Journalism* 10, (Summer/Fall 1993): 17–25.

———. *Oral Histories Relating to Journalism History*, 2nd ed. American Journalism Historians Association (originally published Winter 1996); available online at http://www.elon.edu/dcopeland/ajha/oralhistory.htm.

———. "The Historiographical Tradition in 20th Century America," 1998 American Journalism Historians Association presidential address printed in *American Journalism* 16 (Winter 1999): 105–131.

Startt, James, and Wm. David Sloan, eds., *The Significance of the Media in American History.* Northport, Ala.: Vision Press, 1994.

———. *Historical Methods in Mass Communication.* Northport, Ala.: Vision Press, 2003.

Stauber, John, and Sheldon Rampton. *Toxic Sludge is Good for You: Lies, Damn Lies and the Public Relations Industry.* Monroe, Maine: Common Courage Press, 1995.

Steele, Janet E. "Experts and the Operational Bias of Television News: The Case of the Persian Gulf War," *Journalism & Mass Communication Quarterly* 72 (Winter 1995): 799–812.

Stempell, Guido H. III, and Thomas Hargrove. "Newspapers Played Major Role in Terrorism Coverage," *Newspaper Research Journal* 24 (Winter 2003): 55–57.

Stempell, Guido H. III, Thomas Hargrove, and Joseph Bernt. "Relation of Growth of Use of the Internet to Changes in Media Use from 1995 to 1999," *Journalism & Mass Communication Quarterly* 80 (Spring 2003): 71–79.

Stephens, Mitchell. *A History of News from the Drum to the Satellite.* New York: Viking Penguin, 1988.

Sterling, Christopher, and John M. Kittross. *Stay Tuned: A Concise History of American Broadcasting.* Belmont, Calif.: Wadsworth, 1978.

Stevens, George E. "Newsracks and the First Amendment," *Journalism Quarterly* 66 (Winter 1989): 930–933, 973.

Stone, Gerald, and Elinor Grusin. "Network TV as the Bad News Bearer," *Journalism Quarterly* 61 (Autumn 1984): 517–523, 592.

Stone, Gerald, Barbara Hartung, and Dwight Jensen. "Local TV News and the Good-Bad Dyad," *Journalism Quarterly* 64 (Spring 1987): 37–44.

Stone, Vernon A. "Changing Profiles of News Directors of Radio and TV Stations, 1972–1986," *Journalism Quarterly* 64 (Winter 1987): 745–749.

———. "Trends in the Status of Minorities and Women in Broadcast News," *Journalism Quarterly* 65 (Summer 1988): 288–293.

Streitmatter, Rodger. "The Rise and Triumph of the White House Photo Opportunity," *Journalism Quarterly* 65 (Winter 1988): 981–985.

———. "The Lesbian and Gay Press: Raising a Militant Voice in the 1960s," *American Journalism* 12 (Spring 1995): 142–161.

———. *Mightier than the Sword: How the News Media Have Shaped American History.* Boulder, Colo.: Westview Press, 1997.

Sundar, S. Shyam. "Effect of Source Attribution on Perception of Online News Stories," *Journalism & Mass Communication Quarterly* 75 (Spring 1998): 55–68.

Swain, Bruce M. "The Progressive, the H-Bomb and the Papers," *Journalism Monographs* 76 (1982).

Taft, William, ed., *Encyclopedia of Twentieth-Century Journalists.* New York: Garland, 1986.

Takaki, Ronald. *A Different Mirror: A History of Multicultural America.* Boston: Little, Brown and Company, 1993.

Talese, Gay. *The Kingdom and the Power.* New York: World Publishing, 1969.

Tankard, James W. Jr., and Bill Israel. "PR Goes to War: The Effects of Public Relations Campaigns on Media Framing of the Kuwaiti and Bosnian Crises," conference paper for Association for Education in Journalism and Mass Communication 1997 Convention; http://list.msu.edu/cgi-bin/wa?A2=ind9709c&L=aejmc&F=&S=&P=3857.

Tebbel, John, and Sarah Miles Watts. *The Press and the Presidency: From George Washington to Ronald Reagan.* New York: Oxford University Press, 1985.

Tewksbury, David, and Scott L. Althaus. "Differences in Knowledge Acquisition among Readers of the Paper and Online Versions of a National Newspaper," *Journalism & Mass Communication Quarterly* 77 (Autumn 2000): 457–479.

Tewksbury, David, Andrew J. Weaver, and Brett D. Maddex. "Accidentally Informed: Incidental News Exposure on the World Wide Web," *Journalism & Mass Communication Quarterly* 78 (Autumn 2001): 533–554.

Thaler, Paul. *The Spectacle: Media and the Making of the O.J. Simpson Story.* Westport, Conn.: Praeger, 1997.

Tosh, John. *The Pursuit of History: Aims, Methods and New Directions in the Study of Modern History*, 2nd ed. London: Longman, 1991.

Trotta, Liz. *Fighting for Air: In the Trenches with Television News.* New York, Simon & Schuster, 1991.

Ullmann, John. *Investigative Reporting: Advanced Methods and Techniques.* New York: St. Martin's, 1995.

Underwood, Doug. *When MBAs Rule the Newsroom: How the Marketers and Managers Are Reshaping Today's Media.* New York: Columbia University Press, 1993.

————. *From Yahweh to Yahoo! The Religious Roots of the Secular Press*. Champaign, Ill.: University of Illinois Press, 2002.

Underwood, Doug, and Keith Stamm. "Are Journalists Really Irreligious? A Multidimensional Analysis," *Journalism & Mass Communication Quarterly* 78 (Winter 2001): 771–786.

————. "Balancing Business with Journalism: Newsroom Policies at 12 West Coast Newspapers," *Journalism Quarterly* 69 (Summer 1992): 301–317.

Underwood, Doug, C. Anthony Giffard, and Keith Stamm. "Computers and Editing: Pagination's Impact on the Newsroom," *Newspaper Research Journal* 15 (Spring 1994): 116–127.

Unger, Irwin. *A History of the American New Left 1959–1972*. New York: Dodge, Mead & Company, 1974.

Utt, Sandra H., and Steve Pasternack. "Front Pages of U.S. Daily Newspapers," *Journalism Quarterly* 61 (Winter 1984): 879–884.

————. "Use of Graphic Devices in a Competitive Situation: A Case Study of 10 Cities," *Newspaper Research Journal* 7 (Winter 1985): 7–16.

————. "How They Look: An Updated Study of America's Newspaper Front Pages," *Journalism Quarterly* 66 (Autumn 1989): 621–627.

Vargo, Karen, et al. "How Readers Respond to Digital News Stories in Layers and Links," *Newspaper Research Journal* 21 (Spring 2000): 40–54.

Walsh-Childers, Kim, Jean Chance, and Kristie Alley Swain. "Daily Newspaper Coverage of the Organization, Delivery and Financing of Health Care," *Newspaper Research Journal* 20 (Spring 1999): 2–22.

Ward, Hiley H. *Mainstreams of American Media History*. Needham Heights, Mass.: Allyn & Bacon, 1997.

Ward, Jean, Kathleen A. Hansen, and Douglas M. McLeod. "Effects of the Electronic Library on News Reporting Protocols," *Journalism Quarterly* 65 (Winter 1988): 845–852.

Weaver, David, and LeAnne Daniels. "Public Opinion on Investigative Reporting in the 1980s," *Journalism Quarterly* 69 (Spring 1992): 146–155.

Weaver, David H., and G. Cleveland Wilhoit. *The American Journalist in the 1990s: U.S. News People at the End of an Era*. Mahwah, N.J.: Lawrence Erlbaum, 1996.

Webb, Joseph M. "Historical Perspective on the New Journalism," *Journalism History* 1 (Summer 1974): 38–42, 60.

White, Marie Dunne. "Plagiarism and the News Media," *Journal of Mass Media Ethics* 4, (1989): 265–280.

Whittemore, Hank. *CNN: The Inside Story*. Boston: Little, Brown and Company, 1990.

Wiener, Jonathon. "Radical Historians and the Crisis in American History, 1959–1980," *Journal of American History* 76 (September 1989): 399–434.

Wilkins, Lee, and Philip Patterson, eds., *Risky Business: Communicating Issues of Science, Risk, and Public Policy*. New York: Greenwood, 1991.

Woodhull, Nancy J., and Robert W. Snyder, eds., *Defining Moments in Journalism*. New Brunswick, N.J.: Transaction Publishers, 1998.

Wulfemeyer, K. Tim. "Perceptions of Viewer Interests by Local TV Journalists," *Journalism Quarterly* 61 (Autumn 1984): 432–435.

————. "How and Why Anonymous Attribution is Used by *Time* and *Newsweek*,"
     Journalism Quarterly 62 (Spring 1985): 81–86, 126.
Wulfemeyer, K. Tim, and Lori L. McFadden. "Anonymous Attribution in Net-
     work News," *Journalism Quarterly* 63 (Autumn 1986): 468–473.
Zehner, Dennis. "Shining the Big Spotlight: Case Studies of Attitudes Toward
     Civic Journalism in American Newsrooms." Undergraduate Honors The-
     sis, Lehigh University, 1999.
Zinn, Howard. *A People's History of the United States 1492–Present.* New York:
     Harper & Row, 1980.

Index

About the Author

JAMES BRIAN McPHERSON is Associate Professor of Communication Studies at Whitworth College. Previously he worked as a newspaper reporter and editor; he also has worked in corporate and non-profit public relations, and hosted a local public affairs radio program.